TWO WORLDS,

ONE ART

TWO WORLDS,

ONE ART

LITERARY TRANSLATION
IN RUSSIA
AND AMERICA

Lauren G. Leighton

NORTHERN ILLINOIS UNIVERSITY PRESS, DEKALB, 1991

© 1991 by Northern Illinois University Press
Published by Northern Illinois University Press, DeKalb, Illinois 60115
∞   Manufactured in the United States of America using acid-free paper
Design by Julia Fauci

Library of Congress Cataloging-in-Publication Data
Leighton, Lauren G.
    Two worlds, one art : literary translation in Russia and America /
Lauren G. Leighton.
        p.   cm.
    Includes bibliographical references (p.) and index.
    ISBN 0-87580-160-9
    1. Translating and interpreting—History.   2. Literature,
Comparative—Russian and American.   3. Literature, Comparative—
American and Russian.   4. Russian language—Translating.
5. English language—Translating.   I. Title.
PN241.L37 1991
418'.02'0947—dc20   90-28531

I would like to dedicate this book to my generation of the Young Leningraders.

CONTENTS

Two Worlds, One Art

Criticism and Theory

Prose

Poetry

Problems

ACKNOWLEDGMENTS

I am indebted to many generous translators and admirers of literary translation for advice and criticism. Among these are William Arrowsmith, James Bailey, David Bethea, Thomas Beyer, H. W. Chalsma, Peter Cobin, Milton Ehre, Donald Fiene, D. Barton Johnson, Simon Karlinsky, Donald Keene, Sophia Lubensky, Robert Maguire, Adam Makkai, John Malmstad, Sidney Monas, Gary Saul Morson, Slava Paperno, Marilyn Gaddis Rose, Nathan Rosen, Munir Sendich, J. Thomas Shaw, and especially George J. Gutsche. My appreciation and respect for these colleagues are strong; but, of course, infelicities are my own responsibility. I thank *Russian Language Journal* for permission to use materials from articles published there in my treatment here of translations of Solzhenitsyn and language-acquisition; *Calamus* for the materials in this study on Walt Whitman; and *Slavic and East European Journal* for the materials on Rita Rayt-Kovaleva's Vonnegut. I wish also to thank the College of Liberal Arts and Sciences and the Institute of the Humanities of the University of Illinois at Chicago for the 1985–1986 Fellowship that enabled me to complete the first draft of this study, and my fellow Fellows of the Institute for the intellectual aggravation that made our year in the luxurious basement of Stevenson Hall a good memory.

■■■■■■ In 1970, under the auspices of the Gertrude Clarke Whitall Poetry and Literature Fund, nine poets gathered at the U.S. Library of Congress to listen and to respond to an address by Allen Tate on "The Translation of Poetry." The ideas and opinions offered during the lecture and discussion that followed are of marked interest to translators and admirers of the art of translation. But in at least one respect the event has more meaning as a symbol than for what was said and accomplished there. During the entire history of American letters—the letters of a nation literally founded on foreign languages and cultures—translation has been considered a low art, and the translator has been assigned to an obscure place on the outskirts of American literature. Foreign languages are such a low priority in the United States that Americans were once described as the most complacently monolingual people on earth. In the 1960s, however, literary translation began to receive greater respect, translators, especially poet-translators, began to move closer to the warming fire of literary esteem, and translations began to be recognized as a consequence of creative activity.

In the 1980s translators are sometimes flabbergasted at finding themselves courted. Where so many previous efforts fell sadly by the way, we now have a national Translation Center and a journal, *Translation*; we have the American Translators Association and the American Literary Translators Association working to establish standards and respect for translation; and PEN American Center has strongly supported the idea that translation is an art. Several universities offer degree programs in translation. One of the most vigorous research organizations is the National Resource Center for Translation and Interpretation at the State University of New York at Binghamton. Academic, scholarly, professional, and intellectual journals now feature translations regularly and even show an interest in theory and criticism of translation. Recent bibliographies show that whereas American letters once possessed not a single book-length study of literary translation, there are now many major studies, some of which have even attracted national attention. In fact, the new field of translation studies has made such remarkable advances over the past quarter of a century that the American translation theorist Marilyn Gaddis Rose recently predicted that we are within reach of positive achievements in translation theory, and even a metatheory of translation (1987:1, 8).

There is a dismaying irony in that, as translators know all too well, the teaching and learning of foreign languages fell into a national depression during the same two decades of the 1960s and 1970s when literary translation finally came at least part way into its own. This does not bode well for the future of the art, and, despite all the encouraging events that have moved the art from beyond the horizon of national awareness, it is clear that American letters do not yet have a defined and permanent place for translators and their contribution to world literature. Still, beggars should not be choosy, and translators can appreciate that their art has come further in the past twenty-five years than in all the years before.

The Tate address is not the only indicator of this heartening development, of course—PEN American Center sponsored a highly influential Conference on Literary Translation that same year. But the address can be seen as a cultural sign of the moment when it occurred. And the character of the event—the attitudes revealed there by ten prominent poet-translators in America—can be taken as indicative of the moment, a moment of pause after what began to happen in the 1960s and has continued with greater force since.

What is remarkable about the Tate event is that many things that should have been said about literary translation were said. Most of the problems that have troubled translators since Babel were touched on, most of the familiar questions were raised, most of the opinions translators derive from their vexing work were expressed: The possibility—or impossibility—of translation, the notion that only a poet can translate poetry, and skill versus art. The belief that a poem should be a poem in its new language, the questionable validity of the reinterpretation known as the imitation, the contempt for the literal crib or trot, and the realizability of a faithful literary conveyance that falls between these two extremes. The word versus the poem as a whole, the immortality of a work of art in relation to the temporariness and contemporaneity of its translation, and translation and traduction. These and many other age-old questions were raised, and what was said makes the event symbolic. Two aspects of the discussion there reveal much about the state of literary translation in America at that moment.

First, everything said had been said before. The questions raised and the problems discussed were discussed in the same terms by Virgil in his time and Dante in his, Pope and Dryden in their time, Pound and Eliot in theirs. And second, these elegant users of the English language were perceptibly inarticulate when they got to the fine details of translating poetry. They searched for words to represent the concepts they had to express and found instead established formulas. They expressed strong ideas, they revealed insights, but when they confronted the concepts and principles of literary translation—its intricacies, its techniques—they had to search for terms and often did not find them. Or when they did find them they used them interchangeably and in other ways arbitrarily.

These poet-translators did not lack eloquence. Rather, that was the state of theory and criticism of literary translation at that time. It was a time of assessment and searching for new directions. That was also the condition of the American translation vocabulary at that time: translators possessed new, more complex ideas about their art, but new concepts were only barely visible, and, more cogently, there was a sharp gap between concept and vocabulary. A critical vocabulary existed, but it was a conventional vocabulary. Critical terms—"accuracy," "precision," "word-for-word," "faithfulness," "fidelity"—were not matched correctly with the quite different concepts designated by these words. Principles of translation had not been so convincingly argued as they have been since; strategies had not been successfully revised; the process of translation had not been as extensively explored; methods of translation repugnant to these poets had not yet been dismissed. It is not that the participants in the event were themselves inarticulate, therefore. Rather, a rational critical vocabulary was lacking and theory was poorly developed. Little wonder, then, that so many of the problems discussed through the years since Babel were repeated in conventional phrases and predictable terms.

Of course, problems of translation are fairly basic and constant—they do not go away. Whatever the myriads of permutations among and within many languages, cultural assumptions, and historical periods, discussions of literary translation and its theory deal with essentially unchanging dilemmas. Then consider that Americans tend to disagree on terms and principles, preferring almost always to repeat a heresy rather than to concur. Americans are usually the least ideological people in the present world; it is our character not to settle opinions and move on. "Noticeably lacking to the whole American critical movement, even in its theoretical phase, is a philosophical underpinning," F. Will has said (1973:17). To which George Steiner has added, "The theoretical equipment of the translator tends to be thin and rule-of-thumb" (1975:273). So we will keep on discussing, discussing, discussing. We will probably keep on discussing even though we know that, sooner or later, the humanities will have to begin accepting greater responsibility, to the degree possible, for verifiable knowledge.

Still, many new strategies have been demonstrated and many vaguely established concepts significantly clarified during what we can hope will be remembered as the turning point of the art of translation in America. Many problems have been resolved, and at least some common agreement has been achieved. Translation theory has not been discovered by modern literary theorists, but that, too, may happen. Now is a good time to contemplate what has been accomplished and to attempt to show what problems have been or are now being resolved, to suggest more carefully defined terms for a vocabulary of criticism and theory of translation, and to examine translations that prompt answers to questions about literary translation. There are many ways this can be done, but the method in the present study is to compare the state of translation practice, theory, and criticism in the American world, an essentially pragmatic culture in which solutions are traditionally questioned and revised, and in the Russian world, an essentially ideology-oriented culture in which the possibility of solutions collectively worked out and commonly agreed on is considered a normal national condition.

The use of the word *ideological* as a characterization of the Russian world does not here imply *the* ideology, although, of course, Marxism-Leninism is as ubiquitous in Soviet discussions of translation as elsewhere. Instead, reference is to a culture that, historically inclined to authority, is receptive to the optimistic assumption that all problems have solutions from a single orientation, one of any two opinions is wrong, and theory tied to practice offers intellectual stability. Compare this to our own historical experience, where the expression of individual opinions (and self) usually transcends (we hope) any faith in common agreement, least of all if based on proclaimed authority. It is not true that individual opinion counts for nothing in Soviet society, or that authority is present at all times, or that the acknowledged Soviet propensity for the collective invariably discourages individual expression. As it happens, literary translation was unusually free from ideological control in some of the better years before glasnost, and this presumes sometimes fierce discussion at conferences and in journals. But solutions commonly found and accepted are generally considered a positive state of affairs in the Russian and more largely the Soviet world; collective consideration of common problems, including debate, is perceived as a good way to resolve problems; and authority derived from general acceptance of demonstrated efficacy is more readily respected. The political rigidity of Soviet society is not an incidental subject. But it is not the same as the traditional Russian respect for authority (which is one of its roots and not its only cause), and officially imposed restrictions on literary translation must be distinguished from the more socially natural, even if also institutionalized, quest for collective agreement characteristic of the Russian world.

To speak of this authority-oriented culture is not to say that Soviet translators have solved the many problems of the language barrier that vex all translators, or that they claim to have solved them, or that there are no conflicting solutions, or that accepted solutions are fully satisfactory "once and for all," or that Soviet solutions are appropriate to other worlds of translation. This is no more true than to say that American letters are devoid of respected standards, accepted principles, and established answers to questions that characterize literary translation in every culture. But Russian and other Soviet translators have created a forum for discussing their art and debating it on a national or All-Union level. Through an institutionalized process of discourse they have confronted their problems more systematically, achieved consensus on many questions, incorporated solutions into their practice on a broad basis, and thereby freed themselves to move on from decisions to refinements. They are, in this way at least, in a better position than their American colleagues, who do not have an attentive national audience.

An advantage of this national-cultural condition is that, having established standards and developed a stable body of theory, Soviet translators were for many long years ahead of others in the creation of a vocabulary of criticism, in methods of translation analysis, and in knowledge of the history of translation. Until they recently (and apparently unknowingly) lagged, they were far ahead of the world in theory of translation. They possess a consistent language for the discussion of translation that has been rationalized across the hundreds of languages of the Union. They do not flounder for words because their terms are based on a large body of existing scholarship and criticism. Soviet translators do not confuse "fidelity" with "accuracy" or with "precision" because the concepts designated by these terms have been studied and realized to be antonymical. They do not waste time discussing the tedious problem of untranslatability because they have come to terms with the language barrier. They effectively analyze the differences between a foreign text conveyed into literate Russian (or another language of the multinational Soviet Union) and one that "sounds like a translation" because they have developed methods of dealing with departures from the literary norm. Soviet translators are less vulnerable to arbitrary criticism because established vocabulary, methodology, and standards have helped eliminate amateurish reviewers. American translators will be mightily pleased to learn that their Soviet counterparts do not have to put up with the banality of so much of our own translation criticism: "it reads smoothly," or "it sounds like the original," or, even worse, silence.

Soviet translators have, above all other advantages, a national platform from which to speak, one that extends from the art itself to theory and criticism and provides an editorial process that oversees standards. Soviet translators exert strong influence because they are enforced by training institutes, widely read translation journals, collections of studies and individually authored books, and frequent access to the All-Union or local media. There is a translation establishment at the All-Union level, in the republics, and,

centered around Russian, among most languages of the Union. This establishment—called "the Soviet school of translation"—is rooted in a Russian
tradition that has at least since the eighteenth century assured that Russian
poets and writers have considered translation central to their calling. The
Soviet school of translation is a main ingredient of the nationalities policy
introduced by Lenin and continued, despite obvious difficulties, as the chief
means of holding so many different nationalities into a single Union. The
official base of the school is its status as the Soviet of Artistic Translation,
attached to the Directorate of the Union of Soviet writers and affiliated
with the International Federation of Translators (FIT).

The Soviet school is an esprit as well as an organization—an agreement
welded by common principles. "Our Soviet school of the translator's art,"
the pioneer of Soviet translation, Ivan Kashkin, has said, "is not a closed
shop. It is a gathering of those who, while preserving the diversity of their
individual manners, share the basic creative goals of Soviet translation,
which has its own defined character" (1955:132). Not all is perfect in the
Soviet school of translation. Political ideological controls have been present
even though they have not been as rigidly applied as elsewhere in Soviet
letters, and they seem so far to have been only weakened, not eliminated,
by glasnost. Common agreement and uniform standards are sometimes expressed by a kind of conformity that is not likely to be appreciated elsewhere. Translations of foreign works are often censored or edited to meet
indigenous expectations; bad translations reach print despite an effective
system of criticism and editorship. The ugly head of literalism occasionally
rears itself and some translators persist in taking liberties that constitute
disrespect for the original author's rights. Kashkin was not fully frank when
he denied that the Soviet school is a closed shop. In fact it is not easy
to gain entry into the profession, and for many years a group of Moscow
translators enjoyed a monopoly that even Leningraders had trouble breaking. A finding of this study is that the Russian penchant for conformity
of opinion leads to severe limitations and to failures to correct shortcomings.
Another is that not all the claims of the school's members are fully valid.
But the praise of others for the school's overall standards is not unjustified,
and the respect for many excellent Russian translations of world masterpieces is deserved. Precisely because the state of literary translation is so
unlike anything in the American world, a comparative study offers a contrast
that tells us much about both worlds and the world of translation at large.

The word *comparative* suggests that such a study ought to be fairly evenly
divided between Russian and American literature. So far as analyses and
evaluations of translations are concerned, the comparative emphases are balanced—it is as important to demonstrate how American translators treat
Russian literature as it is to show how American literature fares in Russia.
But where secondary materials are concerned, readers will want to learn

more about Soviet translation theory and criticism than about Western ideas, to which they have easier access.

The relatively new theoretical and critical field of translation studies is richly articulated in world letters. However diverse translation studies are in approach, method, assumption, or discipline, they are not so disparate as to resist coherent discussion. To the contrary, even though the field has grown at an amazing rate over the past two decades, a point worth making at this critical time is that translation practice, theory, and criticism have undergone a worldwide convergence, resulting in a significant number of breakthroughs in theory. This convergence of thought and practice of literary translation has reached toward a balance between the extremes of adaptation and literalism—toward a method of translation known in the Soviet Union as artistic translation and in the West as literary translation. The field of translation studies, which greatly relies on stylistic analyses, is oriented toward linguistics and objectivity of text, but theorists have ranged freely, in their convergence, among formal, linguistic, mimetic, hermeneutic, expressive, and reader-response or reception value. This newly modernized field has made remarkable, if not yet fully noted, contributions to literary theory, and its eclectic character offers new ways of looking at text and reception of text.

The use of the word *critical* implies that translation criticism is *literary* criticism. Western translation theory has recently surpassed Soviet theory, which has been developed over a period of more than a half century, but Western translation criticism has yet to master the sophisticated critical methods that are a sine qua non of the Soviet school of translation. American translators are unhappily trapped in what has been called "Gotcha" criticism on the one hand and the "it-reads-smoothly school" on the other. Critical terminology is not well established in American letters. Standards are not agreed on; devices for analyzing the nuances of language are seldom used. Lay critics are often ignorant of foreign languages, and specialist critics competent in one language have not learned how to communicate to specialists of another language. These failings have made translators vulnerable to arbitrary criticism.

Soviet criticism is not free of these shortcomings, but many problems of terminology, analysis, and judgment that continue to plague Western criticism have been addressed with notable clarity. Soviet translation criticism is both detailed and broad, it centers on problems of language conveyance in the immediate instance, and beyond this on values of art, literature, culture, and all else that is essential to discourse about the difficult art of literary translation. Knowledge of Soviet critical methods and the theory underlying criticism can be helpful to translators and their critics elsewhere.

The first section of this study, "Two Worlds, One Art," begins with an introduction to the Soviet school intended as both a description of its origin and development and an assessment of its unique character. It is followed by an examination of the similar and different ways in which Russian and American translators respond to several concerns common to all modern worlds of translation, and by an assessment of the ways in which political demands and censorship influence literary translation in the Soviet school. In the second section, "Criticism and Theory," an exploration of the sensible rules of criticism developed by Soviet translators is followed by an assessment of the development of Soviet theory to a type and method of translation known as artistic translation, and by an explication of a Marxist-Leninist body of theory called realist translation. The section concludes with a comparative examination of American and Russian discussions of translation as communication of cultural values from one people to another. Two sections, "Prose" and "Poetry," are examinations of problems of translation posed by classics of Russian and American literature. Selected Russian translations of American literary works and English-language translations of Russian literary works are analyzed, with a view to discovering how translators of two different cultural traditions deal with problems of language and style. Throughout this study a number of particularly vexing problems of translation are encountered—the kind of problems that have no easy solution and will not go away. The fourth section of this study, "Problems," examines Russian attempts to deal with three of these problems: literalism, colloquial speech, and realia. It is hoped that Soviet experience with these problems can offer other translators at least new insights into age-old frustrations, if not solutions. A conclusion summarizes the similarities and differences between two different worlds of translation devoted to one art, and suggests that ideas about the nature of translation are converging on a worldwide basis toward a unified perception of what literary translation is.

It is not difficult to mark the differences between comparative and national measures of value, or to apprehend the crossings of lines between criticism and theory. Similarly, the inevitable gaps between theory and practice are more easy to detect in the study of translation than in the study of literature, for the simple reason that translation theory is put to the instant test of right or wrong practice. In confronting the esprit of the Soviet school, however, it has to be kept in mind that Soviet translators are enthusiasts who often fail to distinguish between hope and realization of hope. This means that distinctions have to be made, and that care must be taken to discriminate among statements of principle, expressions of ideals, and claims to achievement. A basic tenet and claim to uniqueness in the Soviet school is that theory has been realized in practice. But Soviet translators have not bridged all gaps between theory and practice, and Soviet theory is not as unique as is often claimed. Similarly, expressions of ideals must be distinguished from established principles, and neither should be confused with enthusiastic claims to excellence or innovation. Many Soviet translators are keenly aware of the difference between their ideals and their failure to realize these ideals in principle; they admit that they have not yet eradicated from practice some of the sins of translation they have forthrightly identified in theory. But translation studies must take into account discrepancies between theory and criticism, gaps between theory and practice, and contradictions between principles and ideals. Literary translation has often been defined as the most contradictory of all arts. In fact, contradiction might very well be where the art lies.

TWO WORLDS,
ONE ART

TWO WORLDS, ONE ART

THE SOVIET SCHOOL OF TRANSLATION

The Soviet school of translation is based on a tradition of great respect for the art. This is an attitude central to the process of Westernization of Russia that began in the seventeenth and eighteenth centuries. The process of transforming medieval Russia into a modern European nation—a transformation identified primarily with the reforms of Peter the Great—brought with it feelings of both fear and awe of things foreign. Russia had to be Westernized at all costs; translation was a chief vehicle of Westernization. Translation was therefore granted official status and the high prestige of art. Because Russia opened to the West while French neoclassicism reigned over European culture, the art was founded on the principle of imitation. Like their teachers, the Russian neoclassicists did not sharply distinguish between translation and original creativity. They assumed instead that translation was an integral part of the writer's calling. The eighteenth-century poets who founded modern Russian literature by introducing European aesthetics into their culture did not even question this assumption.

With the turn to romanticism at the beginning of the nineteenth century, the new modern-school distinction between translation and original creativity made its appearance, but translation remained central to the poet's perception of art. N. I. Gnedich, Russia's first translator of *The Iliad*, drew great respect to literary translation as an art. Vasily Zhukovsky, still remembered as a giant among Russian translators, brought romanticism to Russia via his translations of the English and German romantics and pre-romantics. After Zhukovsky came Pushkin, to whose superb translations the Soviet school traces its concern for high standards. M. Iu. Lermontov, Fyodor Tyutchev, Afanasy Fet, A. K. Tolstoy, and other major writers developed the art well into the nineteenth century. Turgenev, Dostoyevsky, and Tolstoy considered translation a legitimate activity for a writer; together with other leading realists they confirmed the assumption that translation is not an incidental skill. The nineteenth century also saw the appearance of translators who made the practice their profession, including Irinarkh Vvedensky, remembered for his virtuoso, if also libertarian, translations of Thackeray and Dickens, and Pyotr Veynberg, Russia's notable translator of Shakespeare, Molière, Schiller, and Heine.

During the modernist period, from the late nineteenth century to the revolution, when poetry returned to its acme after two generations of realist prose and art for art's sake replaced social realism, translation rose to even greater national esteem. Among the great poets of the Russian avant garde who translated were Andrey Bely, Alexander Blok, Valery Bryusov, Konstantin Balmont, Nikolay Gumilev, Anna Akhmatova, and Boris Pasternak. The works of Baudelaire, Rimbaud, Verlaine, Wilde, and other modernist poets made their appearance in Russia during this time, and Russians discovered Longfellow, Whitman, Poe, Henry James, and other writers of world literature. The great works of the Chinese, Japanese, Persians, Arabs, Armenians, Georgians, and Caucasian peoples also were introduced to Russians during this period. By the time of the revolution, literary translation was an esteemed tradition of Russian literature. Standards were not high; they were nearly nonexistent. But what was to become the Soviet school had a foundation that is not typical of many other cultures: translation is an art.

The Soviet school of translation appeared in the 1920s as a natural consequence of this tradition. Its most immediate precedents have been traced by the translator and propagandist of translation V. M. Rossels to two groups of pioneers at the turn of the century. The first group was headed by the literary historian and translator A. N. Veselovsky (*The Decameron*); the classical scholar and translator F. F. Zelinsky (*The Aeneid*); and the scholar F. D. Batyushkov. These "academic translators," whom Rossels calls "the coryphaea of the cultural-historical school," edited and published "a type of edition where the translation of foreign classics is accompanied by a solid scholarly apparatus and represents the fruit not only of talent, but of the most detailed research besides." The second group comprised writers who "turned to the propagandization of the literatures of the peoples of Russia." It included Maxim Gorky, who published collections of translations of Latvian, Armenian, and Finnish poetry; Valery Bryusov, who translated and propagandized the classics of Armenian poetry; and Vladislav Khodasevich, who (although Rossels does not say so) worked with both men on these and other projects before joining the emigration. "Both trends of Russian translation literature in our century—scholarly and literary—merged after October in Gorky's World Literature Publishing House, a publishing enterprise called upon to bring to the popular masses of revolutionary Russia the greatest achievements of world classics in scientifically prepared and highly artistic translations." Rossels names the pioneer translators Kornei Chukovsky and Mikhail Lozinsky among the leading theorists of the new Soviet school and gives special credit to another pioneer, Ivan Kashkin, but he does not include the active poet-translator Nikolay Gumilev, who was soon shot for alleged anti-Bolshevik activity. Rossels concludes his praise of the founding of the Soviet school by noting, "Gorky's demands—that the translator know everything about the original author, his time, and the literature of his country—became in time the legacy of the best, the most talented masters of translation" (1965:12–14; also 1972:9–13).

Rossels was right to emphasize the importance of Gorky's World Literature (known as Worldlit) as the initiator of the Soviet school of translation. Worldlit was founded in 1918 with the support of Lenin, who saw it as a key to the nationalities policy of the new Union. Its aim was to support and to encourage writers during the civil war and to ensure that the revolution established close intellectual and cultural contact with the world and among the peoples of the new Union. To this end, Gorky recruited scores of men of letters and assigned them a straightforward national task: to assemble, to analyze, and to evaluate all existing translations of world literature and to determine which were worth preserving and which should be done anew. Gorky's chief assistant in this task was the journalist, critic, children's poet, and translator Kornei Chukovsky, who has best described the reults of Gorky's broad survey.

> The academicians, professors, and writers enlisted by Gorky for the realization of this task subjected to the most stringent possible scrutiny the old translations of the works of Dante, Cervantes, Goethe, Byron, Flaubert, Zola, Dickens, Balzac, and Thackeray, as well as the classics of the Chinese, Arabs, Persians, and Turks. . . . And they came to the most sad conclusion that with very few rare exceptions the vast majority of these translations was utterly useless and would have to be done over again on the different basis of solid scholarship that would exclude the previous methods of unprincipled amateurishness. (1984:4)

Russians should never be accused of lacking ambition for large achievements; Gorky's World Literature belongs among the most ambitious Soviet Great Projects. The goal of the newly founded Soviet school was the translation of all world literature—every world classic in all languages of all times, peoples, and cultures. Worldlit did not complete this task—in fact, as the American translator Mirra Ginsburg has noted, Gorky's "magnificent catalogue" turned out to be more for show than an actual realization (1971:355). But by the time it closed in 1927, Worldlit had laid the groundwork for its ambitious, and now fully realized, program by publishing some 120 single and multivolume editions of major world writers. By so doing, it showed the way to future publishing enterprises such as State Literature (*Goslit*), Artistic Literature (*Khudlit*), Foreign Languages Publishing House, and "Academia," the publishing imprint of the Academy of Sciences.

The task of constructing a base of scholarship, theory, criticism, and methodology on which to found a national school was assigned to Chukovsky, who has described it in personal terms:

> Once, at a meeting of the editorial board [of Worldlit] Aleksey Maksimovich turned to me with a question intended for all present:
> "What do you consider a good translation?"
> I was nonplussed and mumbled a reply. "That . . . which . . . is most artistic."
> "And what do you consider most artistic?"
> "That . . . which . . . faithfully conveys the poetic qualities of the original."
> "And what do you mean by faithfully convey? And what do you mean by the poetic qualities of the original?"
> Here I fell into utter confusion. I already had the literary instinct to distinguish a good translation from a bad one, but I was not yet prepared to articulate the theoretical basis for my judgements. At that time there was not a single book devoted to theory of translation in existence. When I undertook to write such a book, I felt like a lonely traveler wandering along an unexplored road. (1984: 4–5)

Thus, the foundations of Soviet theory and criticism of translation were laid together with the foundations of the practice of translation.

At that time there were no book-length studies of literary translation in any world literature. Chukovsky, however, "was expected to come right out with a fully formed and strict theory covering all aspects of this enormous problem." He was unprepared to do any such thing, of course, but he did make a start: "The creation of such a theory was beyond me. But so far as working out a few pragmatic rules of thumb which would offer translators a dependable working system—this I could do" (1984:5). The result was a small in-house manual, *Printsipy perevoda* (Principles of translation, 1918), composed of an essay on translation of prose by Chukovsky and one on translation of poetry by Nikolay Gumilev. The following year a more extensive manual appeared with an essay by F. D. Batyushkov in place of Gumilev's contribution. This was printed, again for in-house use, under the title *Teoriia i kritika perevoda* (Theory and criticism of translation). This pioneer work was developed in subsequent years into a book known as "the bible of the Soviet school," available in English translation as *The Art of Translation: Kornei Chukovsky's "A High Art"* (1984).

Chukovsky has acknowledged in introductions to *A High Art* that the manual he helped write has been followed by many major studies in theory of translation that have gone beyond his lifelong work-in-progress. Among the theorists whose works he considers most important are Ivan Kashkin,

O. L. Kundzich, A. V. Fedorov, E. G. Etkind, and V. M. Rossels. Among other leading Soviet theorists are the Georgian translator Givi Gache-chiladze, A. V. Kunin, Yury Levin, P. M. Toper, Ya. I. Retsker, and V. E. Shor. Beginning in the late 1950s Soviet translators were given an excellent and, as it has turned out, highly influential outlet for their theory and criticism in two annually appearing collections. *Masterstvo perevoda* (The craft of translation) is widely read for its critical studies of literary translation by leading Soviet translators, while *Tetradi perevodchika* (Translator's notebooks) contains technical studies devoted to the social and natural sciences, as well as to literary translation. These collections have been augmented by several other collections published since 1955 and by frequent studies of translation in such leading publications as *Inostrannaia literatura* (Foreign literature) and *Literaturnaia gazeta* (Literary gazette). We do not know how well attended these works are in the Soviet Union, but each issue of *Masterstvo perevoda* sells out immediately, and the tenth edition of Chukovsky's popular work has been reprinted several times. In 1986 a year-long celebration of the anniversary of Chukovsky's birth featured nationally televised discussions of translation.

Soviet letters are not devoid of bad translations. In the 1930s, when the so-called literalists (*bukvalisty*) almost dominated the art, this was especially the case. Soviet translation literature is filled with the same complaints made by American and other translators: deadlines that pressure translators into sloppy work; translations done through informants by writers who do not know the original language; poorly prepared amateurs who know neither the language nor the culture they presume to convey; "improvement" of literary works to make them appeal to a mass audience; capriciously "creative" rather than faithful conveyances. But the Soviet school is widely admired for its overall high standards, and one of its strengths is that translation has attracted remarkably talented people. The pioneers of the Soviet school are Kornei Chukovsky, known for his translations of Dickens, Twain, Defoe, Kipling's prose, Oscar Wilde, G. K. Chesterton, Taras Shevchenko, and especially Walt Whitman; Samuil Marshak, known for his translations of Nursery Rhymes, Kipling's verse, Keats, Blake, Burns, and Shakespeare; Valery Bryusov, the coryphaeus of Soviet poet-translators who brought the French decadents and symbolists along with the classics of Armenian literature to Russia; Ivan Kashkin, who both translated—Dickens, Chaucer, Thackeray, Sandburg, Frost, Hemingway—and taught a whole generation of Anglo-Americanist translators; and Mikhail Lozinsky, known for his highly regarded literalist translations of Dante, Shakespeare, Lope de Vega, Cervantes, Corneille, Molière, Cellini, and Romain Rolland.

The five pioneers and their contemporaries were succeeded by many people who have contributed greatly to the Soviet school's reputation for excellence. There are so many contributors that only a few can be mentioned by way of a description of the school and its chief literary interests. Among the most frequently praised translators of Central Asian and Caucasian literatures are Arseny Tarkovsky, Mark Tarlovsky, Vera Potapova, and A. Adalis. The poet Semyon Lipkin has been cited for his translations of the Uzbek poet Alisher Navoi, and N. I. Grebnev received the Lenin Prize for his translations of Caucasian folk songs. V. V. Levik is valued for his free renditions of European poets in many languages, including La Fontaine, Hugo, Baudelaire, Shakespeare, Byron, Goethe, Schiller, Lope de Vega, Petöfi, and Mickiewicz. Lev Ginzburg is considered an excellent translator of German literature, and V. E. Shor has been similarly versatile in translating French literature. Two of the most highly rated Ukrainian translators are Oleksy Kundzich and the poet Leonid Pervomaysky, while Levon Mkrtchian is considered one of the best Armenian translators and the novelist Jaan Kross one of the best Estonian translators. Givi Gachechiladze is known for his translations of Shakespeare into Georgian, and the Lithuanian poet Antanas Venclova is admired for his translations of Pushkin. Two excellent contemporary Russian translators are the critic and scholar E. G. Etkind (French poetry) and the Nobel poet Joseph Brodsky (John Donne and W. H. Auden). One of the most remarkable achievements in the history of translation is Tatyana Gnedich's version of Byron's *Don Juan*, a substantial portion of which was done in her head from memory while she was a political prisoner. Rita Rayt's translations of Salinger's *Catcher in the Rye* and four novels by Vonnegut were literary sensations of the 1960s and 1970s, respectively. Another major event of the 1960s was V. N. Markova's translations of Japanese poetry and folklore.

English and American literatures are by far the most popular among Russian and other Soviet readers. The generation of Anglo-Americanist translators has done exceptional work in this area. Dickens is a special favorite who has received the attention of no less than six of the most highly admired Russian translators: Marya Lorie, Nina Daruzes, Tatyana Litvinova, O. P. Kholmskaya, Nora Gal, and E. D. Kalashnikova. Among these translators, Lorie is known for her versions of Twain and Galsworthy; Daruzes for Kipling, Twain, and Shaw; Kholmskaya for Hemingway, Faulkner, Hardy, and Joyce; Gal for Joyce, H. G. Wells, Poe, and Joyce Carol Oates; and Kalashnikova for Dreiser, Hemingway, Steinbeck, and Shaw. Viktor Khinkis is known as a superb translator of Faulkner and Updike. His translation of *Ulysses* is one of the most ingenious literary achievements imaginable (and had to be, of course). Slava Paperno's translations of James, Warren, McCuller, and Melville made him one of Leningrad's best translators. R. E. Oblonskaya is a major translator of Thackeray, Galsworthy, Twain, and Whitman, and N. P. Golyshev is a favorite translator of Melville and Warren. Among the best translators of Steinbeck, Hemingway, and James is Natalya Volzhina.

An excellent source of translators and translations has been the seminar —a continuous school and workshop directed by master translators, usually under the auspices of the Union of Soviet Writers, but often at universities. For example, Ivan Kashkin's seminar produced some of the Soviet school's best Anglo-Americanists, and Elga Linetskaya's seminar in French poetry in Leningrad continued its work for over three decades. Decidedly unlike loosely organized American group work on anthologies and collections are the Soviet *kollektivy* (collectives), groups of translators who work together over a long period of time to prepare complete collected works. Collectives have translated scholarly editions of Dickens, Whitman, Twain, Shakespeare, Flaubert, Zola, and Thomas Mann, among others. These collective projects are major efforts that reach a large readership. For example, *The Collected Works of Charles Dickens* was prepared in 30 volumes by 11 translators, and a total of 600,000 copies were printed—an impressive effort even though many sets had to be given away.

The Anglo-Americanists are by far the largest group of translators in the Soviet school, followed by the Orientalists or "Easternists," a rubric that is intended to cover the Soviet Central Asian nationalities but is often extended to cover the world from Japan and China to Turkey. European literatures are a dominant Soviet interest, and the standards for translating Scandinavian, German, French, Italian, and Spanish literary works are high. Polish and Ukrainian currently are the two Slavic literatures of greatest interest in the Soviet school. Within the Union all national literatures are important, but special attention is given to the oral and written works of such exotic peoples as the Koryaks, Laks, Uzbeks, Kirghiz, Kazakhs, and Tatars, whose literatures are not well known elsewhere. The Soviets' interest in "folk" literatures has led to a large-scale project to collect, to transcribe, to translate, and to publish with lavish commentary the "national epics" of the peoples of the world, with a special emphasis on native American oral literature. After 1945 the literatures of the "Fraternal Socialist Nations" became important, and the newly incorporated Baltic countries provided major translators for the Soviet school. Interest in Latin American, Asian, and African literatures grew with interest in Third World countries.

The Soviet school experienced its most rapid period of growth in the 1930s and after the death of Stalin in 1953. In the 1960s Russians were generously endowed with translations of new and previously neglected foreign writers and poets. It is not yet clear what the effects of glasnost and perestroika will be on the school, but several observations can be offered. Chukovsky, Marshak, Kashkin, Pasternak, and many other great translators are deceased, and the generation of Anglo-Americanists and Easternists is now well advanced in years. Several translators joined the emigration in the 1970s, most notably Etkind, Lipkin, Brodsky, and Paperno. *Tetradi perevodchika* has not appeared in print lately, and even *Masterstvo perevoda* has been inactive. Now that Soviet publishing houses and journals have been given unprecedented autonomy, foreign works previously unacceptable to authorities have been appearing in response to demands for literature. This interest pales in comparison to the demand for works proscribed in Russian and other Soviet literatures during the past fifty years. The recent publication of Pasternak's once proscribed novel *Doctor Zhivago* and Vladimir Nabokov's Russian novel *The Gift* is a sign of this, even though the former has been edited for domestic consumption and the latter published without its lampoon on the revered nineteenth-century radical critic N. G. Chernyshevsky. Exactly what these recent developments signify cannot be measured at this time, but it seems prudent to say that the record is mixed and to wonder aloud whether the present generation of specially trained professional translators will uphold the achievements of the cultured amateurs who established the school.

One of the most conspicuous differences between the Russian and American worlds of translation is in attitude. It is wrong to say that Soviet translators believe they can lightly overcome the language barrier or that American translators are overwhelmed by the impossibilities of translation. It is accurate to say that Soviet translators approach the problem of untranslatability with greater certitude than American translators. This has enabled them to acknowledge the reality of the language barrier, put the question itself behind, and concentrate attention where it belongs: on what should be done to convey a literary work from one language to another as faithfully as languages permit. Soviet translators addressed the questions of literal conveyance and individualistic reinterpretation before translators elsewhere, and they resolved many problems inherent to this age-old question with greater assurance and less pointless debate, although solutions may not be satisfactory to translators worldwide. Presently Soviet theorists have fallen behind other theorists who have more effectively clarified what is called spectrum theory—gradation of translation methods between the extremes of literal and free conveyance—but they have achieved agreement on their own particular type of translation called the artistic translation, and they have described a process or a method they call artistic translation. Early definition of the concepts and terms for this type of translation and method of translation have enabled Soviet translators to achieve the standards on which their reputation rests. The character of the Soviet school is to recognize difficulties, try to resolve contradictions, and settle on solutions. Soviet translators are optimistic in this respect, and their enthusiasm is apparent.

The theoretical and practical problems most often discussed in the Soviet school parallel concerns elsewhere but are given different emphasis. Among the Soviet emphases are tactics of choice and decision—the sacrifices translators must make in this least of all perfect arts. Soviet translators constantly complain about "translation language" (what American translators call translationese) and express contempt for editors who persist in saying, "It sounds too Russian," and for translations that are not literate in Russian or other Soviet languages. Definitions of artistic translation exclude both literal and free translation, and for examples of the latter sin, wide departures from the original, they have devised a pejorative—"concoctions" (*otsebiatina*, a compound word meaning literally "something from one-self"). Among the problems that have been particularly well resolved are those concerning the concept of distance of time and space, the condition that where a work of the poetic art is immortal, its translation lasts only for its generation (if that); the implications of archaisms ("the word in its time and place," anachronisms); and the decision whether to attempt to recreate a work in its temporal and cultural context or to nationalize and modernize it. The practice of reinterpreting and rewriting a work in order to make it appeal to a new audience is considered dishonorable in the Soviet school. With regard to translation of poetry, close attention has been paid to the word versus the total poem, the image as image versus dynamism, the efficacy of equilinearity, equirhythmics, equimetrics, equistrophics. Emphasis has been placed on questions concerning the rights and duties of the translator and the rights of the original author and the reader. Not unexpectedly for a multinational country, problems of preserving national-cultural values in translation are a matter of concern, especially regarding realia and idioms. The problem of conveying colloquial style—slang, dialect, jargon, vulgarisms—has proved to be as vexing to Soviet translators as to others. Much discussion has been devoted to the importance of finding, through analysis, the "key" to conveying a style or styles faithfully—an area of theory and practice that has led to the development of such critical terms as *blandscript* (*gladkopis'*), *signal-translation*, *protocol-translation*, *dilution-translation*.

Since Soviet translators have made a strenuous effort to base practice on theory, many discussions are devoted to criticism, theory, and methodology. Attempts to define a translation method that is uniquely Soviet have led to definitions of such types of translation as adequate, full-valued, faithful, artistic, and realist, and to arguments against such types as the linguistic, formalist, scientific (equilinear, equimetric), and literalist translations. The method known as artistic translation is considered the crowning achievement of the Soviet school. Less well accepted is a method called realist translation to denote its basis in Marxist-Leninist theory. The phraseology of both definitions shows that they are founded on an unquestioned, but not unquestionable, assumption that the favored Soviet method of translation is new and unique.

According to Rossels, the Soviet school is based on four accepted postulates. First, Soviet translators accept the principle of translatability, at least *in principle*. Second, translation as a literary process is accepted over translation as a linguistic process. Third, translators consider themselves writers and are thus concerned with reality as well as text. Fourth, the process and result of translation are understood in relation to functionality: the process should lead to a text that has the same effect on its readers as the original has on its readers; a translation should be not a copy or an imitation but an artistic work in its own right (1974:12). The last postulate is prized most highly and is the basic value for those who most readily use the generic term *artistic translation*. In his well-known essay on "Translating Shakespeare," Boris Pasternak declared, "I believe, as do many others, that closeness to the original is not ensured only by literal exactness or by similarity of form; the likeness, as in a portrait, cannot be achieved without a lively and natural method of expression. . . . Like the original text, the translation must create an impression of life and not of verbiage" (1983:125).

Seen in another way, the givens that shape particular questions into the body of theory underlying the Soviet school comprise two principles so powerful that translators seldom question their value: the integrity of the original text is sacred and translation is an art. The first principle requires that a text be submitted to exhaustive analysis by an artist having the best possible command of both the native and foreign language. The method of using an interlinear, a crutch the Russians call a *podstrochnik*, is frowned on and continually decried. Although native informants' cribs are still widely used in the Soviet school, the original text is considered supreme: translators must submit to the original author's work—and manage to do so without compromising their own artistic integrity. Implicit in the second principle is an insistence that a translator is not simply a person who knows a foreign language and has the ability to convey a foreign work. Translators must be fully professional. Because they must be analysts, translators must have mastered stylistics. In addition, translators must have a scholar's knowledge of literature, geography, ethnography, history, social science, and philosophy. Soviet translators are in many cases not only original poets and writers but also authors of scholarly studies, literary histories, biographies, and standard historical-cultural works on the country of their foreign language. Western translators often possess similar skills, but only in the Soviet school has this ideal been so widely established as a professional demand.

Where literary translators and poets who translate in America often sneer at cognitive—nonintuitive—praxis, many poet-translators of the Soviet school advocate a scholarly approach to their work. As the translator of Central Asian poetry Semyon Lipkin has put it, "When a poet (a true poet!) translates a work of the national poetry of one of our republics, he must be a historian, and a traveler, and an ethnographer, and a linguist, and a recorder of mores. . . . After all, only a poet-copyist translates only what the author has written. A true poet—one wants to repeat that notion—

translates both what the author has written and that which he has written about" (1964:35). The ability to find the connotations of a single word of a text in its cultural, historical, and lexical context—all of a word's possible associations—is a highly prized ideal. Kashkin was a scholar and critic of the writers he translated and of American culture in its entirety. Linetskaya's Leningrad seminar was not only a workshop for translators but also a full experience of world culture and literatures. Etkind is not only a translator and critic-theorist of literary translation but also a scholar and intellectual of the broadest cultural diapason. An often used word is *printsipial'nost'*. In the Soviet school it signifies a demand that translators must be highly principled artists who know everything and convey it in their language as faithfully as possible.

The value of a knowledge of the foreign language from which one proposes to translate ought to be self-evident. The text of a lyric poem cannot be comprehended without complete knowledge of the nuances of its language; poetic intuition becomes mere guessing when not accompanied by language competency. Since language-acquisition is a key value of the Soviet school its necessity is regularly emphasized. This has not always been so —as late as the 1950s Soviet translators had good cause to complain about the lack of trained language specialists and the general lack of the appreciation of the importance of a knowledge of foreign languages. The poet Pavel Antokolsky once complained that critics "are apt to forget one necessary prerequisite without which the business of translation is impossible. I speak of the necessity of knowing (or at least studying) a foreign language! A foreign language is mentioned at most in passing, as of some difficult to acquire but desirable possibility of auxiliary value" (1964:9; see also Lipkin 1964:49). "It is better not to know the language from which one translates at all than to know it badly . . ." A. Gitovich has said. "People like this work with a dictionary in one hand, plainly misunderstanding what they are doing," and they believe they are translators because they look like translators (1970:381). Such complaints have subsided, however, and translators are trained more effectively on a national scale. Levik's assumption that "it is impossible to judge the accuracy of a translation without knowing the language of the original" (1964:96) is a prevailing view, and Lev Ozerov spoke for most Soviet translators when he asserted that "the translator is the most attentive and, one may say, meticulous reader of the poet he translates . . . the translator is obliged to know to perfection the text he intends to convey into his own language" (1959:285; see also Opulsky 1973:174). The continued use of the interlinear shows that language-acquisition is still a weak area of the Soviet school, but this ideal is being realized by the establishment of a standard.

A knowledge of foreign languages is not always considered an absolute value in the American world, and poets commonly convey poetry into

English without possessing a knowledge of its original language. It has even been said that a poet is better off not knowing a foreign language at all. The assumption that a poet's giftedness can vanquish language is widespread, as is the notion that a poet's talent need not contend with linguistic nuances of a foreign poem. Burton Raffel has argued,

> [L]inguistic difficulties are indeed vastly overrated, especially in land-locked, largely monolingual America. It is not hard to learn a language; with good sense and proper tools (dictionaries, grammars, all the carefully annotated editions which the professors of French and Chinese are to be blessed for) you too can turn out a volume of Urdu in English, or chase vainly after Arthur Waley. You may not want to make the effort. You may even feel that something more is needed. And again, you would be right—linguistic knowledge is not the best or even a good road toward a good translation.

In Raffel's opinion, "the translator's problems are verbal, it is the words into which he is translating, not those from which he is taking his leave, that create his problems" (1971:104–5).

Raffel's view runs counter to the stress laid on the need to know the original language by the Soviet school. It is also contrary to the Soviet insistence that mastery of foreign language must be enhanced by a scholar's knowledge. Even when Gitovich stated that it is better not to know a language at all than to know it poorly, he immediately added that translators need more than a dictionary for their work: "Somewhere nearby lives a scholar who is in love with Chinese poetry, who knows everything about it, understands everything, and is always ready to help the translator. One ought to make friends with him instead of the dictionary" (1970:381). No matter how strongly Soviet translators stress the value of language mastery, such mastery is considered deficient without knowledge of the context of an original poem. A. Opulsky has said regarding analysis of a poem's language, "Genuine research work lies before the translator, and it consists not only of studying the work . . . its ideas and the form of expression of its ideas, but also of studying the peculiarities of the poet's *Weltanschauung*, the entire arsenal of his artistic means" (1973:174).

Here succinctly stated is the conviction that the translator must know everything and be everything. Opulsky restates this ideal by quoting well-known words of Kashkin: "The translator must be a poet—that is indisputable. But 'it is naive to think that any art can do without knowledge. . . . The poet who works in the area of translation of poetry, that is . . . in a very complex and responsible art, cannot manage without philology in the widest sense of the concept, including linguistics, aesthetics, the history of science and literature, poetics'" (1973:173; see Kashkin 1959:116; for an eloquent endorsement in the United States, see Bennani 1981:136).

Inseparable from the value of foreign languages is the conviction that a translation must be a complete work in its new language. Few Soviet translators would agree with the dogmatic literalist Vladimir Nabokov's assertion that "we must dismiss, once and for all, the conventional notion that a translation 'should read smoothly,' and 'should not sound like a translation.' . . . In point of fact, any translation that does *not* sound like a translation is bound to be inexact upon inspection" (1958:xii). More would agree with Donald Keene, who emphasized that a translated poem must be a contribution to the new language: "The chief requisite of a person who would translate from any foreign tongue is, I feel sure, a love for the English language and a sensitivity to its possibilities and limitations. The translator must not belittle the possibilities of the English language" (1971:322–23). And more translators would agree with the poet-translator Nikolay Zabolotsky, who anticipated Keene when he noted, "If a translation . . . does not read as a good Russian work, the translation is either mediocre or inept" (1959:251–52).

Together with respect for one's own language goes contempt for translationese. N. M. Lyubimov, a translator of Cervantes and Rabelais, once complained, "In recent times some editors have begun using the stereotyped phrase, 'It is too Russian.'" Lyubimov believes that Russian translators must be aware above all else that "the Russian language will vanquish any difficulties, that it is capable of conveying everything, expressing everything, that it acknowledges no limits. Without this awareness, without love for one's own language, the translator risks shrinking from difficulties. More than that, the translator risks falling prisoner to the foreign language." (1983: 6) Translation language, G. Falkonovich has said, shows that the translator has failed both the native and the original language: "Not infrequently when good poets undertake to translate, they suddenly begin stuttering. They somehow work out an awkward, clumsy 'translation language' which has nothing in common with the natural, light constructions of their own work" (1970:287; see also Kashkin 1959:121).

As can be seen from the force of conviction of these statements by Soviet translators, translation is not an unattended art in the Russian world. Translations outnumber original works in Soviet publishing, and critical-theoretical studies are read on a wider basis than is typical elsewhere. According to official statistics cited by Antokolsky in a speech on Soviet translation, 44.6 percent of all books produced in 1953 were translations of foreign fiction. He points out that this is not by chance: "Behind this figure stands the demand of readers and an intense daily labor—the activity of publishing houses, both central and republic, the work of translators, editors, and compilers of dictionaries. Involved in this work are thousands and thousands of literary, scientific, and organizational workers" (Antokolsky, et al. 1955:6; see also Kalashnikova 1966:9, 10; N. K.

Chukovsky 1970:388). A. Leytes once surveyed the leading journal *Novyi mir* (New world) for the year 1953 and found that its issues contained twenty-five original poems and forty-nine poems translated from eighteen languages (1955:100–101). Nor is work in theory and criticism neglected. Data offered in *Masterstvo perevoda* (1972) show that prior to 1961 the number of publications on translation during the Soviet period amounted to between 100 and 120 separate items. In 1961 there were 154 items published, and thereafter publication of critical and theoretical studies skyrocketed. By 1968 the number had reached 493 items (1973:4; for similarly impressive data, see Bazhan 1973:20, 25–26; Sobolev 1973:28, 32; Ananiashvili 1973:60).

There are good reasons why literary translation has been accorded national attention in the Soviet Union, and why the Soviet school of translation was able to progress so far and so quickly. One reason has to do with the already mentioned attitude Russians have toward things foreign. Add to this the well-known Russian fascination with ideas, the fact that Soviet citizens were for so long starved for information and thus all the more determined to obtain global information, and the zeal for the notion of the intellectual as the bearer of culture that constitutes one definition of the distinctively Russian class known as the intelligentsia—and it should come as no surprise that Russians have an enormous appetite for all that goes under the name of world culture.

Another reason for the enormous value placed on translation is the previously mentioned nationalities policy of Lenin. Translations help hold the many republics and nationalities into a single Union and constitute a chief means of communication among the many different cultures. The role of the translator as a propagandist is often asserted in Soviet translation studies. Zabolotsky considers this role an important principle of the Soviet translator's code: "The translator serves the cause of friendship among peoples, their mutual enrichment in the area of culture. All his labor and all his professional skills are defined by this basic goal" (1959:251). The translator's propagandist duties are clearly perceived in the Soviet school and unabashedly elevated to the lofty level of a national and international mission. "The Soviet translator," Rossels has said in an influential article on translation and the national distinctiveness of original works, "is a propagandist of friendship among the peoples of our country, called upon as a writer, as an active figure of Soviet literature, to struggle against all manifestations of bourgeois nationalism." In Rossels's view, "the translator has no right to forget his writer's mission. The role of the Soviet translator, an active figure of a multinational socialist culture, is distinguished and honorable" (1955:166, 166–167; also see Ananiashvili 1973:72). According to Antokolsky, *"translation is an act of the highest friendship between writers."* He adds,

The significance of friendship among peoples in our country is truly immense. Friendship among the peoples of the Soviet Union has penetrated all areas of our labor, social, and cultural life. Friendship among the peoples of the Soviet Union is one of the firm bases of the existence of Soviet society. Always and everywhere, in years of peace and in years of war and again in years of peace, we have been aware of and continue to be aware of this friendship, as we are aware of the air and daily bread of our historical being. (Antokolsky et al. 1955: 43, 5; emphasis in original)

The mission of the Soviet school goes far beyond the Union, for it must include the task of building world socialism. "An artistic translation," Lipkin has said, "can no longer confine itself to the noble aim of 'acquainting peoples with peoples.' It now has an aim even more fine, an even more difficult and distinguished aim . . . to establish the community of socialist nations" (1964:14; see also Lyubimov 1983:7).

Such patriotic assertions are common. Often these comments are made at public gatherings where positive ideological claims are obligatory. Nevertheless, to deny the unifying power of translation is to be guilty of undermining the humanizing aims of art. And the ambition of the Great Project for translators—its task of helping to unite peoples by making available the major works of all nationalities in all languages of the Union—should not be underestimated. Translation has meant the success or failure of the Soviet nationalities policy. An indication of the contribution made by the Soviet school is provided by a reminder that the policy brought a written language to many peoples and that a great effort has been made to propagandize the oral and written masterpieces of peoples brought into contact with the world for the first time. Soviet publishing is a large industry to which considerable natural resources are allocated. Journals and other periodical publications are well financed, as are such enterprises as Foreign Languages Publishing House, which translates Soviet literary works into many languages of the world and foreign works into Union languages. Courses and programs for translators are prominent in higher education curricula. Training centers such as the Moscow Institute of International Relations have long waiting lists for would-be translators along with the diplomats, bureaucrats, and others trained there. The Soviet school's organization base, the Union of Soviet Writers, has a large number of major writers in its Soviet of Artistic Translation. The Soviet art of translation is indeed valued, and not least for reasons of high state import.

Clearly, many different factors enter into the creation and development of the Soviet school of translation. In the end, however, it is to artistic factors that literary translation is indebted in the Russian world. Translation is an art by tradition in the Russian world. Chukovsky, Marshak, Bryusov, Kashkin, and Lozinsky made translation a high art at the beginning of the

Soviet period, but they were able to do so because their predecessors had already raised it to high literary esteem. Many prerevolutionary translations of world classics are still read today, and the translations of French, German, and Italian poetry by Pushkin and Lermontov, among other poets, are still emulated. On this solid literary tradition the Soviet school of translation was built, and on artistic standards the Soviet school developed.

It is not easy to imagine a condition of the art of translation so different from the one known to American translators and admirers of literary translation. No other culture lays claim to a completely organized, coherently defined national school of translation. However, we need not covet the Russian condition. Soviet translators pay a high price for government sponsorship—not all is perfect with a system in which art is affected by sponsorship. The gap between proclaimed ideals and established principles requires critical attention, as do contradictions between theory and practice. The Soviet school is, in significant part, a set of high ideals of a high art; but faith in ideals does not always signify success. But because the state of the art is so different in the Russian world, it offers a contrast against which to assess the state of the art in our own world. A comparison of the two worlds provides examples and insights in sharp relief and indicates the potential of our own art. A comparative study of literary translation in Russia and America also suggests solutions to theoretical problems of translation, together with examples of both failure and success in practice, and provides us with the more effective critical vocabulary we need in our criticism. Moreover, whatever the differences between the two conditions, there is ultimately only one art of translation. And whatever the differences among views of the art, translation is an international art that, despite its countless linguistic, literary, and cultural manifestations, has been undergoing a worldwide process of convergence in theory and practice. What has been happening to the art in the two worlds—both differences and similarities—needs to be understood in relation to this convergence.

2

COMMON CONCERNS

■■■■■■■ A chief point of this study is that Soviet translators have resolved problems and moved on to refinements while Americans continue to debate the same problems. The Czech theorist of translation Jiří Levý, an attentive observer of the Soviet school. concluded that the remarkable development of translation practice, theory, and criticism has given Soviet translators an assuredness not typical of their colleagues worldwide. Levý did not believe that Soviet translators are superior to others. Rather, he acknowledged that they possess a unified body of theory that enables them to solve problems more systematically (1974:30–31).

In what ways does the Soviet school differ from the American world of translation? Conversely, in what ways are the two worlds similar in their pursuits of the art? One way to answer these questions is to examine the common concerns of translators in the Russian and American worlds. Three common concerns can be usefully explored here: the process of translation, including the question of convergence of ideas that has occurred along with the rapid growth of translation studies; commercial conditions; and defense of standards.

Levý did not live to witness the remarkable development of translation studies in the West, but even in the 1960s he detected harbingers. His research showed him that literary translation had begun to converge in both theory and practice on a worldwide basis. The validity of this observation is indicated by an unusually similar development in American and Russian letters that has a discernible context in the worldwide convergence of ideas about translation: recent attempts to define a strategy or strategies of translation, to describe the *process* of translation. In the Soviet school translation strategy first became a concern in the 1950s, in the works of Kashkin (1955, 1959), Rossels (1955), Kundzich (1955), among others, and was continued in the 1960s by such scholars as Etkind (1963), Fedorov (1968), and

Gachechiladze (1967). In the West translation strategy came to the fore in the 1960s in the works of Theodore Savory (1968), Mounin (1963), Nida (1964), and Levý (1963); it reached a peak in the 1970s in the work of Lefevere (1975), Steiner (1975), and Kelly (1979). The similarity between Russian and American contributions can be seen in a comparison of two ambitious prescriptions for the process of translation: the hermeneutic motion advanced by George Steiner in his 1975 study entitled *After Babel* and a "working method" enunciated by V. V. Koptilov in 1971. Because these prescriptions were stated independently of each other, they suggest that translators are converging on a common perception of a specific, and perhaps universally valid, pattern of the process of translation.

According to Steiner, the process of translation, which he calls "hermeneutic motion," comprises four acts of transfer of meaning from one language (and culture) to another: trust or faith, aggression or penetration, incorporation or embodiment, and restitution or compensation (or reciprocity). "All understanding . . . starts with an act of trust," with the translator's faith that the act of translation is "coherent," that translation is possible and desirable. "After trust comes aggression," an act by which "the translator invades, extracts, and brings home" a text from another language. Then comes an incorporative movement, the act of bringing meaning home, "the import of meaning and form, the embodiment of the work in and into a context that is both linguistically and culturally faithful." Finally, the hermeneutic act of movement must compensate, there must be an "enactment of reciprocity," a restoration of the balance between what has been lost in the transfer of meaning and what must now be restored (1975:296–300).

The act of trust, as Steiner explicates it, is "an assumption that there is a sense to be extracted and retrieved" from a literary work in another language. Steiner's act of trust is a rejection of the literalist or monadic view of translation that says that since the transfer of a literary work from one language to another is impossible, the translator has no choice but to mechanically copy it. Translators have no right to reinterpret freely a work in order to carry it into the new language, and any attempt to seek a compromise between the extremes of literalism and libertarianism is certain to fail. (Steiner explicitly rejects the notorious literalist Vladimir Nabokov here.) By penetration/aggression Steiner means that translators invade the foreign language, find meaning there, and bring it to their own language as best they can, without regard for elegance. Because the result is raw, translators are obligated to incorporate the foreign text into their own language by placing it in its correct new linguistic and cultural form. Where they have previously been concerned with what might be termed a breakthrough, they must now concentrate on artistic fidelity to the original. Steiner approaches a chief point made by Levý, namely, that translation is an art of indirectness—form does not equal form (1974:129). And, finally, "the paradigm of translation remains incomplete until reciprocity has been achieved, until the original has regained as much as it had lost." Otherwise stated, it is not enough to retrieve meaning in its correct context. The transfer across the language barrier has resulted inevitably in loss and distortion. Translators must now work to restore in their own language what they failed to recover from the original text. The art—that which is lost in translation—must now be recreated (1975:333–34, 353–54, 395; also see Kelly 1979: 56–62).

Where Steiner elucidates translation strategy as part of a philosophy of language in its broadest sense of humanistic communication, the Russian theorist V. V. Koptilov recommends a similar four-stage process of translation as a practical working method: analysis, search, synthesis, and verification. The first stage in translation is "a thorough *analysis* of the original, an examination of its content, its semantics and style, that is, of the linguistic means the author has used to express content." This stage requires attention to "the determinant features of rhythmic, phonetic, syntactic, and other structures," and equally to the original work's cultural context—its place in its literature and the author's place in his time and literary movement. Koptilov's second stage is "a *quest* in the language of the translation and in the traditions of literature for the equivalent means of recreating the most important features of the original." At this stage the translator must define the method of conveyance he believes to be most effective. The first two stages are related to the third, "the stage of *synthesis* at which the separate parts of the original work are transformed into an artistic whole in the new language." The basic task here is "the recreation of the original in all the power of its artistic immediacy and the force of its effect on the reader." And, finally, Koptilov's fourth stage, *verification*, corresponds to Steiner's compensatory or restorative movement at least to the point that he suggests translators return to their variant and recreate it. By this Koptilov signifies not an external polishing of the translation but what he emphasizes as *"the moment of analytical verification of the degree to which the translation corresponds to the original."* The translator is again an analyst at this stage but must now analyze, search, synthesize—verify—both the original and the translation (1971:154–68). The process is circular: it proceeds at continually higher stages of betterment. The translation process is a return to a beginning—a pattern that is explicit and implicit in both Koptilov and Steiner.

Both translators describe this pattern by dividing the process of translation into initial analytical, "working-draft" stages and subsequent stages of restoring or polishing early texts into more faithful and accomplished final versions. Translators generally seem to work in accordance with this pattern, and strategy theorists usually speak of preliminary work followed by artistic and linguistic refinement. Well known here is the decoding-recoding process developed by Eugene A. Nida and Charles Taber, according to which the text of the source language is analyzed, transferred to the receptor language, and restructured as the translation text in the new language (1969:484; also see Bassnett-McGuire 1980:16–17).

In an elaboration of Steiner, Marilyn Gaddis Rose has prescribed a six-step strategy that begins with "preliminary analysis" and "exhaustive style and content analysis," goes on to "acclimation of the text" and "reformulation of the text," and concludes with "analysis of the translation" and "review and comparison" (1977b). Rose's preliminary and exhaustive analyses correspond closely to Koptilov's single initial stage of analysis and more generally to Steiner's trust and aggression. Her restorative step parallels Steiner's restitution/compensation stage and Koptilov's synthesis stage; her analysis of the translation and review and comparison steps cover Koptilov's verification stage. Steiner, whose brilliant reluctance to settle on terms has been criticized, has been defended by Rose, who sees in his hermeneutic motion an "encompassing" or "enclosing" action. She likens his strategy to two "mental boomerangs," one of which starts from the translator, the other from the text. "Their flights retrace each other, although they cannot always coincide." In her opinion, Steiner is correct but not complete; she offers her six steps as a completion of his four actions and unknowingly but even more closely completes and refines Koptilov's four working stages. In her view, her "preliminary analysis" step corresponds to Steiner's notion of trust because it is at this point that the translator decides whether materials are "judged worthy of translation." Preliminary analysis is followed by "exhaustive style and content analysis, a process through which the translator discovers what makes an artistic text literary or a scholarly text authoritative. By "acclimation of the text," Rose means the point at which the translator moves from the "internal" to the "external"; that is, "we now work out our strategies—perhaps compromises—with the form of its message." The actual process of translation occurs as a "reformulation of the text." Translators reformulate because preliminary analysis now confronts actual practice and brings closer familiarity with text. Reformulation is followed by "analysis of translation." In Koptilov's terms, translators now analyze their own work as they previously analyzed the original text; in Rose's terms, "by this time we have become the original author's mirrored alter ego, and we subject our work to self-criticism to see whether we have been faithful to our other self." And, finally, "review and comparison" is the stage where translators turn their product over to someone else, an editor, instructor, or colleague, "because we are simply too close to our own work" and need someone else to compare the translated text to its original.

Although she is more direct (and practical) than Steiner, Rose rightly claims that she has not altered Steiner's strategy, but "expanded and completed the hermeneutic motion." There is, however, "a further mental motion encircling" the process of translation, "the dynamic framework of translating." Translators must "become the mirror of the original author," and "with a serious text this is a willed transformation." Translators must contend with language as the basis of text; they recode the original text. "Our recoding is a wider hermeneutic motion enclosing Steiner's, for we circle the text. We work out from it and back to it" (1977b:1–5). Clearly, these three contemplations reveal a similar sense of what the process of translation is. We can see in them a convergence of both practice and theory of translation. Steiner, Koptilov, and Rose all perceive the process as movement from the original text to the text of the translation and back to the original text. Presumably, by moving back to the original, translators comprehend it in a new, more profound way; they are more deeply involved in the text and have a higher understanding of it. And when they return to the text of the translation, their circular journey carries them to a still higher level of perception. Strategies or descriptions of the translation process thus seem to be converging on a perception of a circular pattern or a notion of a return to the beginning where work resumes on a higher level. The terms and elucidations of these strategies differ, but they do not disagree in any essential way; and the strategies do not contradict Levý and others who have attempted to describe the process. Nida and Taber's straightforward transition from source to receptor language would seem to be an exception here (1964), but they too have revealed a perception of a circular pattern by adding another step to the process, a return to the source language where the translation is "tested" (1969:163–73).

A second point of common concern is in commercial arrangements. Although differences in American and Soviet conditions might be expected to be great in this area, translation is a free-lance, even in some ways a free-market, activity in the Soviet Union, and certain arrangements between publishers and translators do not differ greatly from those of their counterparts elsewhere. Contracts are signed, advances are given, royalties and flat fees are paid, negotiations are conducted, disputes are submitted to arbitration or taken to court.

Slava Paperno, a very good Leningrad translator now at Cornell University, reports that he received assignments either through his own initiative or, after he became established, by calls from publishers. His first work in 1968 was a children's edition of *Moby Dick*. Paperno received a fixed fee per printed page, which was doubled when the printing exceeded 50,000 copies (the so-called mass printing; not an exceptionally large number under Soviet publishing conditions). He received 25 percent of that fee as an advance, was paid another 35 percent when he submitted his manuscripts and the remainder when the books went to the stores. His income was relatively high when calculated on a short-term, per-assignment basis, but, because assignments were often far between, his average annual income was poor. At the end of his career in the Soviet Union, before he emigrated, he supplemented his income by working as a free-lance editor; during much of his career he earned additional income as a private tutor of English. In one instance, Paperno was obliged to hire an attorney to discourage a republic journal from republishing one of his translations without paying royalties. In another instance, he experienced economic difficulty when publication of the book version of his translation of Robert Penn Warren's *Meet Me in the Green Glade* was delayed after Warren spoke in defense of Solzhenitsyn.

Like most Leningrad translators (and not only Leningrad translators) Paperno feels strongly that Moscow translators usually get the choice assignments. From the point of view of Leningraders, certain Moscow translators have monopolies—Rayt on Vonnegut and Salinger, Volzhina on Steinbeck, Golyshev on Warren. The best opportunities, so far as making a living is concerned, are collected works of particular foreign authors. Paperno worked as a translator and editor of collections of James and Shaw. He notes that collected editions are sometimes a kind of pork-barreling—properly arranged, they provide a hefty source of support for translators.

Here, perhaps, the similarities end, for Soviet translators do far better financially than their American counterparts. To begin with, the enticing sound of the word *monopoly* should not be missed. Soviet translators, unlike the vast majority of their colleagues in other countries, have in a very real sense bested the market. Kashkin would have been correct in saying that the Soviet school is not a closed shop if he had meant that management does not have the upper hand over labor. Soviet translators have been successful at preventing publishers from playing free-lancers against each other. Fees, commissions, and royalties are respectable; translators can initiate publishing projects; master translators are hired as editors or contracted as free-lance editors; writers cannot always dictate the terms of royalties. The position of Soviet translators changed when the government signed the international copyright agreement in 1973. At that time Soviet publishers had to begin paying royalties to foreign authors, and the newly organized All-Union Agency for Author's Rights (VAAP) took control of the selection process from the publishing houses. (The power of VAAP was such that it could —and did—exercise legal right to prevent or to delay publication of translations agreed on between Soviet writers and American translators.) Prior to 1973, when foreign authors received royalties only in rubles or were not paid at all, Soviet translators often enjoyed handsome incomes.

Worth mentioning here is that prior to glasnost Soviet translators enjoyed a distinct advantage in that profit was not the immediate necessity for Soviet publishing enterprises that it is for publishers in free-market economies. Soviet publishers were not particularly concerned with the risk of financial loss, and editors were not held responsible for large stocks of unsold books. But this means that large numbers of unwanted books were pulped and significant resources wasted, with no one held accountable. Now that publishers are financially autonomous—they keep their production surplus and accept their losses—it is hoped that they will be more accountable. This may not prove true. According to a recent Soviet visitor, Soviet readers are still so hungry for information that they snap up whatever appears on the shelves. The demand is so great that there is little incentive to heed the effects of poor supply-side economics. The market for translations seems to be inhibited only by a shortage of foreign currency to pay royalties to foreign authors and by a shortage of paper. Recent newspaper reports indicate that publishers could not meet the demand for foreign and domestic literature even if the paper supply were to be increased tenfold!

Translators elsewhere should hope for such good luck. Lewis Galantière explored some of the most frequent complaints of American translators and concluded that they are discouraged by two factors. The first is "the neglect of publishers to make known their [translators'] part in the works they advertise." The second is "the infrequency with which literary editors assign translated works to reviewers able to judge of the merits of the translations." Indicative of the first condition is that a publisher noted for developing a business "on the backs of translators" advertised six French novels by three authors without mentioning the names of the translators. As a sign of the second condition, a reviewer for the *New York Review of Books* praised the style of Pasternak's letters in English translation without giving credit to the translator, David Magarshack, while another reviewer praised Céline's "wonderful English, cascading, sputtering, rhythmic, a delight to read aloud" without mentioning that the English belongs to Ralph Mannheim, not Céline (1970:30, 31–32). Mainline outlets such as the *New York Review of Books*, the *New York Times Book Review*, and the *Times Literary Supplement* now try to assign translations to reviewers who know the original language, but far more typical are the monolingual "it-sounds-like-the-original" comments added at the tail end of reviews in *Time* and *Newsweek*.

As for commercial arrangements, in the 1960s the standard technical translator's fee was 12 dollars per 1000 words. By the early 1970s it was only 15 dollars, and in this post-inflationary day it is still as low as 35 dollars even though the American Translators Association recommends rates at 85 to 125 dollars per 1000 words in English. In a recent article Marcia Nita Doron and Marilyn Gaddis Rose reported that "despite persistent efforts of the American Translators Association . . . and the recent complementary efforts of the American Literary Translators . . . translators are not generally regarded as members of a profession." They report a case in which "one government agency unabashedly admitted to paying $2.50 a page for

English-into-Spanish translations" and discovered that "other agencies were charging anywhere from $20 to $350 for translating 1000 words of English into that language. Since most translators are quick to agree that they are grossly underpaid, one can only guess into whose pockets the bulk of that $350 falls" (Doron and Rose 1981:162, 165–66; also see Astley 1971; Gross 1971; Purdy 1971).

As for literary translators, it is not likely that many American translators receive as much as $10,000 for translating a promising novel, and they have little hope of sharing profits should the book become a best-seller or be made into a movie. As Galantière noted, authors usually insist that their agents obtain the best translators, but authors often do not offer to share their royalties with translators (1970:32). H. W. Tjalsma reports that much of his energy as a translator of Russian novels was dissipated by economic pressures—it is extremely difficult to insist on fair fees when others will do the job for less money. One of the best translators of Russian literature, Mirra Ginsburg, had to give up translating and turn to children's books to make a living. A Moscow translator told one American translator that she could live comfortably for a year on the fees paid for a translation of a medium-length novel; he, on the other hand, would have to translate as many as ten novels per year to make ends meet.

Soviet translators are convinced that crass commercialism and hasty deadlines are the sole defining factor of translation in America. The belief was established by Kornei Chukovsky in *A High Art* (1984:234–35) and therefore remains an indisputable conviction in the Soviet school today. But American commercial conditions have never been as bad as the Soviets believe, and certainly they are far better now than ever. PEN American Center passed a strong resolution and issued a "Manifesto on Translation" at its Conference on Literary Translation in 1970 calling for contractual arrangements whereby the translator "shall enjoy a *continuing* share in all earnings of his work" and shall be given the copyright, together with a voice in the future disposition of the work (*World of Translation*, 376–84). Just how effective this resolution has been is not clear.

There are other, more important common concerns, regarding standards, that ought to be examined here. Indicative are some Soviet complaints that American translators will recognize as their own. A frequent complaint is that too many hacks still find a way into print. The poet-translator A. Gitovich once complained about what he called a surfeit of dilettantes in the Soviet school, a group of translators he divided into two categories—amateurs and professionals. The amateurs are attracted to the profession because they happen to know a foreign language and desire literary fame, which they hope to achieve by what seems to them the easiest path. Their standards are stated in their belief that they are in no way less talented than some translators who are published, and this claim is often substantiated. As for the professionals, Gitovich testifies that he knows of a group of Sinologists who hired an interlinearist to do their dictionary and research work (1970:369).

Evgenya Kalashnikova, translator of Hemingway, Steinbeck, and Dickens, has also been critical of the Soviet school in this respect. At a conference of the International Federation of Translators she testified that the high demand for translations resulted in low standards, at least in the earlier days of the Soviet school: "There were not enough translators of real literary talent and sufficient philological grounding; people recruited by chance, often totally devoid of talent and lacking knowledge, were drawn into the business. Their translations were no more than hackwork—concoctions of sheer ineptitude and elementary ignorance." Kalashnikova went so far as to say that this pressing need for translations was a chief reason for the rise of the literalist and scientific translations of the 1930s; it was hoped that easily applicable rules of translation would facilitate the mass production of accurate translations on demand (1966:11). The use of the interlinear (*podstrochnik*) or informant translation persists to this day because the demand is so great and the supply of rare-language translators is so small.

How well do American and Soviet translators protect their profession from hacks? To ask this question is to raise the question not only of defense of standards but also of the integrity of foreign authors. How well do Russian and American translators defend each other's literature? As it happens, both worlds provide examples of bad translations that were apprehended by standards-conscious critics, and they seem to have arrived at essentially the same language-oriented methods of analysis. The best-known defenses in the Soviet school are found in Chukovsky's *A High Art*. These include sharp attacks on a certain Fedotov's embarrassingly poor translations of the poetry of Robert Burns, on an extreme literal translation of Dickens's *Oliver Twist* by Evgeny Lann and A. V. Krivtsova, and on equally extreme scientific (direct form for form) translations of Shelley by V. D. Merkureva, Shakespeare by Anna Radlova, and Shakespeare's *Hamlet* by Mikhail Lozinsky. E. G. Etkind's *Poetry and Translation* (1963) contains many critiques of bad Russian translations of French poetry, and Marya Lorie's exposé in 1970 of a poor Russian translation of Joseph Heller's *Catch 22* is particularly well known.

In the Anglo-American Slavic field we have many outraged reviews in 1964 of Vladimir Nabokov's literalist translation of *Eugene Onegin*, the criticism in 1956–1957 of Max Hayward's rushed version of Pasternak's novel *Doctor Zhivago*, and the indignant reaction in the mid-1960s to Robert Lowell's free imitations of poems by Anna Akhmatova and Osip Mandelstam. We also have three thorough defenses of badly treated Russian authors—a review of five translations of Gogol's *Dead Souls* by Carl R. Proffer (1964), a critique by Munir Sendich of a translation of the first volume of Konstantin Paustovsky's *The Story of a Life* (1971), and an evaluation of translations of Alexander Solzhenitsyn's *One Day in the Life of Ivan Denisovich* by Alexis Klimoff (1973). The English-speaking world was startled a few years ago by Simon Karlinsky's exposé in 1982 of D. M. Thomas's unacknowledged use—in many instances word for word—of published crib translations in *The Bronze Horseman: Selected Poems of Alexander Pushkin* (1982) and by Michael Heim's discovery of still other unacknowledged "borrowings" in the collection (1982; see also Thomas 1982).

We can here usefully compare two of these critiques, Marya Lorie's defense of Heller and Proffer's defense of Gogol. Joseph Heller's novel *Catch 22* was first published in 1961; the Russian translation was published in an abridged version by the Military Publishing House in 1967; Lorie's critique, entitled "Translators' Catch," was published in *Masterstvo perevoda* (*The craft of translation,* 1970). In Lorie's opinion the translation, done by two little-known translators, M. Vilensky and V. Titov, "reads well," the translators show professional ability, several parts of the novel are done very well, Heller's slang and jargon are conveyed effectively, and his "cruel humor" comes out very well in Russian. "But nevertheless the translation is bad, very bad." To begin with, the errors of sense and meaning throughout the translation are so abundant that they are typical, not incidental. The translators seem not to have realized that "to train soldiers" means "to instruct" them, not "to transport" them; a "lunatic" is not a *lunatik*, meaning sleepwalker; a "pineapple" is not a kind of "apple"; the English word "satin" is not equivalent to the Russian word *satin*, which means silk; a "supermarket" is not an "outdoor" market in America; and "a crooked trader in the Levant" is not a Lebanese. When Heller writes simply, "Yossarian thought he was dead," the translators embellish, "Hadn't he given his soul up to God?" (1970:334, 337, 343, 345–46).

According to Lorie, the translators continually misunderstand the meaning of simple English expressions. As a result, they create characters and situations that are not true to Heller. Where Heller says that the men of Yossarian's bomber group suffer a mysterious epidemic of diarrhea "on the one clear day (they could see the target)," Vilensky and Titov say that the men forced still another postponement "one fine day." Where in the original General P. P. Peckem "had nothing better to do while he schemed against General Dreedle," in the translation the general "could think of nothing better to do than scheme against General Dreedle." Where Heller's doctor says, "I used to get a big kick out of saving people's lives. Now I wonder what the hell's the point, since they all have to die anyway," Vilensky and Titov's doctor says, "You know, more than anything else I take joy in saving lives. And here's what's interesting to me about it: what the devil's the sense of treating them if they're going to die one way or another anyway?" By changing the tense and mistaking the word *wonder* for *interesting*, the translators change the doctor from an intelligent cynic into a sarcastic fool. The translators miss the point and the tense again when they change a question to a dying man, "Did you have a priest?" into "Do you have a priest (here)?" The question, which of course means, "Have you confessed yet?" becomes pointless in the translation. Where in the original someone thanks someone "crisply," in the translation it becomes "ardently"; "eyed him sharply" becomes "threw a mean look at him"; a simple remark such as "Oh well, what the hell" is taken literally to mean "we went to the devil in hell" (1970:339–44).

The translators persistently miss the literary allusions and parodies in Heller's novel. They do not realize that the beginning of chapter 24 is a paraphrase of well-known lines from Tennyson, they turn T. S. Eliot into Elliot and miss the point of a discussion of Eliot, they identify E. A. Robinson's poem "Miniver Cheever" as a verse tale. Even though they state in a note that certain lines are an almost word-for-word recitation of Shylock's monologue, it did not occur to them to use a Russian translation of *Merchant of Venice*, and their translation does not even sound like Shakespeare. They are unaware of Heller's many paraphrases of the Bible, so that when Heller says of Major Major: "He never once took the name of the Lord his God in vain, committed adultery or coveted his neighbor's ass. In fact, he loved his neighbor and never even bore false witness against him," they convey it as: "He never took the name of God in vain, did not commit adultery, loved his neighbor and never bore false witness against him." The commandment "Honor thy father and mother," is understood as "Respect your father and mother" (1970:350, 342, 340–41).

Worst of all, the translators drastically change Yossarian's character. Understandably, a Soviet military publishing house would be attracted to *Catch 22* because it develops the war into an international cartel where, among other things, the Germans contract with the Americans to bomb their own base. Equally understandable for a culture where Socialist Realism demands that heroes be positive and literary works optimistic, the character of Yossarian is certain to seem rather too eccentric, particularly since he is supposed to be fighting to destroy world fascism in an alliance with the Red Army. This is the view of Yossarian expressed in the introduction to the translation by the writer S. Mikhalkov, a Writer's Union apparatchik well known for his insistence on straightforward reproductions of a heroic, positive reality. According to Lorie, Mikhalkov disapproves of Heller's overly warm regard for his hero—and "proves in various ways that the hero is unworthy of such regard." In Mikhalkov's view, Heller has not properly understood Yossarian; consequently he is too kind to him.

The translation often has Heller reproving his hero—to the point that Yossarian is sometimes indistinguishable from the idiots who run the war. Where in the original Yossarian is consistently developed as a man who was once the best bombardier in his group but has since suffered an attack of sanity in a war managed by madmen, the translation turns him into a coward, thus radically changing the meaning of the novel. Where Heller says several times that Yossarian has "lost his nerve," the translators write that he "completely lost his courage," and wherever Heller says simply that he "was unnerved," the translators say that he "begged for mercy" and "his heart fell to his boots." Where Heller says that Yossarian was "in incipient panic," the translators say that he "saved his own skin" (1970:344). A meaning of *Catch 22* is that war—all war—is so grotesque that reason itself becomes the most irrational of all perceptions of reality. In Soviet terms, this can be said about some wars, particularly imperialist wars, but it cannot be said about the war against fascism, at least not in a Soviet novel and apparently not without modifications in an American novel translated into Russian.

The five translations of Gogol's *Dead Souls* reviewed by Proffer are by Bernard Gilbert Guerney (1948), Andrew R. MacAndrew (1961), Helen Michailoff (1964), David Magarshack (1961), and Constance Garnett (n.d.). On the basis of careful comparative analyses of the texts of the translations and the scholarly Russian edition of Gogol's novel, Proffer demonstrates that Guerney, while generally a careful translator, grafts castoffs and variants onto the canonical text of *Dead Souls* without credible textological justification. MacAndrew, whose version is the worst, fails to translate in full, mistranslates many parts, and translates many parts poorly. Michailoff translates in full, with only a few omissions and errors, and frequently with idiomatic liveliness. Magarshack is the most conscientious and careful translator, and the most accurate in substance if not always in style. Proffer believes that Garnett's translation has stood the test of time very well, even though here, as elsewhere, her translation does not account for differences in style among Russian writers. Proffer recommends the Magarshack translation as the best, noting that it is the most professional and faithful and the least plagued by omissions, liberties, or carelessness (1964:420–33).

Proffer criticizes Guerney not for being a poor translator of Gogol but rather for "unconscionable textual juggling." The structure of *Dead Souls* is awkward, or "shaky," and its failings in this respect cannot be amended. Nevertheless, Guerney selected passages and whole chapters from the six hundred pages of variants to the novel, and his intercalations are in many instances artificial, requiring changes and omissions in the text. In one instance he restores castoffs to the text of Gogol's "Tale of Captain Kopeykin," even though this part of the novel—the only part censored from the first editions and specifically requested by Gogol to be restored at a propitious time—is almost the only passage denoted complete and accurate by the author (1964:420–23).

In contrast to Guerney's sins of textology, MacAndrew's translation is careless and error-ridden. Proffer demonstrates, on the basis of four chapters chosen as a representative sample, that sentences and clauses are systematically abridged or omitted. Thus, one passage of fifty-six words has eighteen words omitted, while another passage of sixty-four Russian words is reduced to forty-three words in English. Where Gogol catalogs systematically throughout his oeuvre, MacAndrew often abbreviates. Thus, "among the three-branched candlesticks, flowers, candies, and bottles" becomes "among the three-branched candlesticks and the bottles." MacAndrew's version of *Dead Souls* includes such mistranslations as "but even more striking" for "incomparably more remarkable"; "was essential" for "(it) was most sacred"; "as it was called in the town" for "to use the expression of local society"; "deterioration" for "unpleasantness"; and "doors" for "cheeks." Among the poor choices, which Proffer characterized as "dull and spiritless," the pungent expression *pliunesh'* 'spit on it,' in the sense of "to hell with it," or "forget it," is conveyed turgidly as "in the end you get tired of the whole business." *Drugoe zapoesh'*, 'you'd sing out something else again' or 'you'd soon sing a new tune,' is given as "you'd talk differently." Proffer concludes his analysis saying, "I can think of no surer way of ruining Gogol' for those who are reading him for the first time than to recommend such a clumsy, careless, uninspired translation as this" (423–25).

There are differences, there are similarities. Ideas about translation are converging; making a living is a constant consideration regardless of economic system; translators can be fierce defenders of their chosen foreign literatures. Whatever the different conditions of two different worlds, it is clear that they are converging at important critical and theoretical points and that they share common interests. The point should be made again, however, that the official, national status accorded the Soviet school sharply separates it from translation groups in other cultures and lends Soviet translators powers not available to others. Not the least of these powers is that the Soviet school's centralized organization gives its members a stronger, more effective voice to articulate its concerns. This can be seen in the Soviet school's better control of the market and, more important, in regard to defense of standards. It is one thing for critics to defend standards, and still another to gain the attention needed to give force to a defense of standards.

Nabokov's reputation brought widespread attention to problems of translating Pushkin's *Eugene Onegin*, and the D. M. Thomas scandal caused an uproar too, but these are virtually the only times in recent American letters that literary translation became a subject of international debate. The translators of the Soviet school, on the other hand, speaking from a national platform, are attended by the mass media not only in Russian, but in scores of other languages of the Union. This makes Soviet translation critics more effective than their counterparts elsewhere, where translation criticism is published in specialized language journals or limited-circulation journals of translation.

This is especially true of critiques of translations of Russian literature, which, like Proffer's critique of translations of Gogol, appear in small professional journals that are not read by major literary critics. Reviewers for mass-circulation outlets such as the *New York Review of Books,* the *New York Times Book Review*, and the *Times Literary Supplement* comment in general terms on the quality of translations, but they seldom take advantage of the reliable—the stylistic—analyses available to them, in specialized journals, and they do not apply the language-oriented critical method so useful to Lorie's and Proffer's defenses of standards. Stated simply, mainstream American letters remain complacently monolingual because translators and other language specialists have not won a voice to express concerns for standards. Russian apples should not be compared to American oranges here. Soviet translators are heeded by an information-starved public; American translators are among many who are trying to gain the attention of their information-saturated compatriots. There is even a certain irony in the fact that Soviet intellectuals, to whom glasnost is now offering so many books, still believe, as they often naively say nowadays, that "we'll read them later." But the fact remains that no matter how strong their defenses of standards, American translators do not yet exert strong critical influence. We do not want a national school, we do not need a monopoly. But we do envy what might well be the most favorable advantage of Soviet translators.

3

TRANSLATION AND POLITICS

One disadvantage of the formation of a national school is that it requires conformity. Demands for conformity are often accompanied by politicization. A noteworthy source of pride in what Soviet translators call artistic translation is its definition in terms of artistic process. Art is not always the dominant factor, however, because there have been many advocates of ideological considerations in the Soviet school. For every Kornei Chukovsky and E. G. Etkind whose works are short on ideological slogans, there are many other translators for whom political implications are essential. Political factors are central to an understanding of the Soviet school of translation, all the more so because some members have insisted that translation be considered a political, as well as an artistic, act.

"It has been known for a long time, incidentally, that the translator's work has its purely political aspect too," the Armenian critic Levon Mkrtchian said. He continues, "The translator always takes part in the socio-political life of the country. In the modern world a translation can even be a powerful factor on behalf of progress, and a weapon in the struggle for progress. Through their work Soviet translators of artistic literature bring cultures and peoples closer together by facilitating their mutual understanding and progress" (1970:44, 45). "Translation, like any other inspired work, is the highest joy of labor," the poet A. Gitovich has said. "[T]he translator who transforms a poet of another language and another country into a poet of his own language and his own country, performs a Communist feat—and the name of Lenin will shine ever upon him" (1970:367–68). Elsewhere, V. M. Rossels has pointed out that

in the USSR the liquidation of the exploiting classes, whose interests lie in the enflaming of hostilities between peoples, and the destruction of the real inequities of nations in economy and culture, have secured conditions for the dawn of a culture that is national in form and Socialist in content. The Soviet state, guided by the Communist Party, is developing and strengthening all that is progressive in the national culture of the Socialist nations, everything that facilitates their movement forward to Communism.

Rossels here alludes to the Socialist Realist formula "national in form and socialist in content," and he adds that all Soviet translators are called on to struggle against bourgeois nationalism. Soviet translators must always be vigilant, they must not be blinded by the apparent charms of a literary work and thus fail to realize that they might be introducing into their language "all the reactionary essence of a work." In Rossels's opinion, the translator must never forget "his duty to the nationalities policy" or fail to remember that "his every mistake . . . can become a political mistake" (1955:165–67).

Such political statements are usually made in reference to the nationalities policy. It is clear that warnings not to convey "reactionary essences" cannot comfortably coexist with assertions that a translation must faithfully recreate a work in its entirety. While it is true that the nationalities policy has seen such positive developments as the spread of literacy and the preservation of national cultures, the policy has not been entirely positive. Those translators who give it such positive political emphasis have had to overlook less pleasant implications of their declarations.

In the Soviet school, as commonly in Soviet literature, political demands are enforced in the process of selecting and editing literary works, and by censorship. Official censorship has perceptibly influenced the conveyance of foreign literatures into Russian and other Soviet cultures, but the censor is more than an official person or office. One bit of Soviet lore has it that a Moscow writer discovered this when he went looking for the censor one day. Only after a long search did he find a small office near the Metropole Hotel in downtown Moscow. No one was there. A great deal has been written about censorship in the Soviet Union, but the Leningrad writer David Dar needed only a few words to make one of the truest statements: "I know perfectly well, with professional exactitude, what I can and cannot, at any given moment, say in print. The censor is right here in my little head."

The process of censorship in Soviet literature is more elaborate than the writer's conditioned reflexes. There are committees at the Union of Soviet Writers; there are sessions of criticism and self-criticism; there are editors and whole editorial boards; there are methods of selection, revision, and approval of texts. Writers work closely with editors and publishers to negotiate what each interested party thinks can and should, or cannot and should not, be put into print. The negotiations are more often collaboration than confrontation. Russian Soviet translators justify this mode of operation with a formula: *Vse pomogaet* (Every little bit helps). That is, it is better to get Vonnegut, for example, into Russian print minus a few politically sensitive statements than to bar him completely from Russian letters. Everyone knows what will give cause for regret; like-minded professionals sit down together to decide what is to be done: Might this word go better than that word? We know from many testimonies by Soviet intellectuals that censorship is agony. But in the end the process of censorship is indeed simple: it begins with the censor in the writer's head and ends with a cursory stamp of approval in a small Moscow office.

The State Committee on Censorship—known as Glavlit—is also vigilant. Proof of this, as well as a remarkable insider's view of the workings of Soviet publishing, has been provided by E. G. Etkind in an account of the events that led to his eventual departure from the Soviet Union entitled *Notes of a Non-Conspirator* (1978). In his introduction to the two-volume collection *Mastera russkogo stikhotvornogo perevoda* (Masters of Russian verse translation, 1968), Etkind made this statement: "During a certain period, particularly between the 19th and 20th [Party] Congresses, Russian poets were deprived of the possibility of expressing themselves to the full in original writing and spoke to the reader in the language of Goethe, Orbeliani, Shakespeare, and Hugo. Whatever the reason, the 30s, the 40s and the 50s were fabulously productive for the development of verse translation in the USSR" (1978:158). The statement seems casual, but in an ideologically sensitive society it means that Russian poets, unable or afraid to speak unpopular truths during the Stalinist period, looked to foreign poets to express their own thoughts and beliefs. It means that a whole generation of Soviet poets turned to translation as a "safe" art, a way to express dangerous ideas in perilous times and to survive the terrors of Stalinism.

Etkind's statement is not casual, but neither is it in any way radical. Had he said this a few years before, he probably would have been officially praised. If he were to exercise such caution under present conditions of glasnost, he would be considered a fuddy-duddy. But his words were written for publication in 1968, and, because of two short sentences, an entire printing of twenty-five thousand copies of two volumes was rebound; three members of the editorial staff of Poet's Library, which publishes a prestigious series of scholarly editions of Russian poets, were immediately fired; Vladimir Orlov, the Editor-in Chief whose longtime direction of Poet's Library resulted in superb scholarly editions, was soon forced to retire; those held responsible were asked to publicly recant; Etkind was called to a *prorabotka*, a public criticism and rebuke, by his colleagues at the Herzen Institute in Leningrad and was subjected to a series of humiliations and public accountings, including dismissal from his faculty until he emigrated in 1974 (Etkind 1978:112, 129–30, 145–46).

Etkind calls translation a "safe art" to convey the irony that the Soviet school thrived because poets turned to translation of foreign authors to express what they themselves did not dare say in the Stalin period (1978: 146). The Soviet school has indeed been fortunate in both the number and the greatness of the poets who belonged to it, and there is something sad in the fact that an artistic plus was obtained from an ideological minus. Translation became a haven, a place to continue active literary life without incurring the risks of expressing thoughts that could be considered political subversion. It is difficult for outside viewers of Soviet society to comprehend this kind of rigidity, but in his address at the Library of Congress Allen Tate expressed both understanding and sympathy for the dilemma of Soviet poets when he commented:

> One's impression of our contemporary Russian poets is that of a daily struggle for the privilege of writing poetry at all. The hourly existential impact of a closed political system must necessarily make that impact itself the subject of the poem; or the poem would at least have to glance at it, or perhaps be a political counter-offensive against a hostile system. It is a situation that is not unique in Russia. Its permutations are visible in many other superficially different societies (1972:2).

Presumably, a literary work in translation is as "subversive" as its original. Shakespeare, Goethe, Orbeliani, and Hugo ought to be as severe a threat to authority in Russian as they are in their own languages. Yet these and other "dangerous" foreign writers are eminently acceptable in the Soviet Union. The same political leaders who consider translation a key to their nationalities policy and a door to the world, and are thus presumably appreciative of the ideological perils of literary translation, have been indifferent to and at times even oblivious to works in translation that would have enraged them had they been written by a Soviet author. Like bureaucrats everywhere, Soviet authorities can be complacently monolingual: what is said in another language does not exist, and even when it is translated it may not be deemed important.

While foreign works are carefully chosen and sometimes modified for domestic needs—foreign writers such as Gide, Sartre, and Robert Penn Warren have quickly become nonpersons when they have presumed to say something unpleasant about the Soviet Union—translators have been less efficiently subjected to ideological controls than original writers. Sometimes Soviet authorities have paid no attention to translation at all.

This is not to say that political factors are clear and simple in the Russian world. There are many contradictions between what is supposed to happen and what actually happens. Even before glasnost, philosophical ideas contrary to Marxism-Leninism appeared in print more often than is generally assumed. Controversial matters were discussed more openly and seriously than is realized. Free speech was more carefully controlled in the Soviet Union than might elsewhere be considered healthy, but those who think that criticism was not permitted before glasnost are mistaken, and those who assume the country is ruled without concern for public consensus misunderstand how the Soviet system works. Indeed, the use of public opinion to force conformity has proved to be as effective in Soviet society as in any other. Special interest groups have been extremely powerful, and even public interest groups have been allowed to exist. Religious materials have never been encouraged in the Soviet Union, but they have been found and, sometimes, under prescribed conditions, permitted.

Soviet authorities have acquired a deserved reputation for sexual prudery, and the censor has been especially vigilant here. But translations show that censorship is not always effective: ripe expressions sometimes get by while innocuous bits and pieces are excised, so that there seems to be no rhyme or reason to the censor's standards in this area. It makes no sense, for example, that in the Russian translation of Gore Vidal's *Burr* the men who have hired Charlie Schuyler to spy on Burr are allowed to say they "are not interested in a retired whore's marriage to a traitor," but that the censors have not allowed Charlie to imagine "all that aged flesh commingled" when an elderly Burr takes his elderly bride to "the hymeneal couch." When it comes to politics, therefore, it should not be assumed that the course of human events is more direct and symmetrical in the Soviet Union than elsewhere.

Etkind suggested this unpredictability in his *Notes of a Non-Conspirator*, and he suggested also that totalistic views of the Soviet Union are unjust: "In the West one quite often encounters a complete denial of all that the intelligentsia of the Soviet Union has lived by for nearly sixty years—all its literary achievements and all those aspirations which are clearly not dissident in character." Etkind does not deny the importance of the dissident movement in the Soviet Union, but he does insist that there is more to Soviet reality than counterideological negatives. The totalistic view of his country's intellectual life "is an oversimplified and thus a distorted view of reality and it leads to false conclusions and logical blind alleys. Russian culture has made a road for itself, overcoming the obstacles set in its way by those whose aim is to muzzle thought, destroy poetry, and stifle theatre, music, and painting. I will go further: in its struggle for the right to live and breathe this culture has gained strength" (1978:1).

Politics is unavoidable in dealing with the Soviet Union. The subject of political censorship has been well reported by Maurice Friedberg (1977) and Carl Proffer, among others. One of Proffer's findings is that ideological advocacy in the Soviet school has caused foreign works to appear in Soviet letters in a strange sequence. In his introduction to his anthology *Soviet Criticism of American Literature in the Sixties*, Proffer has pointed out that it was not until the 1960s that Soviet translators began to catch up with many foreign works judged unacceptable in the Stalin period. Melville's *Moby Dick* arrived with Robert Penn Warren, Tennessee Williams, Norman Mailer, Carson McCullers, and James Baldwin in the early 1960s; Jane Austen appeared along with Kafka, Rilke, Camus, and Eliot; Hemingway's "anti-Soviet" *For Whom the Bell Tolls* was suppressed until the 1960s (Proffer 1972:ix-xxxiii).

It continues to be difficult to obtain foreign literature. Grace Metalious's *Peyton Place* was commissioned for translation but not published when the publisher read in his own language what it contained, and prior to glasnost only one minor piece by Vladimir Nabokov was published in the Soviet Union. Russians still have trouble finding foreign books in bookstores, and availability of foreign periodicals and literary publications is limited. The only factor that seems to remain constant is that literature, especially American literature, is revered in the Russian world. Sooner or later determined Soviet citizens manage to read what they want to read. Indeed, the lengths to which Soviet readers go in order to obtain proscribed foreign and domestic works are sometimes amazing. One admirer of Edward Albee, after numerous failures to obtain a copy of *Zoo Story*, managed to assemble almost the entire text of the play by collecting quotations from reviews in Russian and Western language sources. Since Soviet libraries classify access to Western sources by an "outer-catalog" and "inner-catalog" system, it should be noted that assembling Albee's play involved not only cutting and pasting but also rigging access to official documents.

Libraries are not the only critical point where flow of information is controlled—and disrupted. In an introduction to a recent collection of Soviet stories in translation, Proffer disclosed that "new books are monitored with special care, but older books—the entire realm of second-hand sales—are also subject to controls so strict they are hard to imagine." The key to controlling book distribution in the Soviet Union is the "Consolidated List of Books Subject to Exclusion from Libraries and Retail Stores," which establishes a system of categories for circulation or noncirculation of books. These categories include, for example, "Secret," "Not to be circulated," "For CPSU members only," and "Distribution by list" (1984:xxx). Given the pragmatic (as opposed to moral) imperative of free flow of information, which communication theory holds as a necessity for the orderly working of a complex, modern, computer-age society, it is easy to perceive the Soviet need for the new policies known as glasnost and perestroika.

Soviet motivations are not always political. Americans do not understand the high regard for Poe in Paris or why the Russians ignore Wordsworth while adoring Byron, but these are matters of national taste, not politics. An examination of Valentina Libman's bibliography of American literary works and criticism in Russian between 1776 and 1976 indicates that not all choices are politically motivated. It is understandable that James T. Farrell suddenly vanished from Soviet attention after 1945 because it was at that time he was denounced by Nelson Algren and other members of the American Communist Party. It is generally known that the liberal writer Mary McCarthy is ignored in Soviet letters because of her notorious feud with Lilian Hellman, whose influence in Moscow was immense (the chief instruments of this expression of disfavor were Miss Hellman's close friends Lev Kopelev and Raissa Orlova). But it would be difficult to find any credible political explanation for Soviet readers' preference of Vonnegut over, to name a few writers underrepresented in Libman's bibliography, Bernard Malamud, Edward Albee, and William Styron. Explicit sexuality can account for official dislike of William Burroughs, Henry Miller, John Updike, and Norman Mailer. Jack Kerouac's lifestyle made him undesirable to Soviet authorities. But why was *Gone with the Wind* left untranslated for so long and its great popularity in America mentioned only once in 1937? And given the attention paid to American black writers—there are almost as many entries for Richard Wright as for Twain and Hemingway—why has James Baldwin been given such scant treatment? It could be argued that Arthur Miller, Gore Vidal, Truman Capote, and Kurt Vonnegut are popular among Soviet readers because of their relations with Soviet intellectuals or their interest in Russian literature. But this popularity has to do with public relations and with the fact that such attention from abroad is flattering. Many reasons could be found for cases of neglect—Baldwin's homosexuality, for example, or Warren's defense of Solzhenitsyn—but how do these square with Vidal's and Capote's acceptability or the lack of retaliation against Vonnegut when he defended Solzhenitsyn? Only a rigidly political viewer would find political reasons for every case.

To what degree do foreign literary works appear uncensored and unabridged in the Russian world, and, more important, in what ways and for what reasons are texts modified in the process of translation? This question can be explored by examining a Russian translation known to have been significantly affected by political considerations. This is the translation done by two lesser known translators, M. Bruk and A. Fayngar, of Gore Vidal's novel *Burr*, first published in four serialized parts in *Inostrannaja literatura* (*Foreign Literature*) in 1977.

Vidal's controversial historical novel, the first book in a trilogy that continues with *1876* and *Washington, D.C.*, deals with the American revolution. The appearance of this translation of *Burr* was viewed by many Soviet intellectuals as an event of political and moral significance, and it caused a stir for two reasons. First, Vidal's sour view of the American founding fathers seems unusual in Russia, where the revolutionary birth of a nation is supposed to be treated respectfully; and, second, the protagonist Burr's worldly view of a political system based from the very start on pragmatic self-interest was believed by Soviet readers to be as pertinent to Watergate as it had seemed to Americans when they read the novel three years earlier at the height of the scandal.

An article in *Inostrannaia literatura* by N. Yakovlev, the leading historian of the American Revolution, and an interview with Vidal in the same issue coincided with the publication of the transaltion of *Burr*. Both the article and the interview present Vidal to Soviet readers as an anti-establishment, New Left, revisionist historian. (In Soviet terms this means that he is a liberal who means well but lacks the scientific knowledge to be a revolutionary.) Both assume that Watergate was Vidal's reason for writing the novel and stress Vidal's wisdom in realizing that Richard Nixon's corruption was inherent to the American system—even though Vidal makes no such claim. Vidal's suggestion that the timely appearance of *Burr* was a coincidence is dismissed (Yakovlev 1977; E. S. 1977).

Soviet authorities might be expected to welcome *Burr* as an exposé of the American political system. Vidal's novel stresses the intimate links between personal ideals and economic self-interest that characterize much of American political history. Vidal has never been accused of lacking sarcasm, and his character Aaron Burr is a master of savage portrayals of his fellow founders. In his view, Alexander Hamilton and Thomas Jefferson are hypocrites. About his enemy Hamilton, Burr says that he "realized better than anyone that the world—our American world at least—loves a canting hypocrite." About his primary enemy Jefferson, he says, "I do remember hearing someone comment that since Mr. Jefferson had seen fit to pledge so eloquently our lives to the cause of independence, he might at least join us in the army. . . . Proclaiming the inalienable rights of man for everyone (excepting slaves, Indians, women, and those entirely without property), Jefferson tried to seize Florida by force, dreamed of a conquest of Cuba, and after his illegal purchase of Louisiana set a military governor to rule New Orleans against the will of its inhabitants." Burr also views Jefferson as a dangerous and sinister madman. Burr tells young Charlie Schuyler and writes in his diary, "Presently I shall deal with the Jefferson who brought me to trial for treason, who fabricated evidence, who threatened witnesses, all on the ground that we could not have won the revolution 'if we had bound our hands by the manacles of the law. . . .' Startling to think that Hamilton thought of me as an 'embryo-Caesar' at a time when Jefferson was that Caesar, born full-grown and regnant."

Burr maligns not only his opponents but also the sacrosanct Washington. His Washington is a hypocrite, a masterful self-propagandist, an incompetent general, and a pompous fool. "Washington's mistakes were always proclaimed with a sort of finality that made one feel any criticism was to deface a tablet newly brought down from Sinai," Burr says. Washington's military genius was that he was always able "to snatch defeat from the jaws of victory," and, although Burr sees him as an excellent politician, he jeers that Washington mismanaged the war "in his own mysterious way." Even while crediting Washington with brilliantly launching Presidency, Union, and Constitution, Burr cannot help adding, "Since General Washington could sire nothing in the flesh, it is fitting that he be given credit for having conceived this union. A mule stallion, as it were, whose unnatural progeny are these states. So at the end, not to the swift but to the infertile went the race."

Not even the American people are spared in this novel. In one instance Burr states, "Before Genêt's arrival . . . Americans were considered the politest people in the world—resembling the British but with greater sweetness and less servility. After Genêt they became what they are today—truculent, sullen and envious."

And yet, however useful *Burr* might seem in terms of Soviet propaganda, there is a discernible tendency in the translation to downplay and even to delete many negative political remarks. Analysis of the text of the translation reveals a distinct pattern of deletion of statements that might appeal to ideologues. For example, where Soviet authorities might be expected to appreciate references to slavery and racism in America, Burr's statement regarding the Santo Domingo uprising, that "no one knows how many thousands of Negroes were executed that year by the frightened Virginians," is omitted from the translation. Where Burr says, "There was something in Jefferson's manner that *held* me as no other man was ever able to do," the translators omit the remark that follows: "I never failed to respond to that hushed voice, to those bright child's eyes, to his every fanatical notion, to his very rich slander. He was a kind of wizard. No doubt about it." The translation thus weakens a key intrigue of the novel—Jefferson's deception of Burr and eventual ruin of him not just as a political opponent but also as a human being.

The translators—or the editors, publishers, censors—allow the interpretation of Jefferson as a hypocrital political intriguer but not as a sinister madman. "Either Jefferson was a fool in his zealotry or an active principle of evil," "Jefferson's high-minded platitudes and cloudy political theorizings"—any of Burr's remarks that characterize Jefferson as evil or mentally deranged are expunged from the translation. So are Burr's meanest characterizations of Jefferson. "It was a curious sensation to look about Monticello and see everywhere so many replicas of Jefferson and his father-in-law," Burr says in both the original and the translation. But in the translation he is not permitted to go on: "It was as if we had all of us been transformed into dogs, and as a single male dog can re-create in his own image an entire canine community, so Jefferson and his family had grafted their powerful strain upon these slave Africans, and like a king dog (or the sultan at the Grande Porte) Jefferson could now look about him and see everywhere near-perfect consanguinity."

Clearly, then, the Russian translation of Gore Vidal's *Burr* does not meet expectations about what Soviet authorities are likely to appreciate, politically, in recent American writing. It is not unreasonable to assume that the novel was officially acceptable for the same reasons that might offend an ideological American, but we do not know this to be the case. All that can be assumed with any certainty is that the parallels with Watergate were as topically important to Soviet readers as they were to Americans. It certainly did not harm Soviet power if Vidal's Russian readers concluded that the Watergate scandal was a logical outcome of American history. This does not explain the tendency to moderate the political sharpness of *Burr*, however, and one must therefore speculate political motivations in other directions.

It might be that modifications of the text were motivated not by immediate political or propaganda advantages but by tradition, namely, the traditional Russian respect for authority. Regardless of who made the changes —translators, editor, or censor—there was somewhere along the line a sense that one simply does not treat authority in this way. One does not liken Jefferson and his father-in-law to king dogs; nor does one suggest that George Washington was a military idiot. Jefferson may be presented as a canting schemer, but the idea of a man of power being mad, and in such a disturbing way, is not acceptable. There is virtue in an American novel that debunks American myths, but such treatment of history, legend, tradition—those values from which authority derives legitimacy—should not be overdone. After all, if Gore Vidal is capable of saying such things about American authority, might he also not be saying them about *all* authority? Thus, whatever the political motivations for selecting, translating, and publishing *Burr*, it could very well be that the reasons for moderating it have to do with feelings of national propriety rather than with politics and ideology.

But this is speculation. We do not know the reasons for moderating *Burr*. A political pattern to the editing of the novel can be seen, but the motivations behind the pattern are unclear. Indeed, despite all the available data on Soviet censorship and selection, almost nothing is known about what goes on in the committee rooms at Glavlit and even less about the actual—the human —factors of the selection process. Quite often, émigrés are able to tell a great deal about inner workings, and in recent times Soviet visitors to the United States have been unprecedentedly candid in response to controversial questions. In most instances, however, Soviet citizens themselves do not know how the inner system works. In other instances, actions belie words. Semyon Lipkin was quoted in the first chapter of this study as an example of translator as propagandist; yet Lipkin later contributed to the literary almanac *Metropole*, whose unauthorized publication led to a harsh official reaction against which he helped lead a brave and, from the point of view of Soviet ideology, unpatriotic protest. Human activities are as contradictory in the Russian world as elsewhere, and the complexities of selection, editing, censorship, and calls for political vigilance are not always predictable.

The Lithuanian poet Tomas Venclova, now in the United States, tried to make this comprehensible in an essay on Soviet censorship in the *New York Review of Books*. In his view, total censorship and complete absence of censorship are inconceivable in any social system. The censor, after all, is human—he must nap occasionally and he is not omniscient. "One can compose something so subtle it will go right over his head." He might even be himself dissatisfied and spiteful enough to overlook what he knows is unacceptable. And beyond this, "the mechanism of totalitarian censorship is so multi-leveled and complex that like any overcomplicated machine it breaks down frequently. One part of the mechanism might fight or compete with another." Standard procedures often change and often contradict one another. "Much depends on the dictator's taste and mood. . . . Objectionable content can squeeze thorugh meaningful pauses, empty spaces."

And then there is the Russian tradition of Aesopic language about which, as Venclova points out, Kornei Chukovsky wrote a good deal (and practiced) in *A High Art* and other works. Aesopic language is indirect, covert expression of proscribed matters. As Venclova notes, a Soviet writer might lambast the Chinese Cultural Revolution and hope that readers draw parallels with conditions closer to home. Metonymy, metaphor, association, breaking off the tale at the most interesting point and allowing the reader to provide an ending—such devices are powerful magic in any political system where authority and censorship are the norm. One can put positive ideas in the mouth of a negative character, "praise the secret police in an unbearably sickly tone, denounce religion to draw attention to spiritual values," vilify Joseph Brodsky and thereby remind readers that a great Russian poet is still alive and writing abroad. There are many games that one can play with the censor and with the state itself, Venclova concludes, and in the end one might be playing—and losing—just the game the censor and the state prescribe (1983). Anything can happen in the Soviet system, as in any system, and even an Etkind, a Venclova, or a Chukovsky cannot be fully secure about the rightness of their testimonies.

CRITICISM AND THEORY

4

CRITICISM IN THE TWO WORLDS

██████ "We speak and speak about language," Heidegger has said. "What we speak about language is always ahead of us. Our speaking merely follows language constantly. Thus we are continually lagging behind. . . . Accordingly, when we speak of language we remain entangled in a speaking that is persistently inadequate" (1971:75). Thinkng about language is like trying to think about thinking. Language and thought are not identical. "If language and thought were one and the same thing," Roger Roothaer has said, "we would be trapped in our own particular language" (1978:133). But language and thought are so close that their intimacy deceives us. Thought about language, George Steiner has said, is "this vaulting across one's shadow and attempt to examine the skin of one's shadow from within and without" (1975:117). Linguists, with their specialized method of thinking, know this. Language is always ahead of their writings, and their seeking merely follows. We can no more grasp language than we can look into our own eyes.

The real language barrier arises in thought about language, not between languages. We can be aware of language and build rules from our awareness, but we cannot penetrate the structural depths, except in glimpses. We are locked away from thought about language, and we do not even know whether thought about language is permitted, for when we think about it we cannot help but remember the biblical prohibitions about the sanctity of language. "The problem is this," Jean Paris has said: "Does not the transforming of a written work from one language to another utterly alter its character? And, in performing this metamorphosis, does not the translator commit, if not a sacrilege, at least an offense against art and spirit?" (1961:57).

This barrier inherent in language, as opposed to the barrier between languages, is one reason why the history of discussion of translation is marked by tedious repetition. Constant repetition of the same old ideas in the same old ways is also one reason why it has taken so long to arrive at the breakthroughs achieved by modern translation theories. In the 1970s, Steiner reviewed the history of translation in *After Babel*, and L. G. Kelly reviewed the history of thought about translation in *The True Interpreter*. The latter surely agrees with the former that "despite its rich history, and despite the calibre of those who have written about the art and theory of translation, the number of original, significant ideas in the subject remains very meagre. Over some two thousands years of argument and precept, the beliefs and disagreements voiced about the nature of translation have been almost the same" (1975:238–39). Kelly concurs, "Except for a continual fascination with the rights and wrongs of literal and free translation, this stream of theory has analysed aims and results without paying much attention to the linguistic operations involved." And he adds, not entirely facetiously, "Fortunately, good translation has never depended on adequate theory" (1979:2, 4). No wonder translators cannot agree on principles. "A statement of the principles of translation in succinct form is impossible," Theodore Savory noted two decades ago. "There are no universally accepted principles of translation" (1968:49). We arrange and rearrange our thoughts about translation; we analyze, evaluate, formulate. But our thoughts are seldom unprecedented; only our age-old fascination with the art continually renews itself.

The field of translation studies has begun to eliminate our linguistic inhibition; translation theorists have begun to provide better understanding of the process of translation. But there remains the basic difficulty of dealing with language, and troubles continue to plague the field. One trouble is that translators are a landlocked minority. Translators in the Romance languages do not speak clearly to translators in the Slavic or Germanic languages, and translators together speak only with generalized authority to those who have no foreign language at all. Nowhere is this inability to communicate more apparent than in American translation criticism. Perhaps this situation is inevitable in a monolingual culture: the few who know are overwhelmed by the complacency of the ignorant. Beyond the intensity of modern thought about language and the remarkable development of theory and criticism of translation lies the "it-reads-smoothly" school of popular criticism. Translators struggle against this type of criticism without making an impression, and so they remain an expert few who talk only to each other. "The only acknowledged judges of a particular translation must necessarily be drawn from the class who have no need of it," John Hollander has said. "As a result of this, translation-criticism gets to be a bandying about of *expertise* among producers, as it were, rather than among consumers" (1966:208).

Because they are landlocked by their expertise, when translators become critics they often succumb to the "Gotcha" criticism for which they themselves have little need. Speaking about translation criticism, Richard Howard has lamented, "My barber advises his bald customers, as I have learned, that there is only one thing they can do: resign themselves, and I counsel a similar stoicism without being very good at it myself. All translators, I suspect, are nervous wrecks unless they have bastioned themselves within the citadel of academic infallibility" (1961:164). This is one reason why translators are reluctant to venture into criticism and to discuss their ideas about what literary translation is. "The translator, if he is human, will deal with most problems as he meets them," Richard Lattimore has remarked. "His principles will come out later, by way of self-explanation, or self-defense" (1966:48). And so translators remain not only landlocked but also silent.

American letters do not possess generally accepted standards or principles for fairly and correctly assessing the quality of translations. Our letters have not developed methods of analysis for translation criticism, as they have for literary criticism. Monolingual critics discuss a foreign writer as if they had read the original. This was also the condition of Soviet criticism some three decades ago. Even in the 1960s, well after Soviet translators defined principles and terminology, they still had reason to complain about arbitrary criticism from unqualified literary specialists. The complaints of Soviet translators about the condition of translation criticism can be appreciated by other translators. Semyon Lipkin expressed the feelings of all translators when he protested,

> We would have been saved from many, quite many defects and shortcomings if our criticism concerned itself with translations. Unfortunately, our criticism offers our business very little attention, unpardonably little. Translators are usually criticized for this error or that, for "fleas," or praised for the absence of them. Extremely rarely does criticism attempt to analyze the work of a translator the way it analyzes the work of a writer . . . the translator's style, his artistic integrity, the novelty of his means of expression, his orientation to the world, his understanding of the original, his knowledge of life, the correctness of his choices. (1964:51)

American translators would surely agree with Nikolay Chukovsky's lament that

> literary critics write about the original author and are silent about the translator, without stopping to think that they can judge the author only if the translation is faithful and good. Because of an absence of criticism, our art of translation . . . is developing as if in the dark, and in the dark, as is well known, all cats are gray. Masters of artistic translation . . . work for years alongside hacks, ignoramuses, petty dealers, and no one says, here is a master, here is a hack who has with impunity ruined one book after another. Many publishers even prefer

hacks who are ready to translate anything indiscriminately and knock out any old work to meet a deadline. (1970:388–89)

Soviet translators used to deplore critics who discuss the original work instead of the translation, and who discuss the work as if they had read the original instead of the translation. The master-translator Marya Lorie once charged that she had read dozens of detailed studies of Hemingway's style, but had never "read a clearly expressed acknowledgement that the assessment was done on the basis of translations" (1959:98–99). When A. Leytes found that two-thirds of the poems featured in the 1953 *New World* were in translation, he noticed that "none of the reviewers . . . ever once mentioned one of the translations." In the early 1950s, critical attention was denied to poetry in translation even though the translations included "some which could and should have been discussed as interesting contributions to Russian Soviet poetry" (1955:100–101).

Looking back on his career from the 1920s through the 1950s, Ivan Kashkin deplored the lack of sound criticism based on careful analysis of texts. During his career there was no "professional criticism that together with the obligatory analysis of the original work could have offered an artistic analysis of the translation" Such criticism could have "influenced the general level of translation by helping the translator manifest his potential and by helping the reader evaluate not only the original author, but the translator" (1965:7). Soviet translators were particularly troubled by the naive kind of translation criticism that compares texts for errors, and even finds departures that seem to be errors to the uninitiated when they are in fact ingenious recreations. "Some reviewers who know the two languages . . . compare the translation with the original and ascertain, now this is a departure, now this is precise—and pass judgment," Lipkin complained. "Reviewers like this have no right to consider themselves critics of literature. . . . They believe, these reviewers, that the word, not the thought, is what should be translated" (1964:19). V. M. Rossels has reported the same condition.

The critic measures the text against its original, painstakingly copies out the lexical substitutions, syntactic departures, all kinds of translation compensations, pronounces them errors and declares: the translation is inaccurate. There is another type of criticism: the critic announces that the translation is smooth, there are no crude errors, and it is even similar to the original; however, the resemblance is superficial, the "spirit" of the original has not been conveyed. In both cases it is difficult to refute the assessment. Most often because neither reviewer has analyzed the aspects of the original work the translator concerned himself with. (1965:15; see Elsa Gress 1971:59 for a similar explanation of why translation criticism quibbles over details rather than evaluates poetic quality).

In the 1950s, Soviet translators faced essentially the same condition of criticism faced by American translators in the 1980s. They had a strong tradition of translation, they possessed well developed theory, and they were well versed in methods of analyzing translations. But they had not propagated their standards and principles among the reading public, and so they spoke only to one another. Complaints about incompetent critics have subsided. One reason for the greater happiness of translators is that they stopped surrendering to the arbitrary tastes of the majority and launched a campaign to teach critics, editors, publishers, and readers to appreciate literary translation. The results of this campaign are difficult to assess, but several statements hold up well as a summation of the present state of translation criticism in the Soviet world.

The duties and responsibilities of critics, editors, and publishers have been clearly defined and are now widely accepted. Translations are submitted to editors who are acknowledged master-translators and who work closely with translators; and Soviet translations are greatly improved through the editorial process before being printed. Soviet critics have been made aware of the difference between a translation and its original text, they no longer judge works as if they had read the original, and they devote attention to qualitative analysis of translations. Handbooks such as the definitive *Redaktor i perevod* (Editor and translation, 1965) have been compiled and made available to publishing houses and other literary enterprises. Thanks to Kashkin's insistence that translations must be faithful not only to the original but also to "the interests of the reader" (1959:106), criticism has moved from textual analysis to include evaluation regarding effect on the reader. The popularity of Kornei Chukovsky's *A High Art* has made Soviet readers aware of problems of translation and taught them to detect quality even though they might not know a foreign language. There are clear signs that bad translators are not tolerated a second time—the bad translations of works by Robert Burns and of Joseph Heller's *Catch–22* became a literary casus belli—and that good translators are rewarded with high acclaim. Soviet translators enjoy a prestige not known to translators in any other culture.

The Soviet campaign to educate the public in the realities of literary translation was launched on a broad front. When Soviet translators began their campaign, they recognized the need to bind criticism, theory, and practice into a single perception of translation as an art. The larger concern of the campaign was the reading public, but translators focused immediate attention on the intermediaries between translators and readers—critics and editors/publishers. The campaign was conducted by many translators working together, largely through the influential publication *Masterstvo perevoda*.

One of the most active campaigners was Ivan Kashkin, who has provided some of the best statements of the tasks and goals of both critics and editors. In a set of prescriptions for critics, Kashkin asserted,

> The task of professional criticism comprises helping the reader to ascertain how closely the translation corresponds to the original, and this can be done only by analyzing *how* the translation was done. It is useful to assess a book by the laws the author imposed on himself, but this has to be done twice for a translation. The critic must ascertain the laws the author imposed on himself, and set by him as his aim. But it is impossible not to take into consideration also the laws the translator imposed on himself and the goals he set.

In Kashkin's opinion, "only a sober calculation of pluses and minuses and a valid summation permit the pronouncement of any given assessment of a translation. If the false notes are incidental, this is a remediable matter— only consultation and editing are needed; but if the falsities accumulate to the point that they turn from a quantity to a quality, when 'no matter where you dig you turn up an example,' one may then cite the translation as a demonstration of typical, rather than incidental, errors." Translation criticism is more than a sum of pluses and minuses, however, for it requires attention not only to readily apparent errors at the surface level but also to the fine details of intonation. The task of the critic is not only to point out errors but also to show translators where they can improve their work and to ensure that the work achieves its full potential (1965:7–9).

Kashkin paid specific attention to the tasks of the translation critic. In another influential article he stated,

> Criticism has a role that is both specific and very responsible. . . . The critic must discover the task the author set himself . . . define how this task has been understood and implemented by the translator (elucidating at the same time the degree to which he has succeeded in this and in what measure the translation has become a fact of our literature, how it affects the contemporary reader and the larger modern tasks of literature as a whole) . . . and succeed in conveying his assessment to the reader.

Kashkin admitted that it is possible to argue about whether the translator has correctly identified and solved a task, "but the stylistic achievements and failures must once again be assessed in terms of the laws the translator has set for himself. One may also agree or not agree with the translator's choice of style, but it would be a mistake to apprehend and judge a translator of a romantic fairy tale in accordance with the canons of, say, naturalist poetics." In Kashkin's view, "with all due respect for the translator's individuality, the success of a translation depends on the degree to which he has conveyed the original." The translation critic is an intermediary: "The critic must help the translator express his creative personality with his assessment and . . . help the reader correctly apprehend the work not only of the author but of the translator" (1959:143, 149–50).

Kashkin was equally systematic in his prescriptions of the translation editor's tasks and duties. He was a firm believer in the legitimacy, and the absolute necessity, of an editor of translations, and his axiomatic assertion of this belief has been quoted many times:

> In olden times it was believed the world rested on three whales. In our days we say an airplane needs three wheels to land. The translator's trade has this triad too. We need three participants to produce a translation: the author of the original . . . then the translator, and finally the editor. Without the first there would be nothing to translate, without the second there would be no translation, and without the organizing work of the third the book would never see light.

He defined three tasks—"the comprehensive organization of both the creative and the production process of work on a book in translation, the comprehensive verification of the translation, and consultation with the translator." The editor must have the same skills and knowledge as the translator and "must perhaps know even more than the translator. In the first place, the language—or more precisely, both languages. This is axiomatic." Kashkin believed that publishers should keep foreign-language editors on staff, that editors should be competent in at least one foreign language, and that translations should be submitted to a competent house or free-lance editor. The editor, like the translator, "must be a practicing philologist, not simply a fixator of mechanical correspondences. He must know the history of the Russian language, the size and specific weight of Russian words. He must know Russian phraseology, which words are customarily conjoined and which are not commensurate with each other. . . . The editor must know the country, the literature, the author" (1959:130–32).

Marya Lorie, a translation editor known for the tactful diplomacy with which she persuades translators of collected works (Twain, Dickens) to accept her revisions of dissimilar texts into a single style, agrees with Kashkin that the editor must know both languages and both literatures, "everything touching on the question of *how* the book was written (as distinct from *what* is written in it)." The editor must work with the translator exactly as an editor works with an author, and the task of the editor is "to bring the translation as close to the original as is possible, help the translator faithfully convey a foreign-language work in its unity of form and content." The editor must ensure that the translator has not omitted anything from the text and has not invented anything. The editor must ensure that the meaning of the original has been conveyed faithfully and must watch for instances where the translator has not correctly understood the meaning of the original and where "the translator has correctly understood the author's meaning, but expressed it poorly in Russian." Regarding the latter shortcoming, the editor must ensure that the translator does not use un-Russian syntax, and thereby turn the natural language of the original into something strained and artificial. Lorie believes that the editor has no right to make changes: "Ideally, the editor must not touch a single word of the text himself, but only *point out* where the translator has in one way or another departed from fidelity to the original." The translator must be free to reject or to accept the editor's suggestions and corrections, and Lorie's work with other translators shows that the best solution to a given problem is found somewhere between the translator's first attempt and the editor's suggested variant. She recommends that the best way for an editor to begin working with a translation is initially to skip over the original and instead read the translation as it is in order to gain an idea of the translator's command of the language and to determine whether the conveyance is too literal and whether the work is marred by infelicities (1959:89–91, 94; see also Lorie's classic exposition of the process of her editing of Vera Toper's translation of Dickens's *Hard Times*, 1965:98–117).

American translators are not likely to appreciate the idea of the editor as a supervisory master-translator, however diplomatic the editor might be. As Donald Keene states,

> Collaboration is often suggested as an ideal solution to the problem of translating from obscure languages, but I can scarcely think of a successful example. What usually happens is that a strong-willed publisher imposes herself (or himself) on the gentle Oriental translator, and over his faint protests sets to work bringing out the exquisite charm of the original she believes she has instinctively detected. (1971:326)

Keene's experience is with publishers and editors who do not know the foreign language, however, and he has not experienced the professional relationship between translator and editor assumed by Kashkin and Lorie. Soviet translators certainly do not overlook the difficulties of collaboration. Lorie emphasizes three instances where cooperation between translator and editor is not possible: when the editor's view of the original author is not compatible with the translator's, when the translation is done by a method unacceptable to the editor, and "when the editor oppresses the translator by in fact replacing him and foists variants alien to the translator and while so doing is unable to justify his corrections." In the end, it is the editor who must be the diplomat—again, the relationship must be the same as between author and editor: "In one way or another the process of editing must be a *communication* between translator and editor" (1959:92, 91).

Rita Rayt, translator of Salinger and Vonnegut, believes that an editor is needed as a guide and teacher by inexperienced translators and as a constant guard by experienced translators, who are still prone to errors. An editor should be able to suggest imaginative and appropriate word equivalents, to point out inconsistencies, and to help move the translated text as a whole closer to the authentic style of the original. Above all, because translators become intensely involved in their work, an editor must be able to provide a fresh view of a translated text, and must know how to make translators see both the translated work and the original work anew (1965:6–7, 9, 19–21). There are excellent translation editors in the Soviet school of translation, and one of them, Nora Gal, states the editor's task emphatically: "The editor must not be a *dictator!*" (1972:159–60).

It is easy to criticize translators purely for the sake of being critical—the search for errors. Translators are vulnerable not only because of their diverse views of language and style, but also because of the unpleasant reality that a single slip—a howler or a boner, what Soviet translators call crabs (*kreb*) or fleas (*blokhi*)—can ruin a reputation won by many years of sensitive work. Translators complain about the deadlines imposed by profit-conscious publishers. Even the best established translators have difficulty resisting deadlines, for they are aware of the army of hacks waiting for the opportunity to join their names with great writers for a cheap fee. Nevertheless, translations do require criticism. As Lessing said long ago, "Bad translations . . . are below all criticism. Yet it is a good thing when criticism stoops down to them once in a while, for the damage they do is indescribable" (Lefevere 1977:28). Literate translation criticism can be accepted when it is reasonable, appreciated when it corrects, and challenged when it is wrong. Arbitrary criticism based on a tedious search for errors is as useless as the bland criticism of linguistically ignorant critics who praise shoddy work because it seems to "sound like the original."

Soviet translators have not eliminated arbitrary criticism, but in the course of their campaign they have managed to establish principles in defense of standards. The most frequently stated principle is that criticism must attend to the overall integrity of the translation, not just to incidental errors or poor choices of words. Lipkin speaks of choice of appropriate style and degree of quality as a more important criterion for criticism than the incessant search for fleas. Kashkin advises critics to distinguish between "incidental" errors which are easily corrected, and "typical" errors, which are beyond remedy. (He uses here the Marx-Engels formula of a quantity raised to the level of a quality.) *All* errors ought to be corrected, of course. But in agreement with Kashkin, Kornei Chukovsky reiterates throughout *A High Art* that only when the quantity of errors affects quality should critics point out poor artistic integrity.

Note also that Kashkin, Lipkin, and Nikolay Chukovsky, among other participants in the campaign, point to the importance of identifying the translator's criteria and method of translation. In Kashkin's words, "it is impossible not to take into consideration the laws the translator imposed on himself and set as his goals." A chief task of the campaign, therefore, was to educate critics about the methods or types of translation and about the merits or failings of these methods or types. This task was essential to the success of the campaign. It required that a variety of terms and concepts derived from theory be made coherent and therefore practical as critical tools.

Translation criticism is usually concerned with quality, translation theory with method or methodology and type or typology. Theorists discuss translation method or methodology in terms of process; they analyze result—text—as type or typology. Soviet theorists use the term artistic translation (*khudozhestvennyi perevod*) to describe both the method and the type of *faithful* translation that they believe has shaped their school and become its crowning achievement. The Soviet artistic translation is not sui generis; it was developed out of or in reaction to types or methods well known to translators. Among commonly described types or methods in both the Soviet school and the West are the mass-appeal or popular (*massovyi*) translation, which accomodates the prevailing tastes of the new culture, and the scholarly or academic (*akademicheskii*) translation typical of scholars and generally considered stilted, artificial, and inartistic. The formalist (*formal'nyi*) translation is defined as a method that places form and style above content, and the cultural or semantic (*semanticheskii*) translation is a method that aims at exchanging national values and thus places content over style and meaning over form. The literalist translation is generally despised for its dull accuracy and its avoidance of artistic good sense, and the free (*vol'nyi*) translation bordering on paraphrase is also unpopular. The scientific (*nauchnyi*) translation uses technical devices, even mathematical formulas, to ensure that the form of the translation is identical to the form of the original, while the linguistic (*lingvisticheskii*) translation uses grammar formulas to convey the structure of a work. Other commonly mentioned translation types or methods include the precise (*tochnyi*) or transcript method, called pejoratively the mechanical copy and used as a pedagogical aid (crib, trot, pony); the information (*informatsionnyi*) method, used appropriately for materials in the natural and social sciences; and the machine or computer method.

Soviet theorists describe essentially the same methods and types of translation, but classify them differently. Kashkin took an early lead in a national effort to establish terms and set a scale for the guidance of critics. He began by excluding from translation proper overly "free" methods, which he defined as periphrastic, expository, and variation, and overly literal methods, which he identified as conventional (outmoded) and mechanical copying of text. He grudgingly accepted a less literal method at one end of his scale, which he called academic, and a less libertarian method he called free. He divided "true" translation proper into reproductive, recreative, and reexpressive translation (1959:121). His types or methods are historical: the romantic urge to recreate reality, the realist demand that reality be reproduced as it actually is, and the modernist aesthetic of a reexpression of reality. "Reality" is his measure, and he made no secret of his preference for the reproduction of the reality contained in a literary work.

The history of translation is rich in methodology and typology. Neither Soviet nor any other translators have settled on a uniform system of classification, and terminology therefore remains diverse. Nevertheless, despite differences in systems of classification, it is clear that translation theorists understand methodology and typology similarly, and that they have worked similarly, albeit separately, toward a coherent system of gradations of kinds of translation process and text. Both the diversity of terms and the coherence of gradation theory, as well as their usefulness as critical tools, can be readily appreciated by examining some of these systems.

"A few of the many degrees on a scale of versions might be named here," Reuben Brower has said, "from the most exact rendering of vocabulary and idiom to freer yet responsible translation, to full imaginative remaking ('imitation') to versions where no particular original is continuously referred to, to allusion, continuous or sporadic, to radical translation, where a writer draws from a foreign writer or tradition the nucleus or donnee for a wholly independent work" (1974:2). "There are two principal approaches to the translation of poetry," M. Cohen has said: "the imitative and the recreative." The imitative translation is the faithful translation, the recreative translation is that verse genre which Dryden called the imitation (1970:29–30).

The three translation types explicated by Dryden constitute an established system of reference in English literature. According to Dryden's system, *metaphrase* is "the process of converting an author word by word, line by line"; *imitation* is when "the translator . . . assumes liberty not only to vary from the words and sense, but to forsake them both as he sees occasion"; and *paraphrase*, "the true road," is where the author's "words are not so strictly followed as his sense" (see Steiner 1975:254–56; Rexroth 1961:22). Equally influential in Germany has been the tripartite division of translation types devised by Novalis. In accordance with his system, "mythical translations . . . represent the pure, completed nature of the individual work of art. They do not give us the real work of art, but its ideal." Thus, Greek mythology is a translation of a religion; the Madonna is another mythical translation of a religion. Mythical translations make up cultural communication in the broadest sense. Grammatical translations are ordinary translations requiring "enormous erudition, but discursive abilities only." By this Novalis meant translations of nonliterary works that require accuracy and precision. Such translations are the opposite of transforming translations, which "require the highest poetic spirit, if they are to be authentic." They "easily lapse into mere travesties," but they are the best translations when they are faithful—that is, when the translator is an artist, when the translator is able to "render the idea of the whole," and when the translator can "speak both according to the poet's idea and to his own" (Lefevere 1977:64).

A profusion of terms is apparent here, but each of these attempts at gradation shows concern for process. Modern translation studies still yield different terms, but this is due more to different approaches to problems of translation than to contradictory perceptions—the concepts are understood, the terminology is multiple. There are signs that the systematic approaches of recent translation theorists have begun to standardize critical and theoretical terminology.

Leonard Forster has recommended a system of translation gradations based on three types of conveyance. When the syntactic unit of conveyance is the individual word, the translation tends toward the interlinear; when the unit is the sentence or phrase, the translation reveals concern for intelligibility and respect for style; when the unit is the work as a whole the translation borders on paraphrase (1958:2–5).

The issue here is gradation or spectrum theory. Western translators are not convinced that they have satisfactorily defined literary translation, but the profusion of terms characterizing translation criticism should not be taken as carelessness. Spectrum theory is an area in which modern translation theorists have surpassed the typology of Kashkin and other Soviet theorists. Western typologists and spectrum theorists seem to have settled on the general rule that the translator—and translation critic—must tend to the word and to the work as a whole; they particularize this by focusing on the intermediate point of gradation where the basic unit is the sentence or phrase. In John Hollander's view, "every literary document that purports to be a translation . . . makes a kind of contract to be correct, but it is traditional to regard any such contract, if filled to the letter, with a bit of contempt and suspicion." That is, translations that vary too far in the direction of literalism tend to be unsatisfactory. Hollander stipulates three points on the gradation scale. A *version* is an adaptation or imitation concerned with result, not process, involving change, transformation, variation. An *interpretation*, concerned with process, is a "heuristic kind of translation in which the new rendering would appear to function more as a process of teaching than as a finished . . . object." Pound's "where the treasure lies" is a chief indicator of this type of translation. A *performance* is a type of translation intended for a reading, stage production, or musical composition (1966:206, 220–21, 214–15, 224–26).

According to André Lefevere, there are six strategies of verse translation.

Through a phonemic translation, the translator tries "to capture the sound of the source text." A literal translation results when the translator decides that the meaning is the most important quality. Some translators "translate what is in verse in the source language into prose in the target language," while others strive to preserve the original in its metric form. There are translators who believe that rhyme is the most important element of poetry, and therefore insist that "only rhyming . . . will do justice to the 'poetic' value of the (not necessarily rhymed) source text." And, finally, organic verse translation disregards the meter of the original verse on the principle that reproducing meter is too direct and literal (1975:4–5).

Marilyn Gaddis Rose belongs among the modern translation theorists who have most effectively clarified types of translation by gradation. Her concept of gradation—which she calls autonomy spectrum—incorporates modern ideas into a definition of terminology and a description of process. Rose divides the process of translation into three different—autonomous —methods: determinative, functional, and synthesizing. Determinative methods are usually binary oppositions. "The two oldest, 'literal' versus 'free' and 'literary' versus 'non-literary,' while persistently decried, are still the most used, and perhaps the most useful. Literal versus free concerns the semantic, often syntactic closeness between the source and target texts." Rose points out that closeness—or fidelity—has not been clearly defined, although translators are intuitively agreed on its meaning, even as norms and tastes shift. "Literalists tend to make form inseparable from content, while partisans of free translation tend to believe the same message can be conveyed in what is perhaps a radically different form." Where the terms *free* and *literal* denote strategy, the terms *literary* and *nonliterary* designate substance. The difference is between how a work is translated and what is being translated (1981b:31–32).

Rose points to several useful attempts to classify types of translation. Translations classified by function are, in accordance with the system elaborated by Katharina Reiss, informative (text book, letter, report), expressive (belles-lettres), or operative (advertisements, speeches, propaganda). According to Juliane House, translations are either overt (bound to the source culture, as, for example, literary works) or covert (the source language and culture are not important, as, for example, commercial, scientific, or diplomatic documents). A synthesizing division of translation types has been recommended by Lefevere. According to him, the two poles of gradation are reader-oriented and text-oriented. The translation is accommodated to reader expectations (prevailing taste), or the reader is expected to accommodate taste to the original. Rose concludes, "All of these divisions point to the autonomy spectrum. . . . The translator, we might say, can go from reverence to reference; the translation, from presentation to adaptation." At one end of the spectrum translators are guided by the text, at the other they translate with their readership in mind (Rose 1981b:32–34; Reiss 1976:12–21; House 1973:166–67; Lefevere 1970).

The autonomy spectrum is, together with Steiner's hermeneutic description of the process of translation, one of the important breakthroughs that have raised modern translation study above the repetitive discourse on translation that characterizes the previous two millennia. For the first time in the history of translation critics have been offered the possibility of a sound yet flexible system on which to base judgements of merit. Methodology has been distinguished from typology, process from result (text). Terminology varies but is immediately comprehensible. The autonomy spectrum is a description of process founded on both practical and theoretical methodology.

5

SOVIET THEORY OF TRANSLATION

■■■■■■■ Soviet translators broke out of their closed circle by educating critics and editors to their basic tasks. All that was needed, really, was a set of prescriptions of goals and functions, and strong determination. Especially advantageous to Soviet translators was the national platform that enabled them to propagate their knowledge and experience. Soviet translators recognized the importance of linking translation criticism with translation theory in the task of educating critics and editors about their respective responsibilities. Definitions of essential duties had to be established along with a knowledge of type and an understanding of method and process —the principles that underlie and inform the practical problems of conveying a literary work from one language to another. It was more difficult to teach theory than to teach criticism. This aspect of the campaign was even more difficult because translators tend to resist theory, and the Soviet school has its share of translators who profess to despise theory. Nevertheless, Soviet ideas about translation were well enough developed by the 1950s to articulate the particular body of theory known as artistic translation and believed to be realized in the type known as the artistic translation.

Ivan Kashkin provided one of the most convincing arguments in favor of theory for translators and those who deal professionally with translations. As Kashkin pointed out, theory makes the difference between a professional and a dilettante, and theory created out of an intellectual vacuum without relevance to practice is useless. "A translator without theory, uninterested in general questions of principle," he declared, "is a handyman, sometimes a marvelous craftsman, but most often a limited amateur who is capable to the extent of his talent of incidental achievements and prone too far from incidental failures and even flops." Theory is necessary, Kashkin insisted, and without this basis to literary translation, translations are arbitrary and unstable. Kashkin also argued that theory must be principled and that principles of translation must be extracted from the practice of translation (1964:452).

When translators tied their efforts so strongly to the need for theory, they were keenly aware that translators would resist not only "theory" per se but also any attempt to impose a body of theory not seen to be immediately useful. Kashkin preferred the translation method he called realist translation, but he acknowledged, with reservations, the contributions of other theorists. In his view, the leading Soviet translation theorists fell into three groups. He argued that theory was developed by scholars, some of whom Kashkin disapproved for their literalist theories, others for purely linguistic approaches; by translators who draw preliminary observations and generalizations from experience and reinforce their hypotheses with exhaustive research and analysis; and by translators who profess to dislike theory but in fact apply it closely to their own practice and contribute to theory in turn by the example of their work (1964:455–56).

"There is no such thing as a law of translation, since laws admit no exceptions," Peter Newmark has said in *Approaches to Translation*, a wide-ranging survey of translation theory. And he added, "There can be no single comprehensive theory of translation, and no general agreement on the element of invariance, the ideal translation unit, the degree of translatability, and the concepts of equivalent-effect and congruence in translation" (1981:113). For all their expressed faith in right and wrong theory, it would be difficult to find Soviet theorists who disagree with this assessment. If anything, Soviet translators favor the subjective character of literary translation—they place their faith ultimately in intuition, talent, and personal judgment. Artistic translation is the pride of the Soviet school, and while it is in many ways a singular, uniform theory of translation, it was developed by rejecting certain methods deemed pernicious to artistic creativity and by synthesizing other methods believed to be conducive to faithful conveyance of a literary work from one language to another. The eclectic character of Soviet theory can be seen by reviewing the history of Soviet experience with earlier theory of translation.

With the appearance of the great Formalist School in the 1920s, formalist-oriented translation enjoyed a vogue in Soviet letters and convinced many translators for a time that the structural components of the text were the only reliable guide to a "true" translation. Russian Formalism, rejected but never successfully suppressed in Soviet letters, has exerted its greatest impact abroad, where it conjoined with Structuralism and New Criticism and eventually merged in both the Soviet Union and the West with communication theory and semiotics. Semiotics and communication theory have contributed significantly to translation theory. In the Soviet school, extreme formalism—the belief that once the meter, rhyme scheme, stanzaic articulation, and such other technical features as alliteration and rhythmics are conveyed, the translation is complete and perfect—encouraged a method called scientific. The theorists of the scientific method emphasized such notions as equilinearity, equimetrics, and equirhythmics, and proclaimed their method a revolution in art.

In the 1930s the formalist and scientific methods culminated in the literalist method that came close to dominating theory and practice in the Stalinist period. The translations of the literalists, or *bukvalisty*, turned out to be so bad, their effects on taste so traumatic, that literalism has been banned in the Soviet school. Translators are so anxious to rid their school of the artistic sins they believe were committed by formalist-scientific-literalist translators, that they often resort to argument—and propaganda—at the expense of the essential questions concerning the translation process. Their animosity is apparent. In Ivan Kashkin's opinion, for example, "it is impossible to replace precision with the naive formalism of a literal conveyance of words and style with a literal conveyance of the language structure by turning both one and the other into a fetish that shunts social, and human, and every other sense aside." Heaping on the pejoratives, Kashkin insisted, "literalism tries to uphold capriciously understood, static, abstract, disparate stylistic signs, and by conveying some sort of excogitated norms through the device of formal precision it provides only a precise plaster cast of the work being translated" (1968a:386).

The same attitude toward literalism was expressed by the Ukranian translator Oleksy Kundzich, who argued that literalism resulted not only from poor knowledge of foreign languages or hack work but also from the "idealist aesthetics" of "art for art's sake" and formalism. The tools of literalist translators are dogmatism, precision, and classification; their results are always mechanical. Kundzich states,

> The unrealizable goal of the formalist translation—conditional precision—stipulates a translation condition whose difficulties are insurmountable. Hence lack of faith in the possibility of conveying an artistic work by means of another language, hence the mechanistic transfer of words and forms from the original to the translation. . . . Transliteration of words of similar sound without regard for nuances of content and style, common copying at the basis of which lies *an inartistic perception of an artistic work* . . . these are the mechanics of literalism. (1955:217–20)

The majority of Soviet translators is convinced that literalist translation harms both original works and the reading public. Kundzich has been quoted for his assertion that "literalism is not only a mangling of words, a deformation of phrases, a destruction of language, but a destruction of artistic images and pictures and a distortion of the actual reality depicted in a work besides" (1955:254–56). Soviet translators do not leave doubt as to where to lay the blame for literalism. The only difference between literalism and formalism, L. N. Sobolev has said, is that "the latter has developed into a method of translation, and this makes it far more harmful than the crude work of neophytes, amateurs, and pedants" (1955:270–71). So much for formalism (and Formalism).

In Soviet letters formalism was a code word for avoidance of social content. The outcry has subsided due to glasnost, however, and even though Kashkin and his contemporaries denied it, Russian Formalist terminology and concepts are an undeniable ingredient of Soviet translation theory. Theorists and critics regularly use such text-oriented terms as *dominant, norm, structure, transformation, functionality, metricity, spatiality, intonation, device,* and *parallelism,* for example. Soviet theorists have also paid close attention to the period concept of literary history, and so they are familiar with the historical implications of such methods as the Neoclassical, Romantic, Realist, Naturalist, Symbolist-Decadent, Imagist, Impressionist, among other concepts of translation. Of these methods, the Romantic and Realist approaches to literary translation are frequently discussed as antecedents to modern theory, but in Soviet national culture, which has made a shibboleth of Realism, Romanticism is played down in favor of Realism. Nevertheless, Soviet theory has taken the concept of recreation from Romantic aesthetics, and Kashkin led the movement to conjoin recreation with the Realist perception of art as a reproduction of reality. The Russian terms for recreate and reproduce (*vossozdat'* and *vosproizvodit'*) appear repeatedly in discussions of theory and practice.

Two other methods or types of translation have been developed in the Soviet school. The first of these is the so-called adequate translation (*adekvatnyi*), credited to the literary scholar A. A. Smirnov. The second type, credited to A. V. Fedorov, is the "full-valued" translation (*polnotsennyi*). The terms for these types are used together to describe artistic translation as a method. Adequate translation is proportionate, equal, and correspondent to the original. Adequate translation is not literally and precisely equivalent to the original, for it is based on the realization that adequacy requires imaginative recreations that achieve an equivalent effect, not a direct reproduction. Choice and decision are essential to adequate translation, and this means, in Smirnov's terms, substitution, sacrifice, and compensation. Smirnov defined adequate translation, in the influential Soviet *Literaturnaia entsiklopediia* (Literary Encyclopedia) of 1934, in these frequently quoted words:

By adequate we signify a translation which conveys all the author's intentions (unconscious, as well as intentional), in the sense of its definitive ideological-emotional artistic effect on the reader, and respects as far as possible all resources of imagery, coloration, rhythm, and so forth employed by the author, the latter being regarded not as an end in themselves, but only as a means for achieving general effect. There is no doubt that all this requires sacrifice. (1934:527)

Although A. V. Fedorov, the author of a widely influential study culminating in a fourth edition entitled *Osnovy obshchei teorii perevoda* (Bases for a general theory of translation, 1983), has expressed reservations about Smirnov's definition of adequate translation, he calls his full-valued translation adequate and pairs the two terms in his own definition: "The full value (*polnotsennost'*) of a translation signifies an exhaustive conveyance of the semantic content of the original and a full-valued functional-stylistic equivalence to it." Full-valued translation requires conveyance of "the correlation of content and form specific to the original through reproduction of its distinctive features . . . or the creation of functional equivalents to these distinctive features." This requires "the use of linguistic means which, often without even coinciding in their formal character with the elements of the original, fulfill an analogous expressive function within the system of the whole by corresponding to the norm of the language of the translation." Full-valued translation presupposes "a balance between the whole and the parts." Some elements of an original are essential and must be conveyed, others may be sacrificed. "The relationship between the whole and the parts is so important because it defines the specific character of a work in its unity of content and form." If the translator does not discriminate between the essential and the inessential, with a view toward the whole and the relationships between the parts and the whole, the translation will distort and ruin the individual character of the original. Language is the basis of literature: it is through linguistic means that a literary work must be conveyed from one language to another. In his emphasis on unity of form and content, Fedorov signifies the dialectic (1983:126–30).

The main objection to Smirnov's definition of adequate translation is that the method too strongly emphasizes substitutions, sacrifices, and compensations, permitting these legitimate devices to endorse arbitrary departures from the norm of the original. Smirnov has been criticized on these grounds by Fedorov (1983:127) and the theorist Givi Gachechiladze (1970:134–37). Fedorov's own definition of full-valued translation is criticized for his strong orientation to linguistics. Smirnov's definition is considered too general, Fedorov's too scientific. Smirnov was accused at one time of moving perilously close to sociologism; that is, emphasizing social content. Fedorov is considered overly insistent on linguistic prescriptions (Gachechiladze 1970:139–42). Nevertheless, Fedorov is known to appreciate translation as art, and Smirnov's definition is accepted as ultimately valid. Adequate, full-valued translation has therefore been adapted into the definition of the all-important artistic translation in the Soviet school.

As a particular type, the artistic translation may be described initially as a flexible yet forthright example of what a faithful translation should be. Artistic translation is adequate, full-valued, and equivalent to its original in form, style, and content, as well as in practical principles for dealing with the permutations among these basic qualities of a literary work. It is founded on a respect that impels translators to learn everything they can about the original text, its author, its cultural and temporal context, and its place in world literature. The value most often mentioned in discussions of the artistic translation is individual creativity; the translator's talent is believed to be the guarantor of translation quality.

When A. Leytes contributed to the campaign to educate critics of translation, he stressed that an artistic translation is an ideal achieved through many years of work. He offered critics a succinct definition of the type: "An artistic translation must be faithful and accurate, that is, adequate to the original. This indisputable position has long ago become axiomatic to the majority of Soviet writer-translators." A translation must be more than simply adequate, however; it must also be alive. "No matter how faithful a translation might be in terms of its equivalence to the original, if the reader receives it badly—so much for that translation! After all, the reader does not need laboratory exercises . . . [he needs] an artistic work that is accessible to him" (1955:101–2, 112). In short, fidelity, or adequacy to the original, is measured in relation not only to the text but also to the reader's response as well. And though Soviet translation theorists did not acknowledge it, the term "adequate" is distinctly a formalist, in fact a Formalist, concept, just as "full value" promises the reader an artistically reliable version of the original.

Soviet artistic translation is a high ideal of a high art based on an optimistic view of the possibilities of translation. The most important principle of artistic translation is, as the term suggests, that the translator is a creative artist. Restated, the basis of literary translation is, as with any other art, individual creativity. The creative character of translation, V. Koptilov has said,

> is comprised of recreating . . . as consistently and naturally as possible the entire system . . . of the links of the original by overcoming the colossal difficulties raised on the path to translation by differences of language and national literary traditions. By sacrificing the secondary (that is, what is not essential to the semantic-image structure) the translator secures himself sufficient operating room for maneuvering his battle units—talent, intuition, knowledge of the stylistic possibilities of language. (1973:260–61)

Because of strong emphasis on the translator's creative ability and talent, artistic translation is a Weltanschauung as well as a method. Gachechiladze, whose Marxist study *Vvedenie v teoriiu khudozhestvennogo perevoda* (Introduction to theory of artistic translation, 1970) wielded great influence, defined the method as "a kind of artistic creativity where the original fulfills a function analogous to that which living reality has fulfilled for the creation of the original. The translator's creative method basically corresponds to his world view . . . the translator reflects the artistic reality of a work in the unity of its form and content, with correlation of parts to the whole." In Gachechiladze's view, "in most instances this world view manifests itself in the translator's general attitude toward the original, beginning with the author and the work he chooses to translate and ending with his understanding of the original and the style of his translation." Above all, "an artistic translation is creativity subordinated to the world view of the translator and done in accordance with his artistic method" (1970:148–49).

To Gachechiladze, as to Fedorov, a full-valued translation preserves the unity of form and content, but not mechanically. "If recreation could be made possible simply by repeating the unity of a work's form and content," then translation is as futile as "idealist theorists" claim. But the process of translation is not direct—translation is a creative act. The creative translator does not seek to convey the unity of form and content by copying the content of an original work in a "new national form," for example, because the result of this misunderstanding would be an old content in a new form. Instead, the translator "must recreate a unity of form and content that is analogous to the original. Only in this way will a full-valued translation be created. . . . It goes without saying that unity of form and content means the artistic whole qualitatively distinct from the mechanical sum of its constituent parts." Gachechiladze (in agreement with Koptilov) says the translator must develop a strategy and tactics for recreating both the artistic whole and the constituent parts of the original. By analogy to the unity of form and content he signifies that "in a given instance the original fulfills the role of live nature while the translation functions as an artistic reflection of this nature." Art is not a copy of nature, it is a *recreation*. Just as art requires change to recreate reality, so translation requires change to convey a work of art: "Change is absolutely necessary if we want to create an analogous unity of form and content from the material of another language. This is why the best translations are comprised of conventional changes on the model of the original."

The transfer of a literary work from one language to another is unavoidably a process of change. A translation need not recreate an identical unity of form and content—this would be mere copying. In the process a translation might become a different unity of form and content, but the unity of form and content of the translation must be *analogous* to the unity of form and content of the original—the new unity of form and content must mean the same to the new reader as the old unity meant to the reader in the original language. Moreover, however necessary change might be, it must be used with caution. In Gachechiladze's words, "in terms of the unity of form and content a minimum of changes provides the so-called adequate translation, a maximum of changes results in an imitation. Changes that go beyond the province of the translation but to some extent preserve the elements of the original, constitute literary influence, and even outright epigonism" (1970:123–24).

Gachechiladze does not reject Smirnov's endorsement of substitution and compensation. Instead, he phrases his definition of artistic translation in terms of Fedorov's prescription for unity of form and content and the necessity of change to ensure a faithful, which is to say, analogous, conveyance. By refining definitions of both adequate and full-valued translation in this way, he endorses Smirnov's assumption that the ultimate test of the quality of a translation is its "ideological-emotional artistic effect on the reader." Not incidentally, he adds impetus to Kashkin's and Smirnov's shift of emphasis from text to reader for critical evaluations of translations. In effect, an artistic translation is to be judged in terms not only of adequate form but also of full-valued reader response as well. Seen in this way, Soviet artistic translation is in both theory and practice a synthesis of translation types: it is both text-oriented (adequate) and reader-oriented (full-valued).

The Soviet translators and theorists who campaigned on behalf of the art of translation have made great claims for the originality and innovation of artistic translation as a method and a theory. In fact, despite claims for its originality, its terms and concepts are derived from preceding tradition. Artistic translation is distinguished by the optimism and idealism of its definitions, the acceptance of the necessity of theory as the basis of artistic translation, and the equally sensible assumption that theory must be derived from practice. Its attainment of theoretical and practical maturity was established well before translation theory was established elsewhere. Artistic translation, the unifying core of the Soviet school, is so widely accepted because it was developed through a process of debate and discussion that ensured its highly principled character. Without this integrity and unity, it would not have been possible for the campaign to educate critics, editors, and publishers to succeed.

Two assumptions inform Soviet theory of translation and distinguish it from Western theory. First, the Soviet school was shaped in part by a group of Marxist-Leninist theorists who advocated a body of theory peripheral to theory elsewhere. And second, the bond between theory and practice is remarkably close. When Soviet translators founded their school, they discovered that their only theoretical heritage was an amorphous collection of statements by eighteenth and nineteenth-century predecessors, primarily in Russian literature. Only in the Soviet period was translation theory developed in unified systems such as those of Kashkin, Fedorov, Rossels, and Gachechiladze. When Soviet translators began their campaign to educate critics, they could point out that theory had been developed in practice.

Much has been done to develop translation theory with attention to the most minute problems of versification and linguistics, Elizbar Ananiashvili has said. But the greatest value of Soviet translation theory is that "it does not prescribe norms and point to rules," but rather "generalizes experience with the intent of helping practice" (1973:65–66). Soviet theory thereby gained credibility, and Soviet theorists were able to propagate their ideas effectively because they could demonstrate their theoretical assertions through examples taken from practice.

Soviet translation theory is complex; Soviet translation criticism appeals to a wide audience because it makes even detailed problems of language comprehensible to the lay reader. Yet the tasks of critics, editors, and publishers, together with the extensive teaching of theory, would have been useless had the campaigners not been able to indicate through existing good translations of foreign literary works the how, the what, and the why of literary translation. Criticism, theory, and practice were bound together in the campaign, and it is in the practice of translation that the efficacy of criticism and theory was most convincingly demonstrated.

6

THEORY OF REALIST TRANSLATION

██████████ Soviet theory of artistic translation is phrased in terms of artistic value, but it is not devoid of a Marxist-Leninist core. The work of Kashkin and Gachechiladze is intensely ideological; Fyodorov adheres to the dialectic. An understanding of this strong, if not dominant, core of Soviet theory of translation requires attention to the distinctive character it lends to the Soviet school and to its topos in the development of modern translation studies. Reference here is to the method and type championed under the term *realist translation*.

In their use of the terms *realist translation (realisticheskii perevod)* or *realist method (realisticheskii metod)*, Soviet Marxists refer not to the historical method developed in Realistic aesthetics but to their own particular type of modern translation, and to what they claim is their own unique and unprecedented method. The Soviet realist translation takes its origins from historical Realism and is thus the translator's equivalent to the doctrine of Socialist Realism in original literature, but it should not be confused with the historical Realist method. The realist translation is in many ways typologically similar to the artistic translation—it is defined as adequate, full-valued, faithful, and artistically equivalent to its original, and it is based on the body of theory articulated by Smirnov, Fedorov, Gachechiladze, and Kashkin. The Ukrainian theorist Oleksy Kundzich defined realist translation as both "a realistic [and a] creative method of translation," thereby identifying it with artistic translation. He also provided an initial definition of the method by asserting that "realism in translation is the truthful conveyance of the actual reality reflected in the original. To translate realistically means to convey by means of one's own language all that was felt and cognized by the author of the original" (1959:11). The chief proponents of realist translation in the Soviet school are V. M. Rossels and Givi Gachechiladze; Ivan Kashkin is its pioneer.

According to Kashkin, realist translation is "a working term" more appropriate than the term "full-valued translation" and more apt "as a generalization" because it describes the "essence" of what experienced Soviet translators "understand and apply in practice." The term *realist* is appropriate because "practically it draws theory of literary translation close to the criteria of realist literature." The term does not signify that literary works should be translated into the style of Realist writers. It means instead that all styles should be conveyed as they really are. In Kashkin's words, "of course, we must agree immediately that we are talking not about a literary-historical concept, not about the Realist style, but about a method of conveying style, and of course, it is not that, say, a Romantic style should be made to conform in translation to Realist norms, but that the style of a work being translated should be faithfully conveyed by the realist method" (1955:125).

Realism in art, Kashkin was careful to note, is a complex and variegated phenomenon. For his purposes, both the term and its essence are specific to the type of translation he had in mind, because they define a particular attitude toward art. This attitude governs the realist method, and it is here that the method departs from definitions of artistic translation. According to Kashkin's early definitions, realist translation differs from artistic translation in that the translator seeks to go beyond the text itself to find and to convey the reality reflected there. While the translation must reflect the reality presented by the text, it must first reflect the actual reality represented in the text. Kashkin is ambiguous here, but he seems not to have meant that translation is a dual process. To him, the translator's ultimate fidelity to the original work is a recognition, in accordance with Realist aesthetics, that art is a reflection of an objective reality (and, in accordance with Marxist theory, a material representation of a concrete reality). A translation may be said to be realist when it "achieves fidelity and approximation to the original, when the translator strives to reproduce by means of language the truth of the reality reflected by the original, which the translator perceives not externally and formally, but creatively, and which he conveys in full, from the basic and prominent to the minute details." In Kashkin's view, "it may be said that realism in art is a truthful and poetic, ineffably distinct and inspired apprehension and reflection of the world."

Where Formalism is static and moribund, Impressionism arbitrary, and Naturalism a lifeless copy, "Realism is life itself reflected in art." A realist translator respects the word but strives "not simply to copy the conventional verbal sign of the original." Such a translator understands that the chief task is to "recreate the objective reality that is expressed by the word and gives life to the word." A realist translator focuses not on the words themselves but on "the particular reality that is contained in the text of the original, with all its semantic-image richness." A realist translator strives not just to recreate the text but also to reproduce the reality that is reflected in the text—the true, objective reality, not the verbal abstractions that make the text. "Faithful conveyance of the ideological-semantic system and creative recreation of the artistic and national distinctiveness of the original demand just such a realist approach." He or she realizes that the text is important not in itself but for the "truth in art" that exists in the text. "The truth of an artistic translation is not a hair-splitting, imaginary verisimilitude of external resemblance to the original, it is not simply a reproduction of all the unimportant components but their realization; it is a truth founded on the internal logic of the image; and above all it is a faithful translation of the definitive essence of the original." Realist translators do not traduce, because their translations are faithful in three ways: "fidelity to the original, fidelity to reality, and fidelity to the reader." And, finally, "the realist method is not a code of abstract conditions and recipes, but a generalization and a realization of the large tasks and creative achievements of Soviet translators. The Soviet school is the realist method in action, a creative incarnation of its aims and precepts" (1955:125–26, 127, 140–41, 142).

Soviet theorists do not recognize the artistic and realist methods to be mutually exclusive. Theorists of realist translation use the terms realist and artistic interchangeably, and those who prefer the former term do not reject translation as art. Spokesmen for realist translation such as Kashkin, Rossels, and Gachechiladze emphasize that translation is an art and the translator an artist, and they join their less ideological colleagues in their assumption of the integrity of the original text. Both methods incorporate the basic definitions of the adequate and full-valued translations; both are antagonists of the literalist method and the extremes of the formalist method; both value fidelity while rejecting precision.

Essentially, then, there would seem to be no difference between artistic and realist translation. The link between realist translation and Realism is not an incidental issue, however, for advocates of realist translation base their aesthetics on Marxist-Leninist ideology and orient their theory to Socialist Realism. "Artistic translation is historically a weapon of the ideological struggle, and consequently it is a class phenomenon in a class society," Givi Gachechiladze has insisted. By artistic translation, Gachechiladze means realist translation, and he continues,

The similarities of the various forms of the realist method are conditioned by a general historical link between realism and progressive social forces, the bearers of advanced ideology. Realism is the style of the dawning class. The dawning class is always linked with the people. . . . The latest stage of realism is expressed in its highest form—in the literature of Socialist Realism.

There can be no doubt that "a realist translation . . . is the result of the realist method, which always reflects historically progressive tendencies" (1970:127, 182–83).

Gachechiladze obtains his definition of realist translation from Kashkin, but his definition differs from Kashkin's when he objects to the master's characterization of the method as merely "a working term." In Gachechiladze's view, realist translation is a new, universal, and revolutionary creative method that distinguishes the Soviet art of translation from all others. In his words,

the realist method means a thorough study of the artistic reality of the original, the study of the historical conditions in which it was created, and of the historical reality reflected in it, its national features, the individual qualities of its author, his world and his method, a penetration into the essence of his manner and style, and a reflection of the original through a selection of its essential, typical, and distinctive qualities while conveying both its characters and the environment in which they act, and finally an accurate conveyance of the details of thought and style.

In addition to this, a translation must be "a realistic reflection of the reality of the original which preserves the individual manner of the translator himself and manifests the basic tendencies of his attitude toward the original" (1970:163–64). That is, a translation is created by the same method that an original work of realist literature is created; the translator must reproduce reality in the very process of translation.

In offering this definition of realist translation, Gachechiladze emphasizes its basis in Marxist-Leninist ideology. "From the point of view of Marxist gnoseology," he has noted,

a cognition of a world populated by peoples who speak different languages, a cognition of the culture of these peoples and particularly of their literature, is possible with the help of translation. This does not necessarily signify that every translation fully reflects the object of cognition, that is, the original. A definition of the conditions that can guarantee the solution of the task gnoseologically posed by artistic translation is the subject of theory of artistic translation. . . . Every translation, including an artistic translation, is a recreation of a work created in one language through the means of another language.

In Gachechiladze's view, the key Marxist-Leninist concepts that define realist translation are the Leninist theory of reflection, the Leninist rule that theory must reflect practice, and the dialectic of form and content. Quoting Lenin's well-known precept that "practice is higher than theoretical cognition, because it not only has the merit of universality but also of unmediated reality," Gachechiladze asserts,

It is from this point of view that we would like to approach the artistic translation. As history proves, an artistic translation, which performs a function equivalent to the functions of other cultural values, fluctuates in the majority of cases between two extreme principles: the conventionally precise but artistically not full-valued translation and the artistically full-valued but free translation that departs far from the original. Theoretically there is nothing more simple than to synthesize these two principles and declare the maximally precise and artistically full-valued translation to be our ideal. But in practice such a synthesis is impossible: two different languages use completely different means for the expression of the same thought. The conventional precise translation does not always reproduce the artistic effect of the original. Conventional precision and artistic quality constantly contradict each other. (1970:114–16)

The task of the Marxist-Leninist is to bring contradictions into a clash. Through this activity a synthesis can be achieved and the progression of history facilitated. This is also, in Gachechiladze's opinion, the task of the realist translator. As he has stated the problem, it is not possible to reconcile the two extremes of translation gradation; a realist translator must seek elsewhere for a resolution or synthesis. In his words,

the necessity therefore arises of finding a method for the dialectical resolution of the problem of unifying these contradictions. We must define the concept of precision or, more precisely, the possibility of violating conventional precision in the name of artistic quality and, on the other hand, the possibility of violating artistic quality for the sake of precision. The goal, a striving toward which balances the degree of both these violations, is the fullest possible conveyance of the unity of form and content of the original into another language. Thus, a definition of the means of achievement of so-called adequacy is one of the basic tasks of theory of artistic translation. (1970:116)

In Gachechiladze's view, then, the synthesis of the two contradictory principles of translation—precision and artistic quality—must be accomplished by a dialectical resolution of the problem of unity of form and content. In this he endorses A. V. Fedorov's definition of artistic translation and turns for a final resolution of the problem to the Leninist theory of reflection. Again he quotes Lenin:

Cognition is an eternal, infinite approximating of thought with object. The reflection of nature in man's thought must be understood not "lifelessly," not "abstractly," not without movement, not without contradictions, but in an eternal process of movement, an emergence of contradictions and their resolution. . . . Cognition is man's reflection of nature. It is not a simple, not an unmediated, not a complete reflection, however, but a process of a series of abstractions, of the formation, the forming, of concepts, laws, etc.

Therefore, Gachechiladze adds, "the creation of an artistic translation is in the same way a creative process of reflection of the objective world, which in a given instance is presented by the original, that is, by what is for the translator the object of cognition" (1970:125–26).

For a realist translator, the adequate, full-valued translation is not sufficient because it is too abstract. "In practice it is impossible to achieve complete adequacy. A realist translation, on the other hand, is practically possible. It theoretically canonizes the factual condition of artistic translation and does not demand from the translation what is unrealizable even from a theoretical point of view." The Leninist theory of reflection, seen as the very basis of Realist aesthetics, is likewise the basis of realist translation:

> In accordance with the Leninist theory of reflection, translation creativity presents itself to us as the following process: an artistic work acts upon the translator who, for his part, manifests a definite ideological-emotional attitude toward it: as a result of the interaction of these factors—the objective and the subjective —an apprehension of the given work, in accordance with which the translation is created, is formed in the translator's consciousness.

The theory of reflection defines the artistic task of the translator in direct correspondence to the artistic task of the original author. "In contrast to the author of the original work the translator is presented with a prepared idea incarnated in artistic form in another language. Therefore he is obliged solely to recreate an artistically whole picture of the original for the satisfaction of his own creative demands in accordance with his psychological make-up" (1970:128–29).

The Leninist theory of reflection provides the dialectical resolution to the problem of unity of form and content. "If the original is a reality, and the translation is a reflection of that reality," Gachechiladze says, "then the method of our reflection must be realistic, it must recreate the original in the unity of its content and form." Realist translation differs from all previous methods of translation because it is true to the original, to the reality reflected in the original, and thus to all the qualities of the original in terms of temporal and national-cultural context. It synthesizes the best elements of previous methods of translation into a total method based firmly on a correct materialist perception of the world:

> We have extracted this concept from a materialist apprehension of the inter-relationship between world view and method which defines artistic translation as a formula of artistic creativity and from the essence of the Leninist theory of reflection. The concept of the realist method explains the facts of full-valued translations of the past on the basis of the advanced world view of translators. By force of the continuity of this world view the realist method exploits the finest traditions of the art of translation, it continues and develops them as fully

as possible. More precisely, the realist method in translation is the same gnoseological concept that expresses artistic reflection as in original creativity, the only difference being that the object of the original literature—actual reality —is replaced by the artistic reality of the original. (1970:150–51, 152–53)

Gachechiladze refined the reality-text-translation relationship that Kashkin expressed ambiguously as first and second realities. If the translation reflects the original text, then it will also reflect the reality in the original text; if the translation reflects the reality of the original text, it will have faithfully reproduced the text. In Gachechiladze's words,

> by unity of form and content of the original we mean its artistic and national distinctive features correspondingly conveyed by the artistic and national distinctive features of the translator's creativity, because he is creating a work for his own native literature. The realistic method presumes both a unity of scientific approach to the study of the reality of the original and the artistic quality of its reproduction in the translation.

Kashkin proceeded from the position that "a translation must realistically and accurately recreate the reality reflected in the original. In our opinion, on the other hand, the specific character of a translation consists of the fact that for the translator the unmediated object of reflection is the original itself—that is, his artistic reality—and not directly the concrete reality that in its turn was reflected and mediated by the original." (1970:164,166)

As is evident from the discussion, much effort is devoted to asserting the uniqueness of both artistic and realistic translation methods separately and together. The methods are at once a synthesis of the best qualities of previous methods and a completely new, revolutionary stage of the art of translation. To the extent that realist translation is defined in terms of Marxist-Leninist ideology, which is generally not influential elsewhere, Soviet claims to uniqueness are valid. But denials of eclecticism are not convincing, and some claims to methodological innovation are dubious. Kundzich, for example, asserted the uniqueness of Soviet literary translation by noting, "Until our time essentially only two methods of translation have existed: the realistic, creative method, as a result of which the original has been truthfully conveyed, that is, *translation proper*, and another method, the consistent copying of words, as a result of which a text not corresponding to the original has been produced, that is, *not properly translation*" (1959:10–11). Literalism has been ousted from both artistic and realist methods, but it has been rejected elsewhere too. To make a distinction between the realist and all other methods of translation, as Kundich has done here, is to do no more than repeat the age-old statement of gradations, in this case between the direct and precise type and the indirect and faithful type of translation.

The same failure to make valid distinctions is evident in attempts to disso-ciate realist translation from historical period-concept approaches to liter-ary translation. The question of realism provokes the question of Romanti-cism, and it is in attempts to distinguish the realist method from the Romantic method that Soviet theorists have encountered particular difficul-ties. "Two trends exist in Romantic translation," Yury Levin has noted. "One strives to recreate the work being translated in full, in all its individual and national distinctive character and unrepeatability." But according to Levin, the Russian literary language was not sufficiently developed during the Romantic period and so the translations of the Russian Romantics "are marked by an inclination toward literalism." Levin states,

> Equally Romantic is that translation whose creator strives toward self-expression, toward a recreation of an ideal he comprehends subjectively. . . . In method this translation is closer to the Classical, for it permits departures from the original in the name of approximation of an ideal. . . . The work being translated somehow becomes the result of the co-creativity of two poets whose rights are equal. (1968:13)

Much of what Levin says is true, but he has simply repeated another state-ment of gradation, this time distinguishing between artistically faithful translation and free translation. Levin is correct to assert the first trend of the Romantic method. The Romantic aspiration to *recreate* an original has survived in subsequent methods, most particularly in the historical Real-ist and the Socialist Realist methods. But Levin does not say this, and he goes on to make an irrelevant link between Romantic departures from the original in the name of an idealist perception of reality and eighteenth-century departures from the norm that were motivated by attempts to make foreign works conform to prevailing taste. Levin, an authority on Russian Romanticism, is correct in his assessment that the Russian Romantics tended to literalism because the Russian literary language was not sufficiently devel-oped in their time, but this is a problem concerning the history of language, not of method. Romantic literalism should not be linked to the very different Neoclassical one-to-one literalism that originates from the sovereignty of mimesis.

Ivan Kashkin devoted special attention to separating realist translation from historical methods. "The provisional Formal approach to translation is prone to codify and freeze the original," he asserted.

> After all, the style of a translation is defined by the translator's world view and features of the literary movement to which he adheres, and his general-aesthetic approach. . . . The Naturalist translator, not satisfied with an accurate description, congests it with a protocol transcript of inessential details. The translator of the Im-pressionist trend, by conveying the original with the pure water of Impressionism,

dilutes it with the rose water of his epigonist subjectivism. But the realist translator, by truthfully and thoroughly reflecting and carefully preserving the typical style features of an original not even to his liking, attempts to find and permit into his translation that which the original does as an authentic work of
art, which is to reflect reality in its particular way. (1959:125)

The translator must convey the style of the original as it is. Fidelity to
the reality of the original text distinguishes realist translators from those
translators who use the prevailing style (or styles) of their historical period.
In this regard, Kashkin is correct—it is a fact of literary history that Romantic translators tended to turn foreign works into Romantic works, just as
Realist translators tended to turn foreign works into Realist works. To the
extent that Kashkin, Gachechiladze, and others have defined realist translation as a method that honors the integrity of the original style, they are
correct. But clearly, in his criticism of the shortcomings of Impressionist
or Naturalist translators, or for that matter of any translators who have
been tied to their time, Kashkin has only alerted strawmen to be wary.
It is not true that all translators of a particular period have conveyed styles
to suit the prevailing aesthetic standards of their time. In Russian literature,
for example, Pushkin conveyed Shakespeare as an Elizabethan, Voltaire as
a man of reason, and Byron as a Romantic.

Perhaps it is difficult for a non-Marxist to comprehend what a realist
translation, as described by Kashkin and Gachechiladze, is in actual print.
It is not difficult to understand their arguments or their dialectical thought,
but analyses of realist translations—Kashkin's translations of American poetry, for example—do not yield evidence of a dialectical realization of a work
of art unless we assume that this dialectical realization is what artistic translators strive to achieve. Realist translations honor the unity of form and
content. They reflect the reality of the original text and, to the degree that
it is reflected in the original text, the reality reflected in the original work
of art. They exhibit to a degree a principled fidelity (in this instance ideological as well as aesthetic) to the original. But these are the qualities of any
good translation, regardless of whether the underlying principles are
Marxist-Leninist. Ultimately, it is not possible to distinguish between an
artistic and realist translation—which is perhaps why Gachechiladze uses
the terms interchangeably. Moreover, nothing is ever said about obvious
questions provoked by his discussions of reflection of reality: what of the
degree to which the original *fails* to reflect reality? what of works whose
basic aesthetic premise is to distort reality? what criteria are to be used
by the realist translator to define the degree, the quality, the character, or
the subjectivity or objectivity of the reflection of reality in either the original
text or in the translation?

Proponents of realist translation will reply that the answer to these questions is provided by the dialectic of form and content—if the translator preserves the unity of form and content in the translation in a way that is "analogous" to the unity of form and content in the original, all other relationships between the whole and the parts will logically follow. The notion of an analogous unity of form and content is indeed promising, if only because it avoids the simplistic reductions of Marxism. But the argumentation on its behalf is faulty because the logic is circular: if reality is accurately reflected, the analogous unity of form and content will be true; if a truly analogous unity of form and content is achieved, reality will be accurately reflected. Moreover, given another Marxist principle, that art has "a very high degree of autonomy"—a principle implicit in the likening of realist to artistic translation—it is difficult not to suggest that prescriptions for an analogous unity of form and content prove too rigid in relation to the dialectical dynamism of art. And when we consider additionally the Marxist assumption that language also has a very high degree of autonomy—an assumption that is both explicit and implicit throughout discussions of the realist method—the suspicion arises that the method risks the perils of interpreting the dialectical process in ways too direct, predictable, symmetrical, *mediated*.

It is difficult to identify a uniquely realist translation in the Russian world. As the persistently proclaimed identity with artistic translation suggests, there is little difference, except in terminology, between the stated Marxist-Leninist concepts of realist translation and numerous theoretical discussions of literary translation occurring elsewhere in the world. Granted that the emphasis on a reflection of reality distinguishes Soviet discussions from others, this is not unlike general discussions of Realist aesthetics or, for that matter, unlike the commonplace assumption that all art is a reflection, one way or another, degree or another, with more or less objectivity, of *some* reality, however that reality is to be perceived, defined, and mediated. The Marxist dialectic would also seem to mark discussions of realist translation in the Soviet school as unique. But, after all, one does not have to accept the validity of dialectical materialism to appreciate the common assumption that a work of art is a unity of form and content. Nor does one have to be a Marxist-Leninist to accept the idea that a successful literary translation in one way or another conveys, restores, reconstitutes, or substitutes the original's unity of form and content. Kundzich's claim for the Soviet uniqueness of realist translation is no more than a restatement of the difference between the precise and the faithful translation methods; Levin's critique of the subjective character of Romantic translations is a repeat of the gradation between the faithful translation and the free translation.

Gachechiladze's explication of the dialectic—a reconciliation or synthesis of the contradictions between precision and artistic quality—is well reasoned and appropriately applied to the process of translation. But his

Marxist-Leninist terms for the concepts he discusses do not differ from the terms for the same concepts discussed elsewhere in the field of translation studies. Many examples could be cited, but perhaps one will serve—an account of the essentials of communicative translation that Peter Newmark has developed from the theoretical work of the well-known Bible translator Eugene A. Nida. Where Gachechiladze states that "artistic translation . . . wavers in the majority of cases between extreme principles: the conventionally precise but artistically not full-valued translation and the artistically full-valued but free translation that departs from the original," Newmark says that "communicative translation attempts to produce on its reader an effect as close as possible to that obtained on the readers of the original" and "semantic translation attempts to render, as closely as the semantic and syntactic structures of the second language allow, the exact contextual meaning of the original" (1981:39). The terms are different, and so are the intents of these two theorists. But both men refer plainly to no more than the traditional difference between free and literal translation.

7

TRANSLATION, COMMUNICATION, AND CULTURE

██████ Translators of the Soviet school often use a word of great importance to a multinational country that claims exceptional international responsibility. The word is *svoeobrazie,* meaning "distinctiveness," "originality." When modified by the adjective "national" it signifies a value best
translated as "distinctive national character." A chief task of the Soviet
school of translation is to communicate the distinctive character of one people to another, to convey mutual understanding across the barriers not just
of language but also of cultural-historical experience. This task is based
on the principle of translation as communication and involves the need for
a theory that will facilitate communication. It involves philosophy of language, linguistics (particularly sociolinguistics and psycholinguistics), and,
in its broadest reaches, semiotics and communication theory. In this context,
the relationships between the Soviet concepts of adequate and full-valued
translation and the Western synthesizing concepts of text-oriented and
reader-oriented translation present a special problem. Not incidentally, the
relationships between formalist and reader-response criticism or reception
theory also present problems for this task.

What is translation as communication, and how does this concept enter
into the formation of a national school of translation? "From the point
of view of the translator at any moment in his work, [translation] is a decision process," Jiří Levý has said. But "from the teleological point of view
translation is a process of communication." (1967:II, 1171) With this remark Levý placed literary translation in its broadest context of language
as communication, pointing to Roman Jakobson's well-known concept of
translation as communication in the widest sense. Jakobson identified three
kinds of translation. Intralingual translation is "an interpretation of verbal
signs by means of other signs of the same language," or, plainly stated, *re-
wording.* Interlingual translation, or *translation proper*, is "an interpretation

of verbal signs by means of some other language." Intersemiotic translation, or *transmutation*, is "an interpretation of verbal signs by means of signs of nonverbal systems," translation of verbal language into music, gesture, game, sculpture and painting, mathematical systems. (1966:233)

Translation as communication signifies transference of value from one person to another, one group of people to another, one culture to another. In the earlier years of the Soviet school, translators expressed despair that their cadres would ever properly understand the difficulties of conveying the distinctive character of foreign cultures. In many of his critical articles, Ivan Kashkin cited a wide variety of translation errors that originated in a misunderstanding of culture as well as of language. What hope for communication can there be, he once asked, in a translation that confuses the title of a novel by Faulkner with Shakespeare's *Hamlet* (1959:117)? In a major critique of a literalist translation of Dickens, he asked the same question about a translator who persistently conveyed the polyseme "regular" in its single Russian meaning of "regular army" and translated "sweet-pea" literally as a sweet legume (1968a:399). If the translator cannot comprehend even these minor instances of idiom, how can he or she be trusted to communicate English culture to Russian readers?

Translation as communication is also important to translators in other cultures, and much effort has been spent elucidating the difficulties of comprehending and conveying distinctive cultural phenomena. Turning attention to problems of translation similar to those that Kashkin pointed out, Robert M. Adams has asked whether the English language is capable of conveying German *Geist*, Spanish *machismo*, and Greek *logos*. Apparently not, for, like Yiddish *chutzpah*, neither British nor American cultural experience can account for the distinctive character of these words, and they have had to be transcribed into the English language (1973:151–52). The concern here is not with translatability, but with cultural-historical experience and the difficulties of conveying it to readers lacking shared perceptions. Adams states the problem neatly by pointing out, "A contemporary Arab novelist who wants to represent a boy and girl boy-and-girling it in a rustic scene, cannot, without shocking his audience out of their wits, make his characters speak the sort of Arabic that everyone knows boys and girls speak in actual Arab villages." Arabs do not write the language they speak, and it is not possible to use spoken Arabic in a literary work. How, then, is such a representation to be translated into English or, for that matter, any other language where the spoken language is highly valued in a literary work? What Adams calls "an equivalently flowery and artificial English" would seem foolish and pretentious to an American or Englishman, and of course it would be equally foolish to "make the young people sound like Thomas Hardy yeomen, or Faulkner crackers, or Lawrence gamekeepers, or anybody's peasants." The problem is therefore that "different cultures have different conceptions of literary decorum, and different stylistic options within that decorum. And there may not be any option in one culture that quite corresponds with a mode of feeling that is instantly felt to be natural and familiar in another" (1973:153–54).

F. Will stated the problem similarly when he asked how an American replies to questions about the United States from a Chinese whose sole notion of the Western world is derived solely from translations of Charles Dickens and Hans Christian Andersen (1973:64). The answer would seem to be that the American could not possibly make the Chinese questioner understand the United States; or, if it were possible, the American would have great difficulty trying to place the distinctive character of American culture in a framework comprehensible to someone whose perception is shaped by nineteenth-century Danish children's fantasies and English social consciousness.

The problem arose in regard to translating Molière in both the Russian and American worlds. How does one convey Molière's Alexandrine lines to Russians or Americans, to whom such lines, spoken on the stage, seem artificial? In a critique of M. L. Lozinsky's Russian translation of *Tartuffe* in perfectly reproduced Alexandrine lines, Kornei Chukovsky pointed out that Molière's humor was lost on Russian playgoers because the unnatural sound of the lines in Russian distracted them. He preferred an older Russian translation that employed the familiar Russian iambic tetrameter line and thereby relieved Russians of the barrier of convention between them and the stage (1984:60–62). The same problem faced the American poet-translator Richard Wilbur when he translated Molière into English. Like Chukovsky, he realized that where the Alexandrine line sounds natural to modern French theatergoers, it intrudes rudely on the hearing of English auditors. Wilbur's translations, also in iambic lines, have been widely praised for their fidelity to Molière.

"To make a good translation from any language is a satisfying experience," reports Donald Keene, "but this experience is all the greater when the success of the translation depends heavily on the ability of the translator to make an alien age and civilization seem immediate and important" (1971:321). Keene is fully aware from his experience of trying to communicate the distinctive character of Japanese culture to the English-speaking world that the task of translation as communication is complex. "Translators are men groping toward each other in a common mist," George Steiner has said in reference to translation as communication of human experience. In Steiner's view, "any model of communication is at the same time a model of trans-lation, of a vertical or horizontal transfer of significance. No two historical epochs, no two social classes, no two localities use words and syntax to signify the same things, to send identical signals of valuation and interference" (1975:61, 45). If translation within a single language—

Jakobson's intralingual translation—is as complex as Steiner indicates it is, think how much more difficult communication becomes when inter-lingual translation is at hand. Translation as communication is an espe-cially difficult problem, says Adams, who distrusts the "itchy tendency on the part of the word 'translation' to expand, or even to explode into the word 'communication'" but believes that indulgence of the problem will at least "reward us with an extra sense of the fragility and intricacy of the process" of translation. "The word 'translation' itself lends some color to our impulse, since 'carrying across' or 'carrying over' is in fact what a good deal of communication amounts to." That a translator is a traitor is true, Adams believes, but it is also "true of any man who opens his mouth, or puts his pencil to paper." Language works against, as well as for, communication, and no human being can perfectly express exactly what he or she means; but language is all we have and the elements of language "have an accepted value and import, a certain lowest-common-denominator meaning, in the marketplace" (1973:6).

So far as communication is concerned, translation reflects the common usage and arbitrarily accepted meaning of language. We do not stop using language because it is an imperfect instrument or stop translating because the process is imperfect. "It is plausible that no translation, however good it may be, can have any significance as regards the original," Walter Benja-min has admitted (1968:70). Nevertheless, translation as a mode of commu-nication cannot be denied, and "translatability must be an essential feature of certain works." Translation is the only mode by which different languages can be brought into a relationship, and it "thus ultimately serves the purpose of expressing the central reciprocal relationship between languages. . . . Languages are not strangers to one another, but are, a priori and apart from all historical relationships, interrelated in what they want to express" (1968:70–72). "Translation is equally essential to humanism, to the contin-ued life of feeling," Steiner has reminded us.

> We translate perpetually—this is often overlooked—when we read a classic in our own tongue, a poem written in the 16th century or a novel published in 1780. We seek to recapture, to revitalise in our consciousness the meanings of words used as we no longer use them, of imaginings that have behind them a contour of history, of manners, of religious or philosophic presumptions radi-cally different from ours.

Translation is communication in the same sense that language is communica-tion (thus again "trans-lation"), and we translate precisely because of the difficulties of communication: "No language, moreover, however compre-hensive, however resourceful and inclusive in its syntax, covers more than a fraction of human realisation. There are, at every moment and on every horizon, worlds beyond our own words. Hence the urge to cross the barriers of national speech, the effort to make other insights, other tools of awareness, available" (1968:49, 50).

Soviet translators discuss translation-communication in ways similar to Adams and Steiner, but they are more concerned with the nationalities policy and Soviet internationalism. For Pavel Antokolsky and others, a basic task of the translator is "to reveal in an original its social essence, its historical conditionality, its native roots," and "not only reveal but show them to the reader with the greatest possible clarity" (Antokolsky et al. 1955:22). To the Estonian novelist and translator Jaan Kross, a national culture is "a phenomenon of national character" and "a national poetry is of interest precisely because it is an expression of national character." Therefore, "the translator must above all penetrate to the essence of the national character of the material being translated." To comprehend the distinctive national character of the work is as important as to understand the individual character of the author, and neither is possible unless the translator is an artist who understands the concept of nation (1970:92). A. Leytes agrees: "Literary translation has become a powerful means for the communication and mutual enrichment of many dozens of fraternal literatures, a tool for giving millions of readers access to the classical heritage, *a school of artistic craftsmanship, a progressive phenomenon of the literature of Socialist Realism*" (1955:119). "If we are to avert a new catastrophe," Evgenya Kalashnikova stated at a meeting of the International Federation of Translators, "it is essential that all the peoples of the world should combine their resources of skill and industry in a friendly collaboration—something which is only possible on a basis of mutual understanding." Translators, she reminds us, are the builders in the Old Testament legend of Babel, and it is to translators that the chief responsibility for intercultural (and interlingual) communication falls (1966:16–17).

Such statements are often rhetoric and are in many instances linked with activist promulgations of the principles of Socialist Realism, which no one takes seriously now. Indeed, such statements are essential to the basic Socialist Realist slogan, "national in form, socialist in content." But statements about distinctive national character are not always mere rhetoric. The communication of human values is one of the most crucial purposes of translation, and Soviet translators reinforce this idea when they stress international communication as a chief basis of the art. Translation as communication is a prominent aspect of Soviet translation theory because the nationalities policy and international interests are so crucial to the school's very existence.

One of the most influential definitions of translation as communication was made by V. M. Rossels in a 1955 article on translation and the distinctive national character of an original work:

As a representative of a nation each person possesses a distinctive mentality *[psikhicheskii sklad]*, features of a distinct national character. It [this mentality] comes across on the pages of a literary work, is enveloped by objects of its environment, by national paysage, by local realia. In this sense national form *as a form of the life of the people* becomes an object of depiction in a literary work, a part of its content.

A national culture comprises

all forms of the artistic activity of a people—architectural style, range of colors in painting, manner of depiction in the graphic arts and sculpture, pace, rhythm, and figures of dance, structure of intonations, verbal expressiveness in literary works, ornamentation of embroidery and molding, form and assortment of domestic utensils, tableware, clothing, and so forth—all of these things bear the shadings of distinctive national character.

All the objects of a cultural environment and their essence are crucial to national character and national form, and the translator must comprehend and convey both object and essence. Translators must possess total knowledge of the life of the people from whose language they translate, and this, Rossels emphasizes, is *"an indispensible condition for the conveyance in an artistic translation of the richness of the real content of the original, including the national form of the life depicted in it."* Above all, the translator must realize that objects are contained in the language of a literary work. The translator must therefore concentrate on such elements of language as lexicon, grammatical structures, intonation, and even systems of versification. These phenomena cannot always be conveyed, but their character and their effect can and must be conveyed (1955:172, 175–76, 205).

Where Rossels sees the problem of conveying distinctive national character as one of *"national form,"* Oleksy Kundzich treats it as an essential ingredient of artistic translation. To Kundzich, it is of primary importance for an artistic translation to enrich one's own culture, and he quotes the Ukrainian writer Ivan Franko's observation that "good translations of the important and significant works of the foreign literatures of every cultured people . . . constitute an appurtenance of the basis of one's own literature." At the same time, Kundzich says, "It is an irrefutable fact that a creative translation enriches the new culture. A creative translation through the means of one language is an *assimilation*, what is assimilated becomes *one's own*, equal to the original." For these reasons, an artistic translation develops one's own literature in the same way as original creativity and "develops the language, broadens the circle of conceptions, enriches the culture of a people." An artistic translation introduces neologisms into a language and develops the grammatical structure of the language; more important, it introduces means for new literary expression (1959:7–9).

Both American and Russian translators turn to language to discuss their art as a problem of communication. Kashkin and Adams use language examples to state the problem, Rossels uses language for his definition of national form, and Kundzich sees in the enriching effects of translation a source of new means of national-cultural expression. But it is one thing for Rossels to list the objects of a national character and say that objects are contained in a national language, and quite another to move from these generalizations to the specific means by which distinctive national character is to be conveyed. In Marxist terms we are back to the dialectic of form and content. E. G. Etkind has reviewed discussions of "keys" to the unity of the parts and the whole in conveying the distinctive character of a foreign literary work and concluded that Soviet translators are hardly in agreement about the correct key. To Kashkin the key is the image; to Rossels it is the "fragment"; to A. V. Fedorov it is the sentence; to most Soviet translators it is, in Kashkin's phrase, "the word in its context"; to Etkind it is a matter of which two languages are involved (1959:71–72).

What Etkind implies is that Soviet discussions about conveyance of distinctive national character are not consistent. This is true even of considerations of such a seemingly simple aspect of the problem as national color or "coloration," a notion that has been widespread in world literature since the Romantic period and, as might be imagined, has remained central in Soviet literatures to the present day. According to A. V. Fedorov, "national coloration is a concrete distinctive quality of a literary work that can be expressed more or less clearly." He agrees with Kashkin that the basis of national coloration is the image and adds that idiomatic expressions are equally important to the problem of conveyance. National coloration is not expressed exclusively in images and idioms, but images most clearly reflect "the material environment and the social conditions of the life of a people," and a people reveals itself most fully in idiomatic expressions. In direct opposition to Rossels's definition of national form as a matter of linguistic means—lexicon and grammar forms—Fedorov believes that "national coloration always implicates a total aggregate of the features in a literary work, a whole combination of distinctive features." Because national coloration imbues a literary work as a whole and involves the links among the parts and between the parts and the whole, it is not even possible to speak of particular keys or devices of conveyance. Instead, any conveyance of national coloration depends on "the full value of the translation as a whole," which is to say, "on the degree of fidelity in conveying artistic images, which are linked also with the substantive meaning of words and with their grammatical formulation" and "on the nature of the means of the language" of the translation. By the latter requirement Fedorov signifies all linguistics means, including idiomatic expressions, and he states that the means must not be tied to specific local coloration or specific national realia of the language into which a work is translated (1983:277–80; also Gachechiladze 1970:171–76).

When he turns to language, Fedorov, like Rossels, does not specify *how* linguistic means are to be used for the conveyance of national coloration. He explains that national coloration, like distinctive national character more generally, is an aspect of the unity of a literary work as a whole, and he is lucid about the image and idiomatic expressions as the basis of the value. But he contradicts himself in denying the possibility of specific keys of conveyance, even while his emphasis on the image and idiomatic expressions amounts to a de facto prescription for just such keys. Fedorov is more definite when he comments that a translation should not be tied too closely to the local color and national realia of its language. By raising the question Fedorov at least reveals the direction of Soviet considerations of the problem of conveying distinctive national character.

Stated again as a problem of translation as communication, there is a distance from the distinctive national character of an original beyond which a translation must not go, and there is a distance toward the language of the translation that it must traverse. The means chosen must somehow convey the distinctive national character of the original while honoring the language of the translation. Kashkin is emphatic on this point:

> An artistic translation must show the foreign reality [of the original] and its "foreign distinctiveness" [*inostrannost'*] to the reader, bring the distinctive stylistic character of the original to him, preserve the text "in its native dress." However, the Russian translator's creative potentials manifest themselves to the reader in his skillful shaping [*oformlenie*] of the materials of the Russian language. As a work in Russian, an artistic translation, while preserving the particular national features of the original in its everyday and historical details and general coloration, simultaneously avoids "foreign-language-ness" by subordinating itself wherever possible to the internal laws of the Russian language. (1968b:457)

The translator must preserve both the distinctive features of the original and the integrity of the language of the translation. This is a matter of balance—of degree or distance. If Soviet translators are vague about the specifics of conveyance, they are at least able to cite convincing examples of a remarkable balance between conveyance of distinctive national character and preservation of the language in the translation. Fedorov and Kashkin cite almost the same examples. In Kashkin's opinion, "Romain Rolland's Colas Breugnon remains a Burgundian while speaking in the language of a Russian buffoon. Burns's people address us in our own language in Marshak's translations without ceasing to be Scotsmen," and Russians accept Lyubimov's Sancho Panza and Daruzes's Huckleberry Finn and Sara Gamp as foreigners even though they speak Russian" (1955:140). To Fedorov, "the example of conveyance of national coloration, of the distinctive national character of an original, provided by M. L. Lozinsky in his translation of *Colas Breugnon*, is all the more convincing and important in that Romain Rolland's work presents great difficulties . . . particularly the sheer force of its plethora of specific images and idiomatic elements." Lozinsky's translation is a masterful achievement endorsed by the similar conveyances of distinctive national coloration in Marshak's Burns, Kashkin and V. O. Rumer's translation of Chaucer's *Canterbury Tales*, and N. M. Lyubimov's translations of Cervantes and Rabelais, among many others (1983:282).

A common feature of these translations is that they strike a balance—they neither go too far in the direction of using Russian colloquial language nor avoid the problem by resorting to the neutral (or neutered) language called blandscript (*gladkopis'*). However, a quite different question of balance is involved here, one that runs headlong into formalist versus reader-response criticism. Kashkin says that the "distinctive stylistic character of the original" must be brought to the reader; when Rossels and Fedorov speak about linguistic means or image and idiomatic expressions, they agree with this demand. Not all translators agree, however, and some raise the question concerning whether the original should be brought to the reader or whether the reader should be brought to the original. That is, should translators reorient the original to the perceptions of reader in its new language and culture or should they recreate the original in its distinctive national character and oblige readers to accommodate themselves to the other language and culture?

As it happens, this is an old question that has been particularly well discussed by German theorists of translation and efficiently restated by André Lefevere. In Lefevere's view, conveyances of distinctive national character should be oriented to the opposite poles of synthesizing types of translation—reader-oriented translations and text-oriented translations. Either the original is adapted to the prevailing tastes of readers of the language of the translation or readers are obliged to adjust their taste to the language and culture of the original, even if the original does not appeal to their taste or they are not able to appreciate it (see Rose 1981b:32–33; Lefevere 1970). In his compendium of critical statements about translation in the German tradition, Lefevere offers an apt comment by Schleiermacher: "Either the translator leaves the author in peace, as much as possible, and moves the reader toward him; or he leaves the reader in peace, as much as possible, and moves the author toward him. The two roads are so completely separate from each other that one or the other must be followed as closely as possible" (1977:74). This is also the view of many modern translation theorists, who insist that readers ought to accommodate their tastes to different experiences, different cultures, different times. After all, if a reader chooses to read a translation of any kind, he or she may be reasonably expected to be seeking something new and different. If the reader turns away, Roger Roothaer suggests, then "in many cases the reader is more to blame than the translator." Likewise, the reader who undertakes to read a work of the past in his own language ought to realize that "he must acquaint himself as far as possible with the cultural background of that past period," and "the same holds for translations" (1978:131).

Those Soviet translators who have raised the question of reader- or text-oriented translations prefer that foreign works not be made to accommodate the tastes of the reader in the new language. In the opinion of E. G. Etkind, a translator has two options for conveying a work into another language. The translator may "accommodate a foreign work of art to the perceptions of the reader, make the unfamiliar familiar, the remote near"; or the translator may "reveal to the reader the richness of art, show him the beauty of diverse national forms, historical stratifications, individual creative systems. [He may] oblige him to experience aesthetic rapture over a remote, unfamiliar, foreign work of art, over the multiplicity of ideals and artistic forms" (1963:414). Etkind's words reveal the option he prefers. As Jaan Kross states,

> There are two principally different roads of approach to the national character of another people, its national culture. One of these roads is a quest of the familiar in what is foreign, that is *a quest for oneself*, the other is when the quest is for *what is unfamiliar* in the foreign, but interesting. In the first instance what the translator seeks is ultimately nothing other than his own personal "I," his translator's personality or a moral confirmation and assertion of that which typifies the character of his own nation.

This approach affirms an inclination on the part of some translators to consider worthwhile only those elements of a foreign culture that resemble their own. The second road, on the other hand, is "a striving to make one's own 'I' more multi-faceted." The translator who takes this approach is not afraid to learn something new and "seeks the opportunity to enrich himself." This is the approach that must define the translator's attitude toward both the original and the foreign culture, and this is the road that will lead both translator and reader to "the national culture that stands behind the author" of the original (1970:92).

This approach does not solve the problem of translation as communication, but it emphatically endorses the Soviet preference for translations whose basic intent is to preserve the distinctive national character of the original and to enrich cultures mutually by conveying value. Together with the other endorsements of both the difficulties and necessity of communicating value, such an approach illuminates two sides of the problem that should be taken into account. It tells the translator to be guided by the text, thereby endorsing the belief that a translation must be a faithful recreation; and it says that valid reader-response must be taken into account when judging a translation. The text should nct be brought to the reader, the reader should be brought to the text. And the best way to do this is to respect simultaneously the integrity of the text, the reader, the original author, the values of both cultures, and translation as communication.

PROSE

8

ARTISTIC TRANSLATION

Vonnegut in Russia

████████ The centerpiece of the Soviet school is, as has been discussed, the artistic translation. Discussions of artistic translation are the core of Soviet criticism and theory. Soviet translators are convinced that they have learned from both practice and theory to reject the worst translation methods and to synthesize from the best methods their own distinctive type of translation. They point with justifiable pride to hundreds of translations of world and Union literary works that reach the level of high art. What indeed, is artistic translation, and why does it merit being labeled as "art"? We can best answer this question by turning from problems of criticism and theory to the actual practice of one of the Soviet school's most highly praised literary translators.

Rita Rayt is a translator whom Kashkin has categorized as among those who dislike theory but pay close attention to theory in their work and contribute to theory in turn through the example of their practice. Rayt is recognized as one of the best translators in Soviet letters and has been an active participant throughout the development of the Soviet school. The appearance of her translations of J. D. Salinger's *The Catcher in the Rye* in the 1960s and four novels by Kurt Vonnegut, Jr., in the 1970s proved to be major events in Russian literature. Her translations, clear examples of the artistic method in practice, enjoy a deserved reputation for excellence, and demonstrate the attributes of artistic translation most often cited by critics and theorists.

Rayt is an experienced translator of German and Anglo-American literatures. She has to her credit translations from English of J. B. Priestley, John Galsworthy, Sean O'Casey (five one-act plays), and Graham Greene's *The Quiet American*. Among her translations of American works are Mark Twain's *Life on the Mississippi*, Sinclair Lewis's *Babbit*, and William Faulkner's *The Mansion, Soldier's Pay*, and, with Viktor Khinkis, *The Town*.

Among other American writers she has translated are Steinbeck, Hemingway, Malumud, Eudora Welty, and Clifford Odets. Her translation of Salinger's novel appeared together with an essay by the leading writer Vera Panova in the prestigious journal *Foreign Literature* in 1960 and later appeared in her translation of Salinger's collected works in 1965. Her four translations of Vonnegut were published as a single book in 1978 (Fiene 1976:166–90). In 1983 Rayt was awarded the Translation Center's Thornton Niven Wilder Prize, given to a distinguished foreign translator of American literature, at ceremonies in New York City and Moscow (Smith: 1985). The close relationship between this Russian translator and her American subject is the most important Russian-American friendship since the Nabokov-Wilson collaboration.

The popularity of Kurt Vonnegut, Jr., in the Soviet Union is a well-known phenomenon. Copies of his works in English are a welcome gift from American visitors, and they bring a high price on the black market. His writings, available to Russians in numerous translations, are often discussed in literary journals, and a version of *Slaughterhouse Five* has been staged by the Soviet Army Theater. Soviet readers covet membership in Vonnegut's karass— many are convinced they share a special affinity with him in his interplanetary order of things. Vonnegut's visits to the Soviet Union, coupled with his expressed admiration for Russian culture, have brought him a degree of official toleration. A personal acquaintance with Vonnegut is a source of prestige in Moscow and Leningrad; those who have discussed his works with Russians know he has touched something in the Russian character, just as he touched American college students. The appearance of Rayt's translations of *Slaughterhouse Five, Cat's Cradle, Breakfast of Champions,* and *God Bless You, Mr. Rosewater* was awaited with great impatience, and when they appeared after many delays, they were an immediate sellout.

Vonnegut's style would present specific problems to any translator, (see Lundquist 1977; also *The Vonnegut Statement* 1973). Although his style is straightforward and clear, his sentences, following each other in a matter-of-fact tone, repeat in structure. This persistent repetition would be monotonous were it not that what is so laconically phrased is so smiting. Vonnegut's style, his voice, is so casual as to seem banal—banality is both his style and the theme most often conveyed in his style—but this casualness actually heightens his irony. The meaning of his words is direct, he uses trite American clichés relentlessly, and he explains the obvious. He repeats nouns, verbs, adjectives, and adverbs in strings of epithets and lists of things. He delivers his punch lines in an even tone of voice, and the intonations of his slang, colloquialisms, sayings, brand names, and dirty words are as level as normal speech.

Words and sentences become a toneless litany of ordinariness. Vonnegut says in *Breakfast of Champions*:

When Dwayne Hoover and Kilgore Trout met each other, their country was by far the richest and most powerful country on the planet. It had most of the food and minerals and machinery, and it disciplined other countries by threatening to shoot big rockets at them or to drop things on them from airplanes.

Many other countries didn't have doodley-squat. Many of them weren't even habitable anymore. They had too many people and not enough space. They had sold everything that was any good, and there wasn't anything to eat anymore, and still the people went on fucking all the time.

Fucking was how babies were made.

If these words and sentences seem manageable, their intonations and connotations—the prosaic quality that makes Vonnegut's style his own—are not easily captured in another language. The connection between banality and irony in his style (a connection that conveys his despair) is a delicate one, so that an incorrect choice of lexical equivalent or ordering of syntax could give Russian readers the wrong idea about Vonnegut. Intonation is derived, stylistically, from a variety of elements and their interrelationships, including syntactic structure, phonetic pattern, rhythm, tone, stress. Soviet translation theorists have devoted considerable attention to all aspects of style, and intonation has been a dominant interest. Rayt has pointed to the importance of intonation, to the absolute that the translator must hear and recreate the original author's voice. The translator of Faulkner must distinguish among the differences in the southern speech of aristocrats, poor whites, and blacks. "One must verify whether one *sees* [Faulkner's] characters, whether one *hears* their voices, even the timbre of their voices." The slightest inversion or other transformation of syntax can make all the difference between a faithful and a false conveyance of a stylist such as Faulkner (1965:8, 17).

A. V. Fedorov and Givi Gachechiladze emphasize that intonation is one of the most crucial aspects of style. Intonation is the most sensitive instrument for conveying the impact of a style and thus the meaning of a work, the author's world view, and even the national character of the author's literature. "Any prose . . . is organized by means of syntactic constructions," Gachechiladze has said,

and therefore great attention has been paid in the process of translation to the semantic relationships which are established in the original among the idea, intonation, rhythm, and syntactic structure expressed in the verbal images. . . . Artistic prose is written not only to be read, it is also apprehended by the hearing, and artistic images, with the help of associations, make it accessible to other human senses too. In speech the immediate reality of an idea is expressed not only in words, but by specific intonation and a rhythm, which are created by specific syntactic constructions in accordance with the demands of the idea being expressed. (1970:195–98)

Gachechiladze cites a list of the elements of intonation compiled by V. M. Rossels, who believes that intonation is "a system of pauses, stops, rises and falls of the voice, semantic stress in phrases, acceleration and slowing of pace of delivery—a system which organizes our emotional receptivity, even when we read 'to ourselves' without pronouncing the text aloud" (1955:179).

How effectively is theory here realized in practice? Rayt sustains Vonnegut's style, voice, and intonations. By capturing these qualities unobtrusively, she demonstrates what Soviet theorists of the art of translation mean when they stress the values of affinity and fidelity. The laconic narrative tone of Vonnegut's style and its conveyance into Russian by Rayt can be compared through a sample from *Breakfast of Champions*. Here the original text is broken into the lines of its intonational pattern and juxtaposed with Rayt's recreation:

> The slaves were simply turned loose without any property.
> They were easily recognizable.
> They were black.
> They were suddenly free to go exploring.

> Rabov prosto otpustili, bez vsiakogo imushchestva.
> Otlichit' ikh ot drugikh liudei bylo neslozhno.
> Vse oni byli chernokozhie.
> I oni vdrug okazalis' na svobode—
> Ustraivaesh' kak znaesh'.

Vonnegut's voice does not pause in the middle of a sentence; his diction continues to the end of each sentence before pausing. There is no emotional variation in the intonations; the sentences are devoid of rise and fall, fast or slow pacing. The punch line is delivered at the same emotional level as the matter-of-fact statements made in the other sentences. Note also how closely the structure of Rayt's syntax, lexicon, and intonational pattern matches the original. She breaks the last sentence into two intonational lines, possibly because she must resort to a more syntactically complex Russian formula to make Vonnegut's point about the slaves being suddenly free "to go exploring," but otherwise there are no marked differences between her structure and his. Vonnegut's Russian voice pauses correctly at the end of each sentence, neither rising nor falling nor changing pace— it is as laconic as it is in English. Rayt has even tried to reproduce the rhythmic patterns of the intonational lines:

> The slaves were simply turned loose without any property.

> Rabóv prosto otpustíli, bez vsiákogo imúshchestva.

The similarity between the American and Russian Vonnegut can be seen by breaking another sample from the same novel into its intonation segments:

It certainly was flat out there—
flat city,
flat township,
flat county
flat state.

Da, za oknom vsio bylo ploskim donel'zia—
ploskii gorod,
ploskie prigorody,
ploskii okrug,
ploskii shtat.

Russian words tend to be longer than their English equivalents, so that the pungent monosyllabic word "flat" loses its sharpness in the Russian adjective *ploskii*; Rayt has perhaps given the word "certainly" too much weight by using the Russian word *donel'zia* '(as flat) as can be,' thereby making the sentence prolix. But her conveyance is otherwise remarkably close to the original in ordering of syntax, in pace of delivery, and in pattern of rising and falling voice.

In her adherence to intonation for the successful conveyance of Vonnegut's style, Rayt has exemplified a frequently discussed methodological concept developed in Soviet theory of translation as it relates to problems of style. The concept, known as the "stylistic key," signifies the need for the translator to discover not only the basic elements of an original author's style but also the correct means of conveying them into the new language, so that they make the same impact on the new reader as they did on the reader of the original. Gachechiladze believes that

the finding of the "key" for the translator's penetration to the essence of the work has great significance. . . . The translator must apprehend the rhythm of the original, the intonation, the manner of communicating thought, the link between these components and the story, plot, and composition of the work, and likewise with other elements of form that serve to manifest the unifying idea of the work. . . . The general form is likewise formed from the unity of its separate elements. The general sound of the work is expressed in the general style of the work, and in this sense all elements . . . are the component parts of a single style. Therefore the aforementioned "key" may be called a "stylistic key." (1970:189)

Boris Pasternak explains his use of the stylistic key in his essay "Translating Shakespeare." To him, "Shakespeare's rhythm is the basic principle of his poetry. Its momentum determines the tempo and sequence of questions and answers in his dialogues and the length of his periods and monologues." Pointing to his best-known translation of Shakespeare as an example of his use of the device, Pasternak adds, "Shakespeare's use of rhythm is clearest in *Hamlet*, where it serves a triple purpose. It is used as a method of characterization, it makes audible and sustains the prevailing mood, and it elevates the tone and softens the brutality of certain scenes" (1983:128–29).

Rayt has found one key to Vonnegut's style in his use of repetition. Vonnegut's use of repetition is so persistent that the device becomes a powerful intonational system. His sentences are often lists of words, so that it is not at all hard to find such sentences in *Breakfast of Champions* as "a lot of citizens were so *ignored* and *cheated* and *insulted* that they thought they might be in the *wrong* country, or even on the *wrong* planet," or "he . . . became again the *insufferably brainless, humorless, heartless,* soldier he had learned to be in military school" (italics are mine). Just how carefully Rayt has conveyed the repetitive character of Vonnegut's style can be seen by comparing a sample from the same novel:

> So here was the new Harry now, *rosy with fear and excitement*. He felt *uninhibited and beautiful and lovable and suddenly free*.

> I vot Garri predstal pered Dveinom, *porozovev ot strakha i volneniia*. V etot mig on pochuvstvoval sebia *raskovannym, prekrasnym, obaiatel'nym, i neozhidanno svobodnym*.

Rayt has eliminated Vonnegut's repeated conjunctions in the second sentence because so many "ands" would not have the same effect in Russian as they do in English. She has introduced a clarification by translating "so here was Harry now" as "so here was Harry standing before Dwayne" because a strong Russian sense of place requires the addition. Despite these modifications, the repetitive word patterns are the same. Rayt is clearly aware of the function of repetition, and she honors this key to Vonnegut's style throughout her translations. Where in *Breakfast of Champions* Vonnegut has "heartless and greedy," she has "*besserdechnye i zhadnye*"; where he has "so cruelly and wastefully," she has "*tak zhestoko i rastochitel'no*"; and where he has "slurps and moans," she has "*chavkan'e i stony*."

Analysis of the texts of all four translations of Vonnegut's novels shows that Rayt concentrates on finding the best ways to recreate her subject's English style in an equivalent Russian style. Her modifications are not motivated by a desire to improve Vonnegut, and she does not succumb to the temptation to create for herself. The samples of her conveyances indicate that her concern is with resources of language and style. The value of choice and decision is essential in the detection and use of the stylistic key, and the correspondence between the author's world view and style—precisely where the stylistic key is to be found—"sometimes demands that the translator introduce a carefully chosen substitute" (Gachechiladze 1970:190). Rayt does substitute, and replace, and modify, and sacrifice. She also compensates —the departures in the examples offered seem to derive from a sense that Russian style usage does not tolerate such inexorable repetition, such determinedly laconic intonations. To this it can be added that Rayt deletes too many of Vonnegut's conjunctions—"and" being one of his most frequently repeated words. But Rayt has not reinterpreted Vonnegut; she has instead exercised tact and taste in her choices, and her instinct for style is good. This can be seen in her changes of word order to accord with what she knows is best for Vonnegut in Russian.

There is a semantic difference in English, for example, between Vonnegut's repetitive phrase "uninhibited and beautiful and lovable and suddenly free" and a random reordering of the sequence into, say, "lovable and uninhibited and beautiful and suddenly free"—Vonnegut's priorities have been changed, and in the intonation and rhythm of this reordering, Vonnegut's voice has been changed. When certain structures are conveyed into another language, a literal reproduction of the original order may result in priorities that are wrong for a reader in the new language. The intonations and rhythms may change, and the conveyance may sound wrong. In many cases Rayt's rearrangements are a simple matter of Russian usage. Russians do not say "the cat and the dog," as Vonnegut says in *Breakfast of Champions*, they say *sobaka i kot* 'the dog and the cat,' as Rayt has said in her Russian version. Where Vonnegut has "a pen or pencil," Rayt has "*karandash ili pero*" in correct Russian order, and where Vonnegut has "unselfishly and trustingly," the order in Russian has been reversed to "*doverchivye i beskorystnye.*" In other instances Rayt's modifications are a result of how Vonnegut's voice sounds in English and what must be done to ensure that he sounds like his American self *in Russian*. Thus, where Vonnegut has "a hunter and a fisherman," Rayt has replaced the nouns with verbs—"to hunt and fish"—since in Russian the verbs more appropriately preserve his intonation than the original nouns would have done.

Sometimes Rayt seems to substitute too readily. Vonnegut's list of nouns, "friends or relatives or property or usefulness or ambition," has been varied by turning the first two nouns into adjectives and adjusting the syntax: *bezrodnye, bespoleznye, bez vsiakogo imushchestva, professii i tseli v zhizni*, literally, 'relativeless, useless, without any property, profession, or goal in life.' Where Vonnegut describes Lincoln as a man of "courage and imagination," Rayt has him as "a man of great courage and breadth of views." Vonnegut's "fast and useful and unornamental" has been modified to read as "a powerful, fast useful thing, without ornamentation." Translated back into English, these samples sound less natural than they do in Russian. But Rayt has deliberately changed word order and varied phraseology because the English order and phrasing would sound as false in Russian as the Russian order and wording sounds in English. The first example above sounds like a distortion of Vonnegut's voice, but Rayt's Russian variation on his theme sounds just like he might have written in Russian: "*bezrodnye, bespoleznye, bez vsiakogo imushchestva, professii i tseli v zhizni.*"

Rayt's rearrangements of syntax do not disrupt Vonnegut's steady narrative tone or vary his laconic voice. Rather, as stated, her substitutions and modifications almost always facilitate her intent to recreate an American writer in Russian. Consider the connections between the banality of Vonnegut's lexicon and his irony. It is difficult to think of any writer who uses American clichés as remorselessly as Vonnegut, or any writer who can turn banality into such sharp irony. The despair that is Vonnegut's Weltanschauung derives from his reduction of cosmic infinity to the most ordinary, and often the most vulgar, details of everyday American reality through trite colloquial language. A single slip in conveying Vonnegut's banality-irony can destroy the immediate stylistic effect. Many poor choices could destroy the entire character of his work.

Does the Russian language have the capacity to convey the triteness of such a common remark as, "Life is sure funny sometimes," or a saying like, "Let the chips fall where they may"? What is a Russian translator to do with the comment in *Slaughterhouse Five* about Billy Pilgrim's profession as an optometrist, "Frames are where the money is"? How is the translator to convey such unmistakable Vonnegutisms as "darling elves," "sweet old poop," "perfectly beautiful trouble," "blubbering thanks," or the description of a sexy woman as "a sensational invitation to make babies"? How is a translator likely to fare with such Americanisms as "raised hell," "stopping on a dime," "bug-eyed with terror," or "pinch every penny till it screams"?

For the most part, Vonnegut's colloquial style fares very well in Rayt's translations. Few of her conveyances are flawed, most are adequate to the original, and many are ingenious. Her skill is especially apparent in her handling of equivalents for distinctive Americanisms. In her translation of *Slaughterhouse Five*, "gutless wonder" is conveyed as *chudo bez kishok* 'a wonder without guts,' and the transformation of the syntax from noun and adjective to two nouns with preposition is in keeping with natural Russian usage. For the reference to Frank Sinatra and John Wayne as "dirty old men" who glorified war without having been so bold as to risk experiencing it, she employs the equally blunt Russian equivalent "*skvernye stariki.*" A memorable World War II phrase, "coming in on a wing and a prayer," is given to Russians as "landing on a promise and one wing." The conveyance reverses the two nouns because in Russian this is rhythmically and phonetically more pungent. The unmistakably American expression "scared shitless" is finessed as *do kolic* 'colic,' and the conveyance can be appreciated as apt. The Americanism "bug-eyed with terror" is conveyed with the sharp Russian equivalent *"pucheglazyi ot strakha."* The use of *"pucheglazyi"* is every bit as expressive as "bug-eyed," and in just the same way as expressive. "Stopping on a dime" appears as "braked on a five-copeck piece," using the Russian slang word *"piatachka"* for the American slang word "dime." The latter conveyance may be a Russification, but the word *"piatachka"* is so intimately Russian that the substitution does not enter the Russian consciousness, whereas as a literal conveyance (*daim*) would provoke the reader's curiosity and thereby dim the clarity of the image. "Raised hell" is represented by the Russian expression *"rugatel'ski rugat',"* a Russian colloquialism derived from the verb "to curse" and its vulgate adverbial form *rugatel'ski*. The representation appeals to the Russian fondness for pleonasms, and it should be noted that Rayt has rejected several Russian equivalents for "raised hell" available in dictionaries. The representation is a concoction, but it manages to be right for Vonnegut's voice.

Many of Rayt's equivalents are ready-made for her in the Russian language—she exploits the banalities of her own language to represent similar American banalities. In the translation of *Cat's Cradle* the Russian expression "fresh as a cucumber" is used to convey "fresh as a daisy." The translator chooses one of many Russian equivalents for the American expression "hoist a few," since Russians sometimes do this too. When Americans think of "go through that song and dance again," Russians think of "play all that music again," as Rayt has it in her translation. Russians do not say "big cheese," they say big *shishka* 'bump,' but it is a perfect equivalent and the sound of the Russian word *"shishka"* is as sharp as the semantics of the American word "cheese" in this colloquial context. In her translation of *Breakfast of Champions* Rayt easily found *skazochnyi dom* 'fairy-tale house,' for its American equivalent "dream house," and she used *"shishka"* again for the "big shot." American slang terms for prison and insanity are based on a mode of thought culturally different from the Russian, but *"v kutuzku"* is effective for "(put me) in jail," and *"v tiuriage"* is close to "in the calabash," and equally expressive. *Cherdak byl ne v poriadke* '(his) attic was out of order' is not only good for "he had bats in his bell tower" but also matches the alliteration and rhythm of the American slang. The commonly used Russian expression *"staryi perdun"* conveys to Russians exactly what Vonnegut meant when he described himself upon turning fifty as an "old fart." Use of the Russian equivalent, *"pesochnitsa,"* would have been a mistake.

In the majority of cases Rayt is as inventive in Russian as Vonnegut is in English, and inventive in the same way as he is. This is especially true where she has to rise to his brilliant use of clichés. The rhymed phrase "babies full of rabies" is conveyed with an equally trite rhyme: *rebiata-shcheniata* 'babies-(rabid) puppies.' The culturally acute American saying, "Up your ass with Mobil Gas!" is not substituted but conveyed with an equally trite Russian rhyme: *Rastudy i vas, Mobil'-gaz*! For an equivalent to the expression "off his rocker," Rayt took the advice of Chukovsky, Kashkin, and others that translators should turn to their own literature for the wealthiest source of synonyms and pulled from Gogol's comedy *The Inspector General* an unconventional verb in the past tense, "*svikhnulsia.*"

Occasionally Rayt strains too hard to convey Vonnegut's phrases as they are, perhaps tempted by a pedagogue's desire to teach Russians how Americans think and speak. In her translation of *Slaughterhouse Five*, "pinch every penny till it screams" is conveyed too literally, and thus with labored syntax, as "squeeze in (his) fist every grosh until it shudders." In other instances the translator seems hesitant to deal with Vonnegut's style at its sharpest and slips toward, if not into, blandscript. The Russian expression "(he) used his connections" does not do justice to "pulled political wires"; "sheer raving" ("*sploshnyi bred,*" the dictionary recommendation) does not justly express "gibberish" (*tarabarshchina* might have been better). In *Cat's Cradle,* "they put prayers into action" misses the inimitable Vonnegutism, "So they gave praying a whirl"; "I had nowhere to spend the time" does not serve the American expression "so I had a night to kill"; "stupid invention of poets" ("*glupyi vymysel poetov*") falls short of "poetic crap." Russians do not give praying a whirl and they do not kill a night, but the blandscript is a bit disappointing here. To Rayt's credit, however, such distinctive Americanisms as "the mind reels," "ding-a-ling associations," "addled by booze," and "higgledy-piggledy" are obviously untranslatable, and she does not attempt to do so.

Rayt is always closer to her best when faced with distinctive Vonnegutisms. She has carefully read her author and analyzed his style, and she has an obvious affinity for him. In her translation of *Slaughterhouse Five*, "the engines began to tootle at one another" reads in Russian as it does in Vonnegut's English, and the location of the British section of the prisoner-of-war camp "dead-center in a sea of dying Russians" is exactly the same in the translation. Vonnegut's "out came shit and piss and language," his description of the boxcars filled with American prisoners of war, is conveyed with sureness as *ekskrementy, mocha i rugan'* 'excrement, piss, and cussing.' In this instance, Rayt has changed "language" to "cussing" because the Russian word *iazyk* also means "tongue," and the Russian reader might read the phrase to mean "out came shit and piss and a tongue." For Vonnegut's description of the shriveled genitals of the miserable American prisoners standing naked in the cold, "reproduction was not the main business of the evening," Rayt conveys the irony with stylistic, as opposed to literal, good sense as "reproduction of the human race was simply not on the agenda that evening." Vonnegut's description of a sexy woman as "a sensational invitation to make babies" is equally rendered with good sense as "and right away he wanted to fill her up with babies." In *Breakfast of Champions* the frequently used Americanism "doodley-squat" defies translation. The only way around this example of the language barrier is to substitute, or explain, or perhaps take Nabokov's advice and add a footnote, or give up and replace it with a standard word. Rayt chooses to substitute—to find an approximate colloquial Russian equivalent—and she finds a fair conveyance in the word *shisha*, which catches the meaning of money and even sounds as scatological as its American equivalent. For the classic Vonnegut statement, "their imaginations were flywheels on the ramshackle machinery of the awful truth," Rayt finds equivalents for "ramshackle machinery" and "awful truth" in the Russian epithets "*rasshatannyi mekhanizm*" and "*zhestokaia istina*." And what could be a more brilliant representation of the item "pooteeweet" in *Slaughterhouse Five* than "*piutifiut*"? In this single onomatopoeic comment, Vonnegut sums up all of *Slaughterhouse Five,* and all his despair over the human condition. Rayt's treatment here is a perfect example of what Gachechiladze and other Soviet theorists mean when they emphasize that both the work as a whole and the entire reality reflected in the work are dependent on minutiae of style.

Rayt's translations are indicative of the highest standards. Analysis shows that choice and decision are basic to her modus operandi. She substitutes, sacrifices, and replaces with professional care; she is clearly familiar with theory and criticism of translation, particularly with such concepts as the stylistic key and questions of intonation. Yet, she reveals an instinct for what is right in terms of both the original language and her own—tact, sensitivity, and talent are as evident in her work as knowledge of theory. Rayt is both imaginative and inventive, but she does not attempt to create for herself; her work is not an opportunity to express her own literary "I." She reveals respect for the rights of the original author and, at the same time, for the integrity of the original text. She knows her own language, and she has mastered the English language. She is familiar with American slang and idioms, is at home with American culture, and seems to know everything about Vonnegut's world. And she is optimistic about her own ability and the capacity of her own language to recreate a difficult American style and therefore confident that good translation is possible. Perhaps the tradition of optimism and thus of problem-solving, as demonstrated by Rayt, is one of the greater values of Soviet artistic translation.

LITERARY TRANSLATION

Solzhenitsyn in English

To ask questions about standards in a comparative study and arrive at the notion of optimism is to provoke speculation about differences of character. The generalizing terms that come to mind in discussing Russian standards are *uniformity, agreement, consistency.* In contrast, a word that occurs quite often in American discussions of standards is *inconsistency.* That is not to say that American translators have difficulty finding excellent translations in their letters. Translators are subject to peer review on an individual basis, and for the most part the review system works. But deadlines—hasty races to market—continue to encourage sloppy work, and translators are unsure of their collective ability to ensure high standards. We readily admit that our criticism is in most instances arbitrary, inconsistent, vague in terminology, and indecisive about what constitutes valid measures of excellence.

Another word for inconsistency is *pluralism.* Soviet views of American culture typically fail to consider this difference in distinctive national character. New Soviet émigrés to the United States are often so overwhelmed by our diversity, contradictions, and arbitrariness that they take what might be vitality for *besprintsipial'nost'* 'lack of principle,' and even, according to Solzhenitsyn and others, moral laxity. But the Soviet school's uniformity of standards is certainly not above scrutiny. Through their monopoly and national platform, Soviet translators do a better job of enforcing standards, but uniformity often means conformity, and plurality does not necessarily mean a lack of standards. We can see this by examining translations of a Russian literary work that show a range of both good and bad translation standards. There is no English translation of a Russian literary work that can be said to be representative, but one well-known work has been translated often enough to provide a large and indicative sampling of standards. This work is particularly obliging in that it is modern and has been translated several times within a short period of time. Five translations of Alexander Solzhenitsyn's short novel *One Day in the Life of Ivan Denisovich*, a work containing diverse language and style phenomena, provide representative examples of solutions to problems of language and style.

Solzhenitsyn's *One Day in the Life of Ivan Denisovich* was first published in November 1962, after the personal intervention of Nikita Khrushchev himself. Within a very few months it had stormed the world in translation. The five English translations are by Bela von Block, Max Hayward and Ronald Hingley, Ralph Parker, Thomas P. Whitney, all in 1963, and by Gillon Aitken (in association with the script of the Group W-Leontes Norskfilm 1970) in 1971. This is probably a one-time occurrence, since it is not likely that literary sensation will again prompt so many translations in so short a time period. The first four translations were severely criticized by Chukovsky in *A High Art* (his critique was censored from the 1968 edition of the book); all five translations have been assessed by Alexis Klimoff (1973). The style and language of *One Day* are of great importance; the peculiar character of the colloquial speech of *One Day* is a chief quality. Due to the existence of dictionaries of Russian prison-camp language (Galler and Marquess 1972; Carpovich 1976; Kozlovsky 1981), it is possible to analyze the difficult language of the text with a considerable degree of accuracy.

One Day is written in one of the most rich and unusual styles ever used in a modern Russian literary work, and it establishes the vulgate character of Solzhenitsyn's style for almost every subsequent work. As we now know from such novels as *August 1914* and from Solzhenitsyn's essay with the saucy title "We are not accustomed to seasoning our shchi with tar, for this we use sour cream" (1969), the style of *One Day* is only the first venture by Solzhenitsyn toward the most basic colloquial Russian as a literary standard. To Solzhenitsyn, the language of the Russian people is the true Russian language; without an appreciation for this conviction there can be no appreciation for the difficulties of translating Solzhenitsyn. Ivan Denisovich's speech standard is essentially folkish: he uses words that Russian peasants have used for centuries and cannot be found in standard dictionaries. His peasant dialect is enriched further by his contact with other areas of experience—his life during the war and in the camps, his association with Moscow intellectuals, and his many years as a collective farmer and carpenter. The result is a colloquial manner created out of soldier slang, convict jargon, peasant dialect, Stalinist bureaucratese, the language of "thieves" (*vory*), and Ivan Denisovich's own way of thinking and speaking.

The structure of the tale is based on its narrative mode, and the mode is based on Ivan Denisovich's colloquial manner. Ivan Denisovich is not the teller of the tale. Rather, the novel is told in terms of his thoughts. He thinks what he says, and we follow him through his day in his thoughts

(Luplow 1971). Ivan Denisovich's speech manner reveals his personality, but just as important, it gives the reader access into the strange world in which a man endures. On the one hand, Ivan Denisovich's speech manner prompts the reader to empathize with him and thus to perceive his world as he himself perceives it. On the other hand, its peculiarity also keeps the reader at a distance—a distance sufficient to ensure that we will be horrified by the events and the institution Ivan Denisovich matter-of-factly accepts. This achievement—both empathy and distance—is lost on the English-language reader to the degree that translators fail to convey the character of Ivan Denisovich's speech.

There is a distinct unwillingness on the part of the translators of *One Day* to deal forthrightly with the colloquialisms of Ivan Denisovich's speech manner. Avoidance of colloquial speech is common among translators, but analysis of these five translations demonstrates a tendency to explain, rather than to convey, some of the simplest and most pungent Russian words, expressions, and sayings. In the expression "*Zakon—on vyvorotnoi*," for example, we have a swift insight into Ivan Denisovich's resigned yet still sarcastic acceptance of his prison-camp world. He states quite simply that under Soviet power, "The law—it's a twistabout," or, "The law—it's a turn-around." There is nothing difficult to understand about this utterance, yet Whitney chooses to explain it as, "Law—that was something the government turned inside out as it pleased"; Aitken explicates it as, "The law can be turned any way you want"; and Hayward and Hingley have it as, "They twisted the law any way they wanted." Only Parker has captured the Russian flavor of the phrase, albeit in a somewhat laborious way, with the conveyance, "The law can be stood on its head." The sharp, simple word "*terpel'nik*" is given by Parker and Aitken as "(one) who had suffered so much," while Hayward and Hingley exaggerate it into "(one who) had really been through the mill." These choices are unnecessarily prolix. Only Whitney conveyed it correctly, if not with requisite pungency, as "long-sufferer." Parker's "luckless fellow" does no justice to "*bedolaga*," but it is better than Hayward and Hingley's outright explanation, "He'd had a hard life."

Throughout, the translators have tended to draw out Solzhenitsyn's style, where it is sharp and to the point in the original. Hayward and Hingley's "be a wreck for the rest of your life" is quite good for one of Ivan Denisovich's unspoken thoughts, but Aitken's neutral "your health had been ruined for the rest of your life" is prolix, and too literal. Aitken's phrase "Pavlo delayed things a little further" is a needless explanation of the single, quick verb *potomil* 'stalled,' and is more aptly conveyed by Hayward and Hingley as "Pavlo kept him dangling." In one instance the desire to explain things leads to the omission of one of the tale's subtle ironies. When

Ivan Denisovich thinks, "These Baptists, they love to agitate," he wittily (or perhaps inadvertently) associates a religious entity with the ideologically acute verb "to agitate." Completely missing the point, Parker converts the verb into "recruiting," Aitken turns it into the religious term "evangelize," and Hayward and Hingley choose to reinterpret: "Those Baptists love to spread a little propaganda." The latter choice unintentionally substitutes one ideological practice for another; given the political ballyhoo that welcomed Solzhenitsyn's work to the West, this inattention to ideology is surprising. In another case, only Parker and Whitney correctly convey the important ideological form of address "*grazhdanin nachal'nik*," as "citizen chief." Hayward and Hingley and Aitken have it as "comrade warder," even though political prisoners were forbidden to use the word "comrade," an important fact for the novel's time and place. The tendency to avoid profoundly Russianate words and phrases by explaining them—a device called protocol translation—prompted Hayward and Hingley, Aitken, and Whitney to convey "law of the taiga" with the geographically absurd "law of the jungle." The comprehensible phrase "old . . . camp wolf" is needlessly reinterpreted into "hard-bitten prisoner" by Parker, Americanized as "old camp hand" by Hayward and Hingley, made too British as "old lag" by Aitken, and transformed into a "tough old bird" by Block.

Happily, all six translators attempt to avoid blandscript. Collectively, the translators have provided apt equivalents, and the translations of Parker and Hayward and Hingley are very good in this respect. Hayward and Hingley convey the verb "*dokhodil*," meaning that someone has reached his limits, as "on his last legs." For one slang expression, "now it hit him" is a better choice by Hayward and Hingley than Aitken's far too British "twig what it was all about" and Whitney's elaborated "only then did Shukhov get what was up." The cotranslators reveal both imagination and good sense in the conveyance of "*tyk-myk*" as "all in a sweat," and "shrewd as hell" is a good solution to the problem posed by another Russianate colloquialism. In another case, their phrase "put a bug in the commandant's" ear is far more effective than Aitken's prosaic and literal "whisper in the commandant's ear" and Parker's "whispered to the chief." Parker's rendition of a Russian phrase involving a colloquial form of the word for "master" (*mastak*) and a verb based on the word for "jackal" (*shakalit'*) weakens the style of the original: "Fetyukov was a past master at cadging." But it nevertheless is short and to the point and in this respect is superior to Hayward and Hingley's elaborate protocol rendition: "You couldn't beat Fetyukov when it came to scrounging." Parker also does well in conveying "*der'mom by ikh kormit*" as "ought to feed them on shit," and he uses such pungent English expressions as "not fucking likely," "learn the ropes," and "what's the fucking sense in washing it?" (Curiously, Parker's translation was published in the Soviet Union [Solzhenitsyn 1963e] in a severely toned down text in which many of his best equivalents are often replaced by an artificial, outdated language.)

In many cases it is unfair to reproach these translators for poor handling of Solzhenitsyn's language and style, because *One Day* is an orgy of difficult Russianisms of all kinds and ages. The word "*bedolaga*," for example, seems to be a variant of an old colloquial word *bedolakha* 'wretch, poor devil,' but the variant root *-laga* sounds a distinct note of the word *lager* 'camp.' This etymological hint based on double-root referents probably could not be conveyed. The verb *fuganut'*, given in the Galler and Marquess dictionary as "to slug, hit, beat," is easily conveyed by the first of these variants, but the initial root *fu* is a clear hint of the Russian word *khui* 'prick,' and would be lost in any conveyance. This is true also of Solzhenitsyn's many other circumlocutions based on the root *fu-*, with a meaning similar to the English "phooey" or "foo on you." The preposterous verb "*fuimet'sia*" is a clear euphemism for the equally preposterous verb "*khuimet'sia*" and is not conveyed by Aitken's "fucking likely" or Parker's "not fucking likely," but both translators do all they can for such an impossible invention. This is also true of the expression "*na fuia ego i myt'*," which Aitken conveys as "what the fuck's the point in washing the place?" and Parker as "what's the fucking sense in washing it?" It would be possible to list scores of words in *One Day* that cannot be taken out of the Russian language, and this applies not only to peculiarized circumlocutions and euphemisms of Solzhenitsyn's invention but also to racy, unrepeatable bits of slang and argot acquired from his experience of the camps.

Regarding curse words, incidentally, Solzhenitsyn was obliged by prudish censorship to resort to circumlocutions. In these cases his translators chose to use what they believe is the intended profanity in English. Perhaps this is good judgment—in subsequent works Solzhenitsyn has openly used words true to a language notorious for dirty words. Nevertheless, a stylistic feature of the work has been lost by spelling Solzhenitsyn out. This is a question of language as communication: readers of English-language literary works are not as shocked by curse words as Russians are when they see them in print. In a related example from our own literature, Norman Mailer's circumlocution "fug" in *The Naked and the Dead* is an icon of the history of American literature—a sign of the time when Americans were prudish. Were the word to be replaced now by "fuck," a record of our literary taste would be erased. Perhaps this applies to *One Day* too. The case for this is even more compelling in that Solzhenitsyn's ingenious circumlocutions are linguistically hilarious.

Ivan Denisovich speaks not only in folk rhythms but also in folk sayings and aphorisms. Only Ralph Parker detects and conveys this aspect of Solzhenitsyn's language and style. Ivan Denisovich does not simply recite

Russian sayings; he adapts them to his Russian experience of the GULag. Aphorisms, aphoristic constructions, or, most often, aphoristic intonations are indispensable to the novel. The importance of intonation to the conveyance of authorial voice has already been shown in the analyses of Rayt's translations of Vonnegut. Capturing intonation is even more crucial to the structure of *One Day*, with its voice that is not Solzhenitsyn's, and not Ivan Denisovich's, even though it is very much like his. If we are deprived of the hero's aphoristic intonations, we are deprived of insight into his personality, which in turn deprives us of entry into his experience and, above all, his perception of his reality Ivan Denisovich does not simply say, as Hayward and Hingley have it, "You didn't feel like talking in the morning"; he says, in Parker's perceptive equivalent, "A tongue doesn't wag in the morning." He does not say, as in Hayward and Hingley's protocol conveyance, "The only thing for you was to put your back into the work—that was for sure"; he says, as in Parker's quick aphorism, "Better to growl and submit." When Solzhenitsyn's hero thinks, "Work was like a stick; it had two ends," as Parker has translated, his thoughts cannot be accurately read in Block's simple statement, "Work was like a stick with two ends."

In some instances, Ivan Denisovich's aphoristic intonations are based subtly on repetition, which Parker catches and brings to his English-language readers: "Does it bother you to wear those numbers? They don't weigh anything, those numbers"; "Easy money weighs light in the hand and doesn't give you the feeling you've earned it. There was truth in the old saying: pay short money and get short value." Block approaches the sound of the aphoristic thought of the second sample here, and some of its repetitive character, but ruins the conveyance by introducing slangy equivalents: "Easy money. But easy come, easy go; easy money won't stay in your hand, it doesn't feel as if you'd really earned it." "If you show your pride too much, he said, you're lost," Parker has it in his adroit conveyance of common Russian sense. "He said if you kicked up a fuss you were finished," it is said, not quite faithfully, in the Hayward-Hingley translation. When it is realized that *One Day* is saturated with such aphoristic observations, then Parker's sensitivity in detecting them can be appreciated. But the failure of the other translators to detect this stylistic device bespeaks lack of attention.

Another aspect of style was missed by Solzhenitsyn's translators in some instances, detected in others—with no consistency whatever. One of Ivan Denisovich's pleasures in life is to make sounds appropriate to what he sees and hears around him. When his work brigade sets off across the brittle cold steppe in the morning, he describes their tramping in the snow as "*top-top, skrip-skrip*." The sound is conveyed by Hayward and Hingley as "tramp-tramp-tramp, crunch-crunch-crunch," by Parker as "shuffle, shuffle, squeak, squeak," and by Aitken as "tramp, tramp, crunch, crunch."

A few lines later, however, when Ivan Denisovich, in a marvelous play on the sound of his surname (Shukhov), describes the whispering in his brigade —"And right away—shoo-shoo-shoo through the brigade"—all six translators report the sound as "whisper," as in Parker's "And at once a whisper ran through the squad" and Block's "That set off a bout of whispering in the gang." In another instance, Ivan Denisovich notices that one foot —the one with the hole in the boot—has frozen numb. Too busy with his work on the brick wall he is laying with pride, he simply advises himself, in his own way, "Top-top for it, Shukhov, top-top." In Hayward and Hingley this becomes, "He kept stamping it on the floor," and in Aitken, "He stamped his foot up and down." Happily, Parker catches the sound and conveys it as, "He stamped his foot, thud, thud"; Whitney also appropriately translates it as, "Tap, tap, went Shukhov with his foot, tap, tap." But there is no apparent explanation as to why those translators who detected the device failed to honor it consistently.

When *One Day in the Life of Ivan Denisovich* first appeared in the United States, a reviewer for *Time* (8 February 1963) reported:

> The importance of the book was not lost on two U.S. publishers who raced to be the first in print. It was a dead heat. Both versions appeared the same day at the same price. Dutton, offering the "authorized" version, is paying royalties to the Soviet government. Praeger is pirating the book on the ground that Russia, which refuses to join world copyright agreements, pirates U.S. books. Publisher Frederick Praeger was so excited by his steal that he locked one translator in his Greenwich Village house for eleven days, and moved in two editors, two typists, and "enormous quantities of Scotch." The Scotch did not help.

The translator for Dutton was Ralph Parker; the translator for Praeger was Ronald Hingley. Max Hayward was apparently called in to doctor the Hingley translation, and the Parker translation was apparently revised in later printings. Early printings of the two versions seem to have vanished into oblivion, so it is not possible to establish how bad the first copies were, but if the *Time* report is accurate, the circumstances of the first translations and publication of *One Day* are a sad commentary on commercial quickies.

To the degree that the marvels of cost-benefit analysis and supply-side economics permeate so much of American culture, the view that our translations are affected by the profit motive has some basis. Economics is certainly a common complaint by American translators. But are commercial considerations decisive? Such a view does not account for federal and state funding of translations, or for the priority given to translation in American arts and humanities. And it bears no relation to, say, the twenty-five years Hal Draper spent on his translation of Heine's *Complete Poems*, or the long years of work spent by other American translators on *The Iliad, The Divine Comedy*, and *Faust*, or the lifetime Vladimir Nabokov spent on *Eugene Onegin*. Moreover, despite the rush to get Solzhenitsyn's *One Day* into print, the publishers did, after all, make an effort to undo the damage. Not only did the first printings vanish, but the weakest translation—Bela von Block's—immediately went out of print. Whitney's translation—judged by Klimoff to be weak, but more highly regarded by Chukovsky—remained available for several years before it, too, went out of print. Of the four earliest translations, therefore, only the Parker and the Hayward and Hingley translations (or their revised versions) survived the most intense competition; since they are the best early translations, it can be suggested that considerations other than profit are operative even in the worst commercial scenario.

Of the six translators of Solzhenitsyn's *One Day*, only Hayward, Whitney, and Hingley are well established in the field of Russian translation. Hayward is remembered as a giant among translators and popularizers of Soviet Russian literature; Whitney is an eminent connoisseur of Russian art and literature; Hingley is a major scholar, editor, and translator of Chekhov. Together with Parker, it may be said that collectively they came up with a potentially superb translation of the novel, although each translation fails individually to reach the mark. There is no lack of quality and standards in these translations; what is lacking is consistency. Even when one of the translators comes up with a brilliant solution to a language problem or an ingeniously chosen equivalent for a difficult word, he may gloss over a crucial stylistic item with a lengthy explanation one or two sentences later. The translators should not be blamed for balking at some of Solzhenitsyn's impossible colloquialisms or for settling for substitutes that do no justice to this aspect of his style. Some of the formulations by the four better translators are even boldly inventive. But none of the translators devoted sufficient time and thought to searching for equivalents consistently through the entire text. The translators were evidently tempted to take over Ivan Denisovich's task of narration wherever his thoughts serve as the narrative. The result is that the translations sometimes read like protocol versions—Ivan Denisovich did this and then went there and said this and did that.

Three translations by four translators reveal talent, imagination, and command of both Russian and English. There is evidence that bad practices are sometimes rectified, and the possibility exists that among the permutations of three and perhaps all five translations lies an opportunity for some translator to produce a major literary achievement. Vitality is not lacking here—there is cultural strength in the pluralistic, pragmatic, individualistic character that separates the American world from the more stable and uniform Russian world of translation. But there is little method apparent in or among these translations, no detectable awareness of methodology or uniformity of standards on the part of these translators. Discipline is lacking. An esprit among translators is missing, and so is a sense of communication among creative people.

Optimism about the possibility of good translation is also missing. The optimism that gives the Soviet school its strength certainly marks a clear difference from the American world. "My principal doubt," Zulfikar Ghose remarked at the Tate lecture, "is that I wonder if poetry can be translated at all." This view was endorsed by Serge Gavronsky, who added, "There is something extraordinarily priceless in an original, which by its nature cannot be duplicated" (Tate 1972:17, 22). Statements such as these are often encountered in translation scholarship, and they are usually made in discussions of a problem called the impossibility of translation, or untranslatability. The impossibility of translation, especially in regard to poetry, is a problem based on the pessimistic view that the translation of a literary work—seen to be an unrepeatable creative act—is impossible. The prevailing American attitude toward untranslatability was expressed most notably by Ezra Pound when he said that the only thing a translator can do is "show where the treasure lies" (Pound:200). Burton Raffel has also expressed the pessimistic view: "Nor do I think the reader of translations should delude himself that a translation in some way is the original. Only the original is the original: it becomes, again, a matter of decision-making. If poetry is what is lost in translation, what is it that one chooses to preserve?" (1971:14). Raffel here seconds Pound's often quoted assessment; he also refers to Robert Frost's notorious statement that poetry is what gets lost in translation.

Only a fool would deny the difficulty of translation. But there is something foolish, too, about translators who complain that literary works cannot be translated while they are busy translating a literary work. Donald Keene, translator of Japanese literature, expressed great exasperation when he declared, "I like to think of the translator's profession as a noble one. The slander of the Italian 'translators, traducers' has gone too long unchallenged" (1971:329). Commenting on the insistence of many theorists that translation is by definition impossible, Roger Roothaer has warned, "We must not try to deny [the existence of translations] any more than a physicist would try to deny the existence of a given phenomenon because it does not fit into the generally accepted theories. On the contrary, when something exists and the theory says that it cannot exist, there can be no doubt that the theory is wrong" (1978:132).

It is time to set the argument for translatability aside. Perhaps this is not possible. When Georges Mounin began *Les Belles Infidèles* with a review of arguments for and against translatability and concluded, "Today it is an anachronism to argue for or against translation . . . translation is *becoming* necessary" (1955:30–31), he apparently did not realize that he was repeating the same argument used by Goethe over a century before. We might therefore be doomed to listen to another century of pessimistic arguments about untranslatability, and the reason for this is that such arguments are the most readily available defense for insecure translators. Roothaer's warning, for example, was issued in a criticism of the use of arguments for untranslatability as an excuse for weak translators and a defense for nervous ones. Nevertheless, the question has remained in discussion far too long, and it is not possible to say that discussions have led to better translations. We do, after all, translate. Translators do well, translators do badly, but they do not do well or badly as a result of arguments for the impossibility of translation.

This point has been made again and again by decidedly more optimistic Soviet translators. "We know that among well-known men of literature in other countries there are not just a few who consider the *translatability of poetry* practically impossible," the Estonian translator Jaan Kross has emphasized. "And even the circumstance that the Germans, for example, often prefer to call artistic translation . . . not *Übersetzung*, but *Nachdichtung*, and the French not *traduction*, but *adaptation*, testifies to a certain degree to this skeptical attitude. Our general point of view is first of all a conviction that the translation of poetry is possible" (1970:89). Soviet optimism was expressed even more strongly by G. Falkonovich, who went so far as to suggest that emphasis on untranslatability is an excuse for poor work. In his view, discussions of the problem are usually no more than sloganeering, "but the practice of translation has shown that it is not a translator's slogans that define his true position. Poor translations, regardless of their authors' eloquent claims, place translators squarely in the camp of the advocates of untranslatability" (1970:286–87). Pavel Antokolsky, who apprehends literary translation in relation to the translator's duties to the Soviet nationalities policy, linked the optimistic Soviet view with the task of communication among peoples when he declared, "We assert the possibility of translation, the *translatability* of a work from any language to any other language. Translatability is adequate to the possibility of contact among peoples. All world culture rests on this assumption" (1964:11).

This does not mean that Soviet translators are so foolish as to deny the difficulties of translation. The visiting East German writer A. Kurella was applauded for telling Soviet colleagues, "Although we consider translation possible intuitively . . . when we examine the question in all seriousness, we are convinced that this is not a self-evident truth. Every translator knows from his own experience how many times he has felt doubt: is what I am doing necessary? is it possible to convey in my language what I have apprehended and understood? Every serious translator constantly experiences doubt as to the possibility of translation" (1959:414). Soviet optimism does not rest on avoiding the difficulty of translation, and Soviet translators do not refuse to acknowledge what is lost when a literary work is taken over the language barrier. Rather, as stated, Soviet translators draw the line else-where—between perfection and a reasonable expectation that translators can honor the artistic integrity of a literary work if they exercise artistic responsibility. They assume that literary translation is no more perfect than any other art. Like Mounin and Roothaer, Soviet translators insist that de-spite the difficulties of translation, we are left with the creative desire to translate, just as we are left with the feasibility, even the absolute necessity, of translation as the only means of communication among human beings of different languages.

Discussions of impossibility of translation are futile precisely because Babel is a fait accompli. The task of translators is not to lament over what cannot be changed but to find effective ways to ameliorate and reduce diffi-culties. V. M. Rossels has clarified this attitude of the Soviet school by assert-ing that "*in principle* there are no insurmountable barriers to the translation of any work from any language. This logical truth is reinforced by the entire experience of the history of culture." Having asserted this optimism, how-ever, Rossels turns from principle to practice and emphasizes, "from a posi-tive solution of the problem *in principle* to concrete, living practice, there is, as is well known, a long road. Practice at any time raises almost insur-mountable difficulties stemming from national realia, the character of the work, the author's manner, and finally from the specific relationships be-tween two given languages." Rossels concludes that the solution to the prob-lem of untranslatability is not to constantly affirm it but instead to devise ways to overcome the language barrier. Indeed, this is the very raison d'être of translation theory: "Theory of translation is called upon, in part, to clas-sify and analyze the barriers" (1963:152).

Nor can it be said that all American translators are pessimists. In fact, one of the most emphatic affirmations of the *possibility* of translation, the difficulties of translation, and the proper context in which to view these difficulties was made in American letters. "But if 'perfect' translation is no more than a formal ideal," George Steiner has said in *After Babel*, "and if great translation is rare, there are, none the less, examples which seem to approach the limits of empirical possibility. . . . There are translations which are supreme acts of critical exegesis, in which analytical understand-ing, historical imagination, linguistic expertness articulate a critical valua-tion which is at the same time a piece of totally lucid, responsible exposi-tion" (1975:407–8). Steiner is fully aware of the difficulties of reconstituting a literary work in a different language, for as he has said elsewhere, "a poem is language in the most intense mode of expressive integrity, language under such close pressure of singular need, of particularised energy, that no other statement can be equivalent. . . . The poem is because nothing exactly like it has been before, because its very composition is an act of unique designation" (1968:48). And he continues, "Add to this the nature of poetic language. The distinctive beat of any given tongue, that sustaining undercurrent of inflection, pitch, relations, habits of stress, which give a particular motion to prose, is concentrated in poetry so that it acts as an overt, characteristic force." Nevertheless, Steiner insists that literary works can and must be translated. "Each act of translation is one of approximation," he has said, echoing Paul Valéry's widely acclaimed definition of translation as the art of approximation, "of near miss or failure to get within range. . . . The case against translation is irrefutable, but only if we are presented, in Ibsen's phrase, with 'the claims of the ideal.' In actual performance, these claims cannot be met or allowed" (1968:48–49).

10

ON CONVEYING COLLOQUIAL SPEECH

■■■■■■■ Soviet translators excel at solving problems of translation. This is one reason for their high standards. They cannot and do not claim to have solved all problems satisfactorily, but it can be said that Soviet translators put many problems in their place. The problem of untranslatability, for example, continues to be discussed, but no longer in futile ways. By putting problems behind them in this way, Soviet translators have freed themselves to address problems that have not yet been approached or that have been avoided in other worlds. One of these problems is the translation of colloquial speech (*prostorechie*). Slang, jargon, dialects—these phenomena present a difficult problem for translators. Not unexpectedly, and despite their optimism, Soviet translators and theorists of translation who have discussed colloquial speech admit that there is probably no solution to the problem. Many Soviet translators are as adamant about refusing to deal with the problem as translators in other worlds.

Translators know the reason for this hesitation. Rita Rayt was fortunate to find an approximate equivalent for Vonnegut's "doodley-squat" in the Russian colloquialism *shisha*; Solzhenitsyn's translators were not so fortunate when they encountered the triple meanings of the simple word *bedolaga*. But most translators, including some of the most optimistic Soviet translators, have balked at the task of translating colloquial language. Literary works laden with slang or dialects are often conveyed with standard words—the device called blandscript—and an occasional attempt at substitution. The basic rule adopted in the Soviet school is that translators should not refuse to confront colloquial style; but when they do confront it they should exercise tact and moderation, never using resources too strongly identified with their own language. Kipling's soldiers three should not be made to speak the dialects of Russian peasants, the Russian writer Nikolay Leskov's immortal Golovan should not use the words of a Nebraska farm boy. Soviet translators do not have many examples of adept handling of colloquial style, but they are proud of a few brave attempts.

Among the most highly praised Russian translations of authors known for their colloquial styles are Mikhail Lozinsky's *The Life of Benvenuto Cellini*, N. M. Lyubimov's Rabelais, and Samuil Marshak's Burns. Praised as frequently are Dickens in the versions by Nina Daruzes, Marya Lorie, and Evgenya Kalashnikova; Kipling in the renditions by Daruzes, Marshak, and Chukovsky; and Marshak's Nursery Rhymes. Rayt's handling of Kurt Vonnegut's banal American clichés, examined in a previous chapter, is widely admired, and N. I. Grebnev is considered a master of colloquial style in his translations of Avarian, Abkhazian, Tatar, Georgian, Armenian, and Kirghiz folk songs. Boris Pasternak is often mentioned as a superb translator of Hans Sachs. Among the American classics that provide difficult problems of colloquial style but are believed to have been handled with exceptional ingenuity are J. D. Salinger's *Catcher in the Rye* by Rayt; Mark Twain by Chukovsky, Daruzes, and Lorie; and John Steinbeck's *The Grapes of Wrath* and *Travels with Charley in Search of America* by Natalya Volzhina.

Translators who have confronted colloquial speech and have attempted to convey it into their language seem to have approached the task either cautiously or boldly. These opposite approaches to the problem are well demonstrated by, respectively, Daruzes's translation of *The Adventures of Huckleberry Finn* and Volzhina's translation of *The Grapes of Wrath*.

Nina Daruzes is well known in Soviet letters as a literary scholar and translator of Rudyard Kipling, George Bernard Shaw, and Sean O'Casey. She was a leading Anglo-Americanist, and her translation of *Martin Chuzzlewit*, which appeared in the thirty-volume *Collected Works of Charles Dickens*, has been highly praised. Among the American writers to her credit are Hemingway, Henry James, John Dos Passos, Bret Harte, Ambrose Bierce, Langston Hughes, Irwin Shaw, Erskine Caldwell, Willa Cather, and Pearl Buck. Her translation of *Huckleberry Finn*, considered the standard text, has appeared with Chukovsky's translation of *The Adventures of Tom Sawyer* (1961) and in collections of Twain's works, including a twelve-volume edition (1953, 1961). Her translations of both novels appeared in a single-volume collection of short stories translated by Daruzes, among others (1971) and have appeared separately in numerous special editions for workers and children. A laudatory critique of her translation appears in Chukovsky's *A High Art*.

To begin the analysis of Daruzes' *Huckleberry Finn*, consider Twain's classic words:

You don't know me, without you have read a book by the name of "The adventures of Tom Sawyer," but that ain't no matter. That book was made by Mr.

Mark Twain, and he told the truth, mainly. There was things which he stretched, but mainly he told the truth. That is nothing. I never seen anybody but lied, one time or another, without it was Aunt Polly, or the widow, or maybe Mary. Aunt Polly—Tom's Aunt Polly, she is—and Mary, and the Widow Douglas, is all told about in that book—which is mostly a true book, with some stretchers, as I said before.

The first important aspect about the opening words of the novel is Huck's voice—his personality and his acceptance of human behavior and of the world as it is. Intonations are as important here as in Vonnegut's novels. However, the concern of the translator in this text is not with the sound of Huck Finn's voice per se but with the role of departures from the grammatical norm and the dialectisms in the conveyance of his voice.

The opening paragraph is not the most striking example of colloquial style in the novel—Huck's colloquial speech does not begin to compare with Jim's far more radical departures—but it immediately establishes the character of the language Twain's translator must confront. Of 107 words in this paragraph, 40 are deliberate violations of standard usage—"you don't know me, without you have read a book," "that ain't no matter," "that book was made by," "I never seen anybody but lied," and so on. An additional 18 words reflect regional nineteenth-century Missouri speech: "and he told the truth, mainly," "but mainly he told the truth," "(there was things) which he stretched," "with some stretchers." Other constructions crucial to conveyance are "Tom's Aunt Polly, she is," "without it was," "is all told about," "mostly a true book." Constructions worth noting as idiomatic expressions for which there are ready equivalents in Russian, are "by the name of," "that is nothing," "one time or another," and "as I said before."

Just how effectively Daruzes has conveyed this passage into Russian may be demonstrated by a comparison of the Russian version (or its English translation) with the original (the essential style components are emphasized in the translation):

Vy pro menia nichego ne znaete, esli ne chitali knizhki pod nazvaniem "Prikliucheniia Toma Soiera", no eto ne beda. Etu knizhku napisal mister Mark Tven i, v obshchem, ne ochen' navral. Koe-chto on prisochinil, no, v obshchem, ne tak uzh navral. Eto nichego, ia eshche ne videl takikh liudei, chtoby sovsem ne vrali, krome teti Polli i vdovy, da razve eshche Meri. Pro tetiu Polli—eto Tomu Soieru ona tetia,—pro Meri i pro vdovy Duglas rasskazyvaetsia v etoi samoi knizhke, i tam pochti vse pravda, tol'ko koe-gde privrano—ia uzhe pro eto govoril. (p. 197)

'You don't know me, *if you haven't read* a book by the name of "The Adventures of Tom Sawyer," *but that's not bad.* That book *was written* by Mr. Mark

Twain, and *he didn't lie, mainly*. There were *things he made up*, but *mainly he didn't lie all that much*. That is nothing, I've never seen anybody *that didn't lie*, one time or another, except for Aunt Polly, and the widow, or maybe Mary. Aunt Polly—Tom's Aunt Polly, she is—and Mary, and the Widow Douglas—are all told about in that book, and *almost everything there is true*, except *there are things made up there*, as I said before.'

Daruzes apparently chose to convey "without you have read" with a conditional construction using *esli* 'if,' because a gerund construction, the only other grammatical alternative, would not represent a departure from the grammatical norm. For the common but difficult colloquialism "ain't" she chose the Russian colloquial expression *eto ne beda* 'that's not bad,' which is close in colloquiality to the original "that ain't no matter." For some reason Daruzes chose to say that the book was written, instead of "made," even though she might similarly have misapplied at least two available Russian verbs to get the same colloquial effect in Russian. For "mainly" the translator chose the Russian expression *v obschhem*, which is neither a sharp departure from the norm or too weak, and she chose to say simply that Mr. Twain "didn't lie" and, adding emphasis by way of compensation for being less colloquial than the original, "mainly he didn't lie all that much." As a rule in polite Russian usage, the indirect and negative is preferred to the direct and positive, but Daruzes might have chosen to specify the notion of not lying, as opposed to not telling the truth, in order to use the effective Russian verb *navrat'* 'to fib a bit.' The choice is good— the Russian verb sounds more like Huck Finn than a literal conveyance would have. The dialectisms "stretched" and "stretchers" are replaced by the Russian verb *prisochinit'* 'to make up,' which is an unusual use of the verb but not as striking as the original. The only other significant departure from the original text is where the translator has translated the phrase "mostly a true book" as "almost everything there is true." But for the Russian reader, the effect of her change of expression is closer to the original than a direct conveyance, which would not have sounded like Huck Finn in Russian. Two grammar usages not marked here—"You don't know me" and "told about in that book"—are conveyed differently but faithfully by an unexpected *pro menia* rather than the standard *obo mne*, for "know [about] me" and "told about."

Daruzes's translation of *Huckleberry Finn* is not as radical in terms of attempts to convey colloquial style as, say, Lozinsky's *The Life of Benvenuto Cellini* or *Colas Breugnon*, where every fracture of language is inexorably conveyed. Hers is a cautious translation, and she clearly prefers to err on the side of moderation rather than of colloquiality. In the scene where Huck and Tom play a joke on Jim while on their way to the graveyard, "Who dah?" is conveyed simply and with perfectly standard Russian as *Kto tam?*

'Who's there'; "Whar is you?" is conveyed as *Gde zhe vy?* 'Just where are you'; and "Dog my cats ef I didn' hear somf'n" is conveyed in Russian as something that would have to be read back in English as "Indeed I did hear it for sure, some sort of dirty trick (it must be)." Elsewhere, "Fetched us a dollar a day apiece" is given in straightforward fashion as something like "We started getting . . ." and "Po' little chap" as *Bedniaga!* 'Poor thing!' In the scene where Jim confounds Huck with his vexingly logical interpretation of King Solomon's wives, Jim's "I doan k'yer" is conveyed as "I don't care"; "Warn' dat de beatenes' notion in de worl'?" becomes "There you are! You'll never think up anything dumber than that!"; "Roun' de which?" is conveyed as "Just what is this thing a harem?"; and "I didn' know dey was so many un um" reads in Russian as something like "And I didn't even know there were so many of them." Often, Daruzes's conveyances of Jim's language become blandscript. "I be dingbusted" is given as *Vot eto da* 'Now that's something!' and "Blame de pint!" as 'So much for your point!' The reason for this moderation of Jim's colloquial speech is obvious. There are not likely to be equivalents in any foreign language for nineteenth-century black American colloquial speech. Had Daruzes attempted to find a colloquial equivalent for every one of Jim's utterances, the result would have been ridiculous.

In his critique of this translation, Chukovsky notes the translator's reluctance to confront colloquial style justified use of blandscript. Compare a nature description identified by Chukovsky as more like Turgenev than Huck Finn (1984:127–29). The passage is important because the nearly illiterate Huck, charmed by the stillness of night on the Mississippi River, becomes almost literary:

Every night we passed towns, some of them away up on the black hillsides, nothing but just a shiny bed of lights, not a house could you see. The fifth night we passed St. Louis, and it was like the whole world was lit up. In St. Petersburg they used to say there was twenty or thirty thousand people in St. Louis, but I never believed it till I see that wonderful spread of lights at two o'clock that still night. There warn't a sound there; everybody was asleep.

Kazhduiu noch' my proplyvali mimo gorodov; nekotorye iz nikh stoiali vyskoko na temnykh beregakh, tol'ko i vidna byla blestiashchaiai griadka ognei—ni odnogo doma, nichego bol'she. Na piatuiu noch' my minovali Sent-Luis, nad nim stoialo tseloe zarevo. U nas v Sent-Pitersberge govorili, budto v Sent-Luise zhivet dvadtsat' tysiach chelovek, no ia etomu ne veril, poka sam ne uvidel v dva chasa nochi takoe mnozhestvo ognei. Noch' byla tikhaia, iz goroda ne donosilos' ni zvuka; vse spali.

'Every night we passed towns: some of them *stood high* on the black hillsides, *all we could see* was a bed of lights—not a single house *or anything*. The fifth night we passed St. Louis, *there was a blaze of lights standing over it*. In St. Petersburg they used to say there were twenty or thirty thousand people living in St. Louis, but *I didn't believe it* till I *saw* that *multitude* of lights at two o'clock. *The night was still*, there *wasn't* a sound from the city; everybody was asleep.'

The only notable changes here are in expressions and in adjustments of syntax. The Russian expression "there was a blaze of lights standing over it" (*stoialo zarevo*) is a reasonable stylistic equivalent for "it was like the whole world was lit up." The translator has shifted "still," of "that still night," to an opening clause of the next sentence ("the night was still") for better syntax, rhythm, and phonetics, and for equivalent effect. In almost all respects—tone, mood, style, metaphor—the Russian version is an exceptionally faithful literary representation of the original. The only feature of the passage that is not conveyed, except sporadically, is Huck's colloquial speech. "It was like the whole world was lit up" is given in standard Russian, as are "till I see" and "warn't." Elsewhere in this nature description Daruzes has used a few colloquialisms: *potikhon'ku* for "on the quiet" and *pogoda v obshchem stoiala ochen' khoroshaia* for "we had very good weather, as a general thing." But "it was kind of solemn" is given in standard Russian as "it was so fine"; "laying on our backs" is conveyed as "lying on our backs"; and "it warn't often that we laughed" reads back "we didn't even laugh very often." The syntax for these conveyances is slightly unusual, but, so far as lexical features are concerned, the translator has been remarkably conservative. The translation of this passage is not as literary as Chukovsky's fanciful comparison to Turgenev suggests, but this is, if not a bland translation, a perceptibly smooth one.

One fault of the translation is that the translator misses an important stylistic key. Twain's novel is so heavily marked by colloquial speech that translators are likely to be overwhelmed by it and overlook the bad grammar that characterizes the language of both Huck and Jim. In Daruzes' translation, more could have been done to convey the radically substandard English that makes *Huckleberry Finn* an American masterpiece. Daruzes attempts to establish substandard Russian through enclitics, (*-to, -te, -ka*), but she uses them too sparingly. Enclitics are such a common feature of the Russian language, without regard for dialect, that they are neutral—they would not intrude on the Russian reader's consciousness to the point of halting attention and seeming unnatural. Incorrect case usage might also have helped. A mark of poor Russian grammar is the use of the dative case where locative or genitive are required. Other possibilities that might have helped to convey Jim's poor grammar would have been mixed tenses or confusion involving the Russian imperfective-perfective aspect, or, as often happens in the original, use of words incorrectly.

Russian dialects do not slur words or stretch them into a drawl, as English dialects do, but Daruzes might have emphasized more Huck's and Jim's mispronunciation of words. Daruzes employs some of these bad-grammar devices in her translation, but she is overly cautious here. Lozinsky was highly praised for fracturing and mangling the Russian language throughout the entire text of his translation of Cellini's autobiography. Perhaps Daruzes could have used this same stylistic key to mark Jim's speech in her translation. American children have to struggle to decipher Jim's grammar when reading *Huckleberry Finn*, so why shouldn't Russian children be obliged to struggle too?

Attempts at recreation of colloquial speech can enrich a translation but can also irreparably harm a translation. Translators around the world warn each other to be leery about undertaking to convey works rich in dialectisms, slang, and jargon. We can appreciate the validity of this advice through an examination of Natalya Volzhina's bold approach to John Steinbeck's *The Grapes of Wrath*.

Natalya Volzhina is, like Nina Daruzes, one of the great Anglo-Americanist translators. She was a member of the *kollektiv* of translators of *The Collected Works of Charles Dickens*. In addition to her 1957 translation of *The Grapes of Wrath*, she has been praised for her popular translations of *Travels with Charley in Search of America, The Red Pony, The Pearl, The Moon is Down*, and *Winter of our Discontent*. The last translation was done with Evgenya Kalashnikova, with whom she also translated the long awaited, long proscribed *For Whom the Bell Tolls*. Among the writers to her credit are Ambrose Bierce, Bret Harte, Henry James (*Daisy Miller*), Stephen Crane, John Dos Passos, and Erskine Caldwell.

The Grapes of Wrath presents considerably fewer problems of translation as a narrative than *Huckleberry Finn*. The colloquial speech of John Steinbeck's Okies of the 1930s is not as extreme as Huck Finn's speech a century earlier and of course does not compare with Jim's speech. Steinbeck's objective narrator is far more literate than Huck Finn—even though he is not above using slang and jargon. Furthermore, where there are few, if any, points of cultural contact between the life described in Twain's novel and the experiences of Russians, the translator of *The Grapes of Wrath* is offered at least a few experiential, and thus linguistic, similarities. Like Americans, Russians experienced mechanization of agriculture, the technology of the new automobile age, displacement of populations, and other cultural changes described in *The Grapes of Wrath*. Certainly there are differences between the two national experiences of these and other social upheavals, but the basic experiences including many of the realia, much of the language, and even some of the colloquialisms, have points in common.

The difficulties of coping with Steinbeck's colloquial style should not be underestimated. The speech of Steinbeck's Okies departs decisively from the literary norm, as, for example, in this statement by the character Muley:

"An' I see my Pa with a hole through his ches', an' I felt him shiver up against me like he done, an' I seen him kind of settle back an' reach with his han's an' his feet. An' I seen his eyes all milky with hurt, an' then he was still an' his eyes so clear—lookin' up. An' me a little kid settin' there, not cryin' nor nothin', jus' settin' there."

But there are some congruences. No Russian would have the slightest difficulty comprehending this bit of Americana, for example:

"Listen, Jim, I heard that Chevy's rear end. Sounds like busting bottles. Squirt in a couple of quarts of sawdust. Put some in the gears too. We got to move that lemon for thirty-five dollars. Bastard cheated me on that one. I offered ten an' he jerks me to fifteen, an' then the son-of-a-bitch took the tools out."

Russians know very well what a "lemon" is, even though they call it an *ogurchik* 'pickle,' and they know about squirting a "couple quarts" of sawdust into the rear end. They might not catch the meaning of "Chevy," and so Volzhina has "Chevrolet," but she does not have difficulty finding colloquial equivalents for "bastard" (*prokhvost*) or "son-of-a-bitch" (*sukin syn*). The realia of automotive technology are shared in common by Russians and Americans, so that Volzhina easily finds such technical jargon as *radiator, kompensator, ventiliator, tsilindry, bloki motorov*. Russians might have difficulty identifying a Chandler a Graham, a Chalmers, and an Apperson—so do most Americans today—but Russians know what a *model' "T," Dodzh, Plimut, B'iuik, Nesh, and De-soto* are.

Where Daruzes faced an almost impossible task of conveying colloquial speech, and therefore chose to lean in the direction of blandscript, Volzhina was working with enough convergences of language and culture to approximate colloquial speech. Volzhina's task differed from Daruzes's, and her translation must be judged on different grounds. Volzhina conveys American colloquial speech as fully as possible in order to give the Russian reader the fullest possible experience of American language and culture. Where the two languages do not coincide, she used Russianisms that are not so inappropriate to the American environment of Steinbeck's novel that they intrude on the consciousness of the Russian reader. The translation problem here is one of balance, of mixing native Russian resources that do not violate the spirit of American environment with Americanisms that are not so exotic as to be incomprehensible.

In the first chapter of Steinbeck's novel, Tom Joad, just released from prison, hitches a ride with a truck driver. The speech of both men is the Oklahoma dialect of the 1930s, their conversation markedly colloquial. For example, Tom Joad says,"Thanks, buddy. My dogs was pooped out." Obviously, because some colloquial items are inimitably American, there are no Russian equivalents. Russians do call their feet *khoduli* 'stilts,' 'walkers,' however, and they mean by this just what Americans mean when they call their feet "dogs." Volzhina has Tom Joad say in Russian, "these stilts of mine have just given up trying to do their bit." Joad also tells the truck driver, "No, my old man got a place, forty acres. He's a cropper, but we been there a long time." Russians would not understand "cropper," and "forty-acre cropper" would have to be explained in a footnote, but they have almost exact equivalents for "my old man" in the word *starik* and for "place" in the word *uchastok* 'piece,' or 'plot.' In addition, an equivalent for the verb "to share crop" is *arendovat'*. Thus, for Joad's statement, "No, my old man's got a place, forty acres. He's a cropper . . ." Volzhina has no difficulty letting him say in Russian what he says in English: "—*Net, u moego starika tut uchastok. Arenduet.*"

Volzhina tries to translate American colloquial speech as fully and closely as possible. When the truck driver protests that he is not curious about Tom Joad's identity, the hypersensitive Joad snaps, "The hell you ain't. . . . That big old nose of yours been stickin' out eight miles ahead of your face. You had that big nose goin' over me like a sheep in a vegetable patch." Russian folklore is rich with expressions involving noses, including expressions about noses stuck into others' business, but the Russian language does not feature a nose that goes over others like a sheep in a vegetable patch. Thanks to Volzhina's decision to convey the Americanism in toto, Russian noses can now go over others in true Okie style. This approach may seem obvious, but translators are seldom this adventurous when dealing with colloquial style. Volzhina often conveys colloquial style in this way —given a chance to introduce American colloquial expressions sensibly and naturally, she usually takes it. For the dialectism "gettin' screwy as a gopher," Volzhina has the faithful equivalent *puglivyi stal, kak suslik*. For "gutache" she has *rezh' v zhivote*, for "wet his drawers" she has *napustit' v shtany*—both perfectly equivalent representations. Thanks to her, Russians can now say "I'm giving you my shirt."

Sometimes Volzhina's approach fails. It was a mistake to convey the expression "seat covers ain't turning no wheels over," because the result in Russian is a long, unnatural sentence. But in most instances her instinct for knowing when to reproduce Americanisms in Russian is dependable. This is especially apparent whenever she encounters the colloquialisms of American religious sectarianism. Where the former Reverend Jim Casey identifies himself as a "Burning Busher" and explains that he "used to howl out the name of Jesus to glory," Volzhina has him say exactly this in Russian, with the explanatory insertion only that "Burning Bush" is a *sekta*. The Russian version likewise has Jim Casey getting the irrigation ditch "squirmin' full of repented sinners" and getting "the people jumpin' and talkin' in tongues an' glory-shoutin'"; and in Russian, when he was done preaching, he would "take one of them girls out in the grass, an' . . . lay with her." Volzhina might have found substitutes for these and myriads of other Americanisms in *The Grapes of Wrath*, but she chose in almost every instance to convey the reality and the flavor of the original cultural environment.

Not all the purely American and peculiarly Okie expressions of Steinbeck's novel are translatable, of course, yet Volzhina has tried to find Russian colloquial equivalents that avoid Russianizing the work, even if they are not fully satisfactory. *S den'goi*, a grammatically incorrect expression for money, falls short of, but does not betray, the inimitable American expression "jack in his jeans." For "die with his heart et out," Volzhina substituted *nogi protianul s toski* 'stretched his legs out with grief'—not a perfect substitute but one that is not prolix in Russian. The translator settled for *udalets* 'daredevil' as a substitute for the expression "hell on wheels," and for "he's nuts" she used *on obaldel* 'he was stunned, he was struck dumb, he's gone off his rocker.' *On ni bel'mesa me smyslit*, roughly 'he has an empty head' or 'he can't think straight,' is too mild for the American expression "don't know his ass from a hole in the ground."

When translation is discussed as interpretation—understood in the sense of both hermeneutic value and communication—it must be appreciated that literary translation removes cultural exchange from the area of politics and diplomacy to the individual, personal level of human experience. Translation is the basic key, perhaps the only effective key, to conveying valid understanding from one people to another. Colloquial speech resides at the roots —in the native soil, to use a notion of nineteenth-century Russian Slavophiles—of national character, national culture, national social experience. Colloquial speech is undoubtedly the most untranslatable aspect of language; but it is also the language that needs to be communicated, illuminated in the sense of hermeneutic value. Almost thirty years ago an article entitled "Impossibilities of Translation" attracted considerable attention because of its stark pessimism. The article was widely read by Soviet translators, who were struck by its contrast to their own very different attitude even though they were unable to deny its validity (see Chukovsky 1984:152). As Werner Winter wrote, "There is no completely exact translation. . . . There are only approximations, and the degree of similarity possible between original and translation depends on the degree of similarity between the systems of form and meaning in the two languages involved." But even Winter held out hope that the language barrier could be overcome, and he held out this hope in terms of the need for cultural understanding: "Transfer of denotative meaning, though difficult and at times impossible, can, as a rule, be extracted in a more or less satisfactory manner; the closer

the cultural bonds between the speakers of two languages, the more acceptable the results become" (1961:69, 76).

Winston Churchill once said something about Russia being an enigma
in a puzzle, but he really said more about British ethnocentrism than about
Russia. Russia is not incomprehensible, and the Russian language is not
impenetrable, even at its most intimate, colloquial level—no more than the
English language proved impenetrable to either the cautious overtures of
Daruzes or the bold approach of Volzhina. Somehow Russians and Americans, above all other peoples, must succeed in communicating with each
other. This must be done at the most basic levels of national experience.
What we both should hope in this regard is that neither of us runs afoul
of the problem of untranslatability.

11

HISTORY OF TRANSLATION

Translation Old and New

██████████ Soviet translators have produced many works on the history of translation in their national letters, but curiously, no scholar seems to have been attracted to the idea of writing a history of translation in America until very recently. Steiner (1975, 1976) and Will (1973) have introduced materials on the history of translation in Western civilization; Kelly's *The True Interpreter* (1979) is a history of Western ideas about translation; Adams (1973) and Brower (1974) have offered historical materials on translation. Susan Bassnett-McGuire has written a brief history of translation theory (1980); Peter Newmark's *Approaches to Translation* is a compendium of translation theory (1981); and Mary Snell-Hornby has reviewed the history of the development of translation studies in *Translation Studies: An Integrated Approach* (1988). Histories of translation in the world at large now exist, but no one seems to have written a history of translation in the United States. Steiner was right when he remarked, "In the history and theory of literature translation has not been a subject of the first importance. It has figured marginally, if at all" (1957:269).

In the Russian and more generally the Soviet world, translators and literary historians have written histories of translation in their letters. Kornei Chukovsky's *A High Art* contains significant historical materials and analyses. A. V. Fedorov's *Osnovy obshchei teorii perevoda* (Bases of general theory of translation, 1983) and its previous three editions contain an extensive history of translation in Russia. Oleksy Kudzich's *Slovo i obraz* (Word and image, 1973) treats the history of translation in the Ukraine, and V. M. Rossel's *Estafeta slova* (Relay-race of the word, 1972) contains a history of Russian translation. In *Masterstvo perevoda 1963* (Craft of translation) Rossels issued a strong call for a history of translation in Russia (1964). G. R. Gachechiladze's *Vvedenie v teoriiu khudozhestvennogo perevoda* (Introduction to theory of artistic translation, 1970) has a large section covering the history of translation in Russian literature and another on the history of translation in Georgia. Yury Levin has almost single-handedly worked out the principles for the study of the history of translation in Russia (1963a, 1963b), and recently he published a major historical study of Russian translation in the nineteenth century (1985). Russian scholars have written major studies of Pushkin, Zhukovsky, Gogol, Fet, and Turgenev as translators and a number of shorter studies of Lermontov, Bunin, Blok, and Pasternak, among others. Rossels has translated other histories of translation into Russian, including Levý and Gachechiladze. Encyclopedias, bibliographies, standard Russian histories of literature, and numerous collections contain historical studies or materials on the history of translation in the Russian world.

The possibility for a history of translation in America in the not too distant future exists. The ambitious bibliographic project currently being established by PEN American Center and the American Literary Translators Association is promising, and the increasing breadth of work by translation scholars sponsored by the Translation Research and Instruction Program, under the auspices of the National Resource Center for Translation and Interpretation at the State University of New York at Binghamton, also offers possibilities. In Chapter 1 it was noted that more has been written in American letters about literary translation in the past quarter century than in all the preceding years. The new field of systematized knowledge called translation studies is bursting in both quality and quantity of ideas, theories, and methods. Certainly, translation criticism and the study of the history of translation need greater acceptance as legitimate activities in American letters. Many translators have declared the world is experiencing a new renaissance in literary translation. Even in the 1960s Rolf Klöpfer was sufficiently optimistic to declare, "Translation appears finally, in the twentieth century, to have gained the position in public life toward which it had been continually and energetically striving for more than two thousand years." More translations than original works are published in most countries, and studies of translation are prominent in the letters of Germany, England, France, and Russia. "If we summarize the contemporary state of translation theory and practice," Anton Popović has observed, "we must conclude that it is in a state of growth. Translation theory is paying back what it has borrowed methodologically from linguistics, stylistics, the theory of literature, and other disciplines that have helped its evolution." There are "flaws and reserves" in modern conditions of translation, but in both theory and practice the outlook for growth and development has never been better (1978: 113, 111). So conditions may be favorable for a history of translation in America; at least the direction for such an undertaking has been marked out.

The basic problem concerning the history of translation is called the contemporaneity and temporariness of translation. "The fact is that levels of diction change over the years," Robert M. Adams has said. "What the nine-teenth century thought scandalous may be for the twentieth century merely commonplace—as what the eighteenth century thought commonplace, the nineteenth century thought scandalous" (1973:92–93). The modern reader must take into account the tastes of a given time in order to understand how a once audacious word becomes ordinary. Adams, addressing the ques-tion of the contemporaneity of translation, points to the need in a history of translation for attention to changing taste and style. His statement raises questions about the period concept of literary history and suggests that a history of translation is a history of changing perceptions of language. "Every period demands new translations," A. Gitovich has said. Styles grow old, language grows outdated, a translation inevitably loses its vitality. But the problem for a translation is especially acute since new "perceptions of the text" make a translation seem "outdated," even as the style of the origi-nal continues to be perceived in terms of its time (1970:371). As Levin has noted,

> In order for a history of translation to become truly a history, it is necessary to trace the changes in the very meaning of "translation," which has never been the same in different periods, and in accordance with which the demands made on translation have also changed. If he wishes to create a reliable picture of historical development, the historian of translation must make an effort to reveal and perhaps even emphasize the moments of change, of evolution of translation principles. He must not allow modern views of translation to eclipse historical perspective. (1963a: 374–75)

Attitudes toward and perceptions of translation have changed radically over the years, just as tastes in literature have changed radically. "There have been so many different kinds of translation," Levin has pointed out, "verse and prose, literal and free, poetic and inarticulate. There have even been curiosities" (1968:5). An important aspect of change in taste has been, in Levin's view, the "change in styles and trends" that has occurred in litera-ture. According to Levin, these styles are directly reflected in translations. "Classicism, Romanticism, Realism, and so forth . . . defined the style of translation literature as well as original literature, and this has revealed itself not only in the selection of works for translation but in the very principles of translation." More importantly, "the very interrelationships between original and translated literature have constantly changed." To the Neoclas-sicists, translations were identical to original works—they were both consid-ered a product of imitation. In the nineteenth century, "translated literature was steadily separated from original literature, and the translator from the independent creator." At any given time tastes in translation are likely to differ, and a striking example of this was provided by Gorky when he published in one volume four completely different translations of Voltaire's *La Pucelle d'Orleans* by Georgy Adamovich, Nikolay Gumilev, Georgy Ivanov, and Mikhail Lozinsky (1963b:6–8).

Each generation translates for itself anew, a condition of historical change that Soviet theorists refer to as "translation old and new." Presumably, the art of translation improves with time. Translators not only build from their predecessors but also learn from them. They devise new methods and principles from their awareness of existing deficiencies and develop methods and principles when they judge models to be sound. In the case of translations developed from previous ones, translators can speak specifically about translations old and new. When a translation is unprecedented, valid rules and principles of development can be extracted from the history of the art of translation. Among the many concerns of scholars working in the history of translation, two may be identified as prominent: the history of the development of the art and the improvement of the art through the creation of a new translation to replace an old one. These problems can be best illustrated by examining translations of Dostoyevsky and Chekhov, whose works have generated much attention over a long period of time.

The six English translations of Dostoyevsky's *Crime and Punishment* are by Frederick Wishaw (1886), Constance Garnett (1912–1913[?]; 1951 text used here), David Magarshack (1951), Jessie Coulson (1953), Michael Scammell (1963), and Sidney Monas (1968). Although the translations of Coulson, Scammell, and Monas are new and modern, Magarshack's Penguin edition and Garnett's Modern Library edition are the standards by which the novel is known to most Anglo-American readers. Wishaw's pioneer translation is useful today for what it tells about the early standards and methods. Even though Garnett was instrumental in the development of standards and methods, a frequent criticism of her translations is that she does not differentiate among individual Russian styles. Magarshack's translation has worn quite well with time, but it is somewhat weakened by his penchant for British language. The Coulson, Scammell, and Monas versions, which set a standard for modernized translations of Russian literature, are proficient. Examination shows that these translators, with the exception of Wishaw, have similar instincts for Dostoyevsky's style in Russian. They all make similar choices of lexicon and phrasing and reach similar solutions to stylistic problems in the text.

Frederick Wishaw's translation of *Crime and Punishment* falls within the category of early translation that Vladimir Nabokov criticized. As Nabokov observed, an early translation often posed as an account of "real" life in the land of snow and muzhiks. Wishaw's translation is even subtitled "A Realistic Novel," not to indicate the novel's aesthetics but to meet its readers' preferences for the quaintly foreign. Yet, while aiming for this true-to-life "Russianness," the translator deracinates Dostoyevsky by resorting single-mindedly to British literary expressions—"She durst not," "Pillages the post on the high road," "Dear sir, excuse me, but I must insist." While it strives to be authentic, a translation of this type often turns out to be half foreign, half English. Wishaw sometimes Anglicizes Russian names—Elizabeth instead of Elizaveta, Porphyrius instead of Porfiry—and sometimes retains the Russian names—Alena Ivanovna, Rodion Romanovitch. In some instances he turns names into English-Russian barbarisms—Porphyrius Petrovich, Catherine Ivanovna, Peter Petrovich. The translator does not have a sense for what is Russian and what is English. He conveys the novel's Russian character by transliterating the names of Petersburg's streets and places, but just as often he translates them. For example, Vasilevsky Island is given variously as Vasili-Ostroff, Vasilyevski Ostroff, and Vasilyevski Is-land. He too often transliterates realia because he does not know the mean-ing of a word. A peculiarly Russian long coat, *poddevka*, is given as "*paddiovka*." Wishaw's command of written Russian is not bad, but he does not know how the language is pronounced. Since he apparently knows that the *e* in *poddevka* is pronounced *yo*, he should also have known that Alena is transliterated as Alyona and Zametoff as Zamyotoff. He confuses the Russian letters for the sounds *zh, z, sh,* and *ch*—Luzhin (or Loozhin, to use Wishaw's outdated method of transliteration) is transliterated as Looshin. His system of transliteration is typical of a time when French was the medium for English systems: *batiushka* is given as "batuchka" and *muzhik* as "moujik."

Wishaw clearly lacks control of language and literature. He attempts to offer authentic national flavor but provides halfway measures instead. His translation is, as the Russian saying has it, "neither like mom, neither like dad, but more like some strapping passing lad." The point here is not that Wishaw is incompetent as a translator but that his translation represents the standard of his pioneering time and is therefore a good measure for analyzing the better work of his successors.

With the exception of Garnett, Dostoyevsky's other translators usually know the names of Petersburg's streets, squares, and canals. Even though Dostoyevsky indicated them only with initials and blanks, they know that Dostoyevsky wanted the names restored in later editions of *Crime and Pun-ishment*. They know that exact place is important to every event in Dostoyevsky's novel A *kalancha* is a "watchtower" (Magarshack, Scammell, Coulson, Monas), not, as Wishaw has it, a "belfry," so that the corrupt Svidrigaylov commits suicide near a police station, not a church. The old pawnbroker woman's house is not vaguely at "waterside" (Wishaw), but "on *the* canal" (Scammell, Coulson), "on *the* Canal Embankment"

(Magarshack),"on *the* canal embankment" (Monas). Except for Garnett, they know that Raskolnikov lives on Stolyarny Street or Stolyarny Place, not on Wishaw's "*pereulok S——.*"

These translators are not always familiar with Petersburg-Leningrad. They do not know the design of Vasilevsky Island—a series of "lines" facing each other across tree-lined boulevards (once canals)—so they turn Dostoyevsky's careful designation of the location of the home of Svidrigaylov's child fiancée into vague conjunctions of streets, avenues, prospects, blocks. They redirect Raskolnikov's oblivious, but physically and metaphysically exact, wandering toward "the Petersburg Side," one of the city's four main quarters, to "the mainland" (Garnett) or "a Petersburg suburb" (Magarshack). But even Garnett, who often gets lost in this city's geometric chaos, has made an effort to orient herself to significance of place. Monas, who knows the city so well that he gets lost only once on Vasilevsky Island, indicates awareness of the symbolically important but seldom revealed juxtapositions of events and places in his introduction and in notes. He knows that Svidrigaylov commits suicide near Petrovsky Island, where Raskolnikov experienced the symbolic dream of the horse, and within sight of the home of his dialectical antithesis Razumikhin. Monas knows why Dostoyevsky has Raskolnikov standing on a particular bridge or crossing at a particular time, and he knows what other event has occurred in proximity to this location and therefore what Raskolnikov is contemplating. (The crossings lead either to the police station, where Raskolnikov might confess, or to a bridge, where he might commit suicide.) Above all, he and the other four translators after Wishaw know when to transliterate (in order to convey realia) and when to translate. They understand they are dealing with a literary classic, not an anthropological document. And they translate a Russian novel as a Russian novel, not as an English-Russian hybrid.

When we speak about translation in American letters, we must keep in mind that our translators are often British. At issue here is the Americanization and Britishification of Russian and other literary works. It has already been noted that Hayward and Hingley used American colloquial style successfully when they translated *One Day in the Life of Ivan Denisovich* and that Aitken used too many British expressions. For the most part, translators in Britain and North America are well attuned to the differences among different standards of English. But while English language readers accept these different standards in original works, in translations the different usages often intrude on the reader's awareness. That is, a translation characterized by overly obvious British words and expressions sounds artificial to an American, while a strongly Americanized translation becomes an irritant to British readers. In either case, the reader begins to question the language of the original text, and, in the case of translations of *Crime and Punishment*, to wonder why a nineteenth-century Russian university student in Petersburg uses British or American expressions. Magarshack, for example, has been criticized for using such inimically British verbalisms as "my dear fellow," "Chuck it, Roddy!" and "hang it all." To a degree, it is difficult to avoid using indigenous words and expressions. For example, various solutions for the Russian expression *opytnaia kanal'ia* are "experienced brute" (Magarshack), "practiced ruffian" (Garnett), "experienced ruffian" (Scammell), and "experienced rascal" (Coulson)—neither too obvious nor too bland. But Magarshack's Britishisms are too obvious. "Oh, rot!" "I daresay," "what a funny crowd you all are"—these choices are too inimitably British to sound natural in a novel by Dostoyevsky. The same shortcoming is apparent to a lesser degree in Monas's American translation. "Down to brass tacks" is an American colloquialism that would not occur to a Russian. "He's really quite a guy," "kid them along," "old pal"— these Americanisms are not appropriate for Dostoyevsky. One aspect of Monas's translation that distinguishes it from his colleagues' versions is that he has attempted to differentiate among the voices of Dostoyevsky's characters by giving them distinct intonations and manners of speaking. But his Americanisms limit an otherwise long stylistic reach by diverting the reader's attention from distinctive speech styles to artificial text. The word *kanal'ia*, for example, is given too sharply as "bastard"; "Hell no!" "damn it!" and "Go to hell" are too strong and too American. The slang term "I.O.U." does not belong in a Russian novel.

Magarshack and Monas are not incompetent translators. In respect to this particular problem of choice and decision, however, Magarshack uses the British standard and Monas the American in so marked a fashion that one's choices intrude on American readers, the other's on British readers. There is a need for moderation here—the balance recommended by Soviet theorists for dealing with colloquial speech. This and other problems of different and changing translation standards can be explored in some of the many translations of Chekhov's stories.

Probably no other Russian writer has been so widely translated in English as Chekhov. D. S. Mirsky has said that Chekhov is an easy writer to translate (1958:382). An extraordinarily nuanced stylist, Chekhov is otherwise a straightforward writer whose techniques are used consistently throughout his oeuvre. Because he is easy to translate, there are remarkably few differences in choice of syntax and lexicon among his translators. Because his style is so subtle, even a slightly wrong choice can become a glaring stylistic violation.

For purposes of historical perspective, it is appropriate to assess translations of Chekhov in terms of Levin's orientation to the evolution of principles, methods, and aesthetics of style and language. How have we treated Chekhov in our world, and how has literary translation developed since the first translation of Chekhov appeared in the late nineteenth century?

Translations can be traced from the pioneer work of R. E. C. Long, Constance Garnett, Marian Fell, and S. S. Koteliansky (with J. M. Murry or Gilbert Cannan) to the later work of Avrahm Yarmolinsky, David Magarshack, Robert Payne, and Ann Dunnigan in the 1950s and the 1960s to the recent work of Ronald Hingley and Patrick Miles and Harvey Pitcher. Analysis of the translations focuses on passages that represent problems of Chekhov's style as a whole and on representative indicators of specific problems of lexicon, syntax, and intonation.

Modern translators know the historical problems of contemporaneity and temporariness, changes of taste, and the need for each generation to translate for itself anew. Chekhov's style does not seem outdated in Russian, because he is read in his time and place. His style may very well seem *dated*, because short-story techniques have become more sophisticated over the years and because style tastes have changed, but not *outdated*. When we read Chekhov in the translations of Long, Fell, or Koteliansky, in contrast, his style seems outdated to us. These translations do not satisfy us and may even offend us. This is due to changing tastes and is not a question of the translator's competence. Whereas Russians consciously or unconsciously suspend their judgment of Chekhov himself, readers of translations customarily make judgments according to their own time.

Even a cursory reading of Long's translations yields marked British lexical choices of his time. In *The Kiss, and Other Stories* (1908), Chekhov's landowners in "The Kiss" become "local country gentlemen" who are served "biscuits" by "footmen," while his army officers are obliged to wear "mufti" and exclaim, "I like his cheek!" Long's version of "Women" features "country gentlemen" again, servants who address their masters as "your honour," and peasants who drop in at the local "drink-shop." The same outdated and out-of-place lexicon is obtrusive in Koteliansky and Murry's *The Bet, and Other Stories* (1915). A character in "The Bet" loses his "last farthing," and in "A Dreary Story" we find such British realia as "navvy," "knight," and "satis" (a student's grade). British expressions such as "high-class," "a nice lot," and "Fire away!" abound in this translation. Similarly, Koteliansky's *Tchekhov's Plays and Stories* (1917) is marked by such expressions as "By Jove!" and "queer fish," and Anglicized names such as "Mr. Cheeky Snout," "Radish," and "Little Profit."

Early translators wisely transliterate such realia as *khalat, shchi, kvas,* but they also use the device to cover up uncertain knowledge of Russian culture. The early translator most severely criticized for mistranslation, misunderstanding, and poor conveyance is Fell. Kornei Chukovsky devotes much of one chapter of *A High Art* to criticism of her "slips of the vocabulary." Chukovsky catches Fell confusing the poet Batyushkov with *batiushka* 'old man,' the critic Dobrolyubov with St. Francis of Assisi (*dobroliubets*, a doer of good deeds), and the French General Jomini with

Germany. Fell mixes up names, dates, currencies, and numbers,"which is deplorable," but "it is far worse that she imputes to Chekhov an insipid, colorless, stingy style by excising from his works . . . every vivid, colorful sentence, every vital intonation" (1984).

We can see the effect time has on translations and begin to appreciate the process of improvement in literary translation by examining two older versions of a difficult passage in Chekhov, the colloquial speech of old Semyon in "In Exile." The first example is taken from Koteliansky and Cannan's *The House with the Mezzanine, and Other Stories* (1917), the second from Long's *The Black Monk, and Other Stories* (1903).

> "You will get used to it," said Brains with a laugh. "You are young yet and foolish; the milk is hardly dry on your lips, and in your folly you imagine that there is no one unhappier than you."

> "You'll get used to it," said Wiseacre, grinning. "You're young and foolish now —your mother's milk is still wet on your lips, only youth and folly could make you imagine there's no one more miserable than you."

Old Semyon's speech is not illiterate, but it is nevertheless substandard. He uses dialect phrases and folk sayings in the original. Long's conveyance of this colloquial standard is better than Koteliansky and Cannan's, at least to the extent that he uses contractions, and his substitution of the word "grinning" for the original word "laugh" helps him to avoid the benevolent tone that ruins Semyon's character in Koteliansky and Cannan's misinterpretation. Semyon's tone is mean; he does not sympathize with the young Tatar in these and other nagging admonitions. Both translations convey literally the saying "the milk's not dry on your lips yet," and both are too literary in choice of lexicon: "youth and folly," "imagine," "you will get used to it," "you are young yet and foolish."

Ronald Hingley's modern version of the same passage in *The Oxford Chekhov* (1965–1980) is superior:

> 'You'll settle down,' said Foxy with a laugh. 'You're young and stupid yet, you ain't dry behind the ears, like; and you're daft enough to think you're the unluckiest man on earth.'

In Hingley's more imaginative approach, Seymon's speech, and thus his character, has been deftly caught. Hingley replaces the Russian saying with "you ain't dry behind the ears," and he even heightens the original by adding the telling colloquialism "like." Long's "you'll get used to it" has been changed to a better English variant, "you'll settle down." Hingley can be criticized for being too colloquial. "Daft" is too British, and in other passages Hingley has Semyon saying "That's all daft, mate," "I ain't just another yokel, mate," "I ain't a bumpkin, like," and "it ain't just us stupid peasants that comes a cropper." Except for these too obtrusive British slang expressions, Hingley's version is successful. He at least recognizes colloquial speech—something that is beyond Long and Koteliansky and Cannan—and his attempt to deal with the problem is brave.

Hingley's version can be usefully compared to Dunnigan's modern version in *Selected Stories* (1960). Dunnigan refuses to reproduce colloquial speech but still catches Semyon's character:

> "You'll get used to it!" said Preacher with a laugh. "You're still young and foolish—the milk's hardly dry on your lips—and in your foolishness you think there's no one more unfortunate than you."

Dunnigan has avoided the stiff literary words that mar the older translations, and her vocabulary is simple like Semyon's. "The milk's hardly dry on your lips," "in your foolishness you think"—these phrases indicate that Semyon is jeering at the young Tatar, not offering him fatherly advice. Dunnigan has erred in the direction of blandscript, as Hingley has erred in favor of colloquiality, but both modern translations are satisfying, as the older versions are not. It is not possible to say whether Dunnigan has consulted existing translations of this story, but some of her formulations are close enough to Garnett's to suggest she consulted her predecessor's texts. Note, however, that Dunnigan's style is her own. Indeed, each of these translators unavoidably and naturally imprints his or her own personality on Chekhov's stories.

Garnett has often been cited as an example of an outdated translator, but her work has nevertheless survived extraordinarily well. Her versions are still selected for volumes by such modern editors as Ralph E. Matlaw, Magarshack, Yarmolinsky, David Greene, and Edmund Wilson (the latter does not acknowledge his use of her texts). A comparison of her first and her later translations shows very few changes: the texts in Matlaw (1979), Magarshack (1964), Greene (1965), and those noted as "newly improved" by her son David Garnett are almost the same. Perhaps we have been conditioned to "hear" Russian writers in Garnett's popular translations, so that we are too receptive to her style, but analysis indicates that her work is far superior to work by contemporaries and that she developed principles of translation far ahead of others

Certainly it would be possible to compile a long list of marked British expressions in Garnett's vast oeuvre, but a search through *The Lady with the Dog, and Other Stories* (1917) yields few examples. In "The Lady with the Dog," Garnett has "he had been so schooled by bitter experience," and in "A Doctor's Visit," there is "have a peep at it." *The Schoolmaster, and Other Stories* (1921) offers only the British expressions "a bit of pie" and "your honour" in the story "The Schoolmaster," and "how queer it is, really" and "flunkey" in the story "Enemies." Aware of the dangers of tying a foreign work too closely to one's own time and place, Garnett has clearly made an effort to avoid strongly marked colloquialisms and to be sensible about realia. A characteristic feature of the early translators is that they tend to swing too far in the direction of either literalism or free translation, often inappropriately, without a strong instinct for when to be more accurate, when to be more imaginative. Modern translators, in contrast, stay close to fidelity; they know when to be more literal, when to be more free. They are also adept at using translation devices, including embellishment, compensation, substitution, rephrasing, lexical equivalency, and reconstitution. If Chekhov in English is any indication, we are indeed living in an age of translation. Chekhov's modern translators, having learned from the pioneers, have resolved problems of realia and colloquial speech. They are not mesmerized by the spell of the original language—they know that the best way to serve Chekhov in English is not to replicate his Russian syntax but to allow him to speak in English as he spoke in Russian. They seem to know that translation is an art of approximation and are aware of the importance of choice and decision. Among these modern translators, Robert Payne is an enthusiastic propagandizer of Chekhov who does not hesitate to invent but avoids modernizing; Ann Dunnigan is a careful, cautious translator; Ronald Hingley's first concern is an accurate text, but he does not lack imagination; Patrick Miles and Harvey Pitcher are conscious modernizers who somehow manage to please the reader of our time without violating Chekhov's rights as the original author.

The standards of modern translators and their improvement over early translators can be seen by comparing Payne's work with the best of the early translators, Garnett. In his eagerness to champion Chekhov, Payne does not always resist trying to help Chekhov along in English, but he does not arrogantly "improve" Chekhov, and his enthusiasm works in Chekhov's favor, not for his own vanity. Compare Garnett's version of the seduction scene in "The Lady with the Dog," in *Select Tales of Tchehov* (the improved 1961 text), with Payne's version of the same scene, in *The Image of Chekhov* (1963):

But in this case there was still the *diffidence*, the *angularity* of inexperienced youth, an *awkward feeling*; and there was a sense of *consternation* as though someone had suddenly knocked at the door. The attitude of Anna Sergeyevna —"the lady with the dog"—to what had happened was *somehow peculiar, very grave*, as though it were her fall—so it seemed, and it was *strange* and *inappropriate*. Her face *drooped and faded*, and on both sides of it her long hair hung down *mournfully*; she mused in a *dejected* attitude like "the woman who was a sinner" in an old-fashioned picture.

But here was all the *shyness* and *awkwardness* of inexperienced youth; a feeling of *embarrassment*, as though someone had suddenly knocked on the door. Anna Sergeyevna, "the lady with the pet dog," accepted what had happened in her own special way, *gravely* and *seriously*, as though she had accomplished her own downfall, an attitude which he found *odd* and *disconcerting*. Her features *faded and drooped* away and on both sides of her face the long hair hung *mournfully* down, while she sat musing *disconsolately* like an adulteress in an antique painting. (Italics are mine.)

Garnett's version is slightly Victorian—the telling embellishment in the phrase "the woman who was a sinner." Payne's version is modernized. He invented the syntax "in her special way," and the phrase "as though she had accomplished her own downfall" is an outright concoction. The Garnett version is more accurate—she retains the key word "angularity" where Payne replaces it with "awkwardness" (and thereby coopts *nelovkoe chuvstvo* 'awkward feeling,' and has to omit it). Garnett's "consternation" (for *rassteriannost'*) is closer than Payne's "embarrassment," which is too weak for what Anna Sergeyevna feels, and his "disconcerting" is too strong for *nekstati*, which she has caught with "inappropriate." Garnett errs by elaborating "here" into "in this case," while Payne recreates the specificity— the seduction has just occurred *here* in this Yalta hotel room. The translators both have the equivalents "faded," "drooped," and "mournfully," but Payne's reversal to create the phrase "faded and drooped away" provides a more graceful phonetic and rhythmic pattern. Payne's choices of "shyness" (for *nesmelost'*) and "disconsolately" (for *unylaia*) are better than Garnett's "diffidence" and "dejected." But he has erred by attributing the sense of Anna Sergeyevna's "strange and inappropriate" attitude to Gurov—Chekhov and Garnett have it as a vague feeling in the atmosphere of the room. Payne's phraseology is more imaginative and graceful than Garnett's, but he has taken liberties to please modern readers.

Garnett and Payne have used the same devices and techniques. They have both embellished (Payne has even invented), compensated, rephrased, substituted. We can argue with a few choices, but both have caught the most important feature of the scene, that Chekhov's words progress carefully— with physiological precision—from shy, angular, and awkward to strange and odd to mournful and disconsolate. We can see how well both translators have served Chekhov by comparing their work to Koteliansky's less successful version in *Tchekhov's Plays and Stories* (1937):

But here there was the *shyness* and *awkwardness* of inexperienced youth, a feeling of *constraint*, an impression of *perplexity* and *wonder*, as though someone had suddenly knocked on the door. Anna Sergueyevna, "the lady with the dog," took what had happened *somehow seriously, with a particular gravity*, as though thinking that this was her downfall and very *strange* and *improper*. Her features seemed to *sink and wither*, and on either side of her face the long hair hung *mournfully* down; she sat *crestfallen* and *musing*, exactly like a woman taken in sin in some old picture. (Italics are mine.)

"Perplexity and wonder" are not what Anna Sergeyevna feels; Koteliansky has introduced with the word "improper" a moral judgment that is alien to Chekhov; the words "sink and wither" are too raw for the Chekhov mood; "a woman taken in sin" is another moralistic concoction. The translator wanders from being overly free to overly literal (he retains the Russian grammatical construction "but here *there* was" [*bylo* in the opening line]), and his use of compensation, substitution, and rephrasing is inept.

Language and taste change; translations lose their vitality. It ought to be true also that art improves, that translators learn from their predecessors' mistakes. A characteristic of old translations of Chekhov is that they are both too accurate, to the point of literal precision, and too free, to the point of sloppy paraphrase. Long's version of the opening in "Sleepy," in *The Black Monk, and Other Stories,* provides an example of unstable control:

> In front of the ikon burns a green lamp; across the room from wall to wall stretches a cord on which hang baby-clothes and a great pair of black trousers. On the ceiling above the lamp shines a great green spot, and the baby-clothes and trousers cast long shadows on the stove, on the cradle, on Varka. . . . When the lamp flickers, the spot and shadows move as if from a draught. It is stifling. There is a smell of soap [sic] and boots.

The translation verges on literalism. In some instances, Long has preserved the original syntax too precisely: "burns a green lamp," "a cord on which hang," "there is a smell," "shines a great green spot." At other times, he has slurred some of Chekhov's delicate phrasing: using "across the room from wall to wall," rather than "across the entire room, from one corner to another"; and "on the ceiling above the lamp shines a great green spot," rather than "the icon-lamp throws a large patch of green onto the ceiling." In these and other cases, paraphrase has led to both error and unclear image. Long's syntax is markedly Russian, his version lacks Chekhovian clarity, and the translation is vague and stilted.

We can appreciate how stilted Long's version is by comparing it with the work by Miles and Pitcher in *Chekhov: The Early Stories, 1883–1888* (1982, 1983):

> In front of the icon burns a small green lamp; across the entire room, from one corner to another, stretches a cord with baby-clothes and a pair of big black trousers hanging on it. The icon-lamp throws a large patch of green onto the ceiling, and the baby-clothes and trousers cast long shadows on the stove, the

cradle, and Varka. . . . When the lamp begins to flicker, the green patch and the shadows come to life and are set in motion, as if a wind were blowing them. It is stuffy. The room smells of cabbage-soup and bootmaker's wares.

Miles and Pitcher's version is accurate without being literal, imaginative without being too free. The translation is not tied to Chekhov's syntax: the phrase "hanging on it" has been shifted to the end of the sentence; "the room smells of cabbage-soup and bootmaker's wares" is natural to English, more specific to what Chekhov is describing. Miles and Pitcher are sensitive to the nuances of Chekhov's style. Where Long has the shadows cast "on the stove, on the cradle, on Varka," repeating the preposition in a way that makes all three equal. Miles and Pitcher have "on the stove, the cradle, *and* Varka," thereby moving from the inanimate and less important stove and cradle to the animate and very important Varka, whose perceptions are the basis of the description. The modern version has caught not only the tone of pathos—pity for the tortured Varka trying to stay awake—but also the sinister hint at the story's ending—her murder of the baby—in the telling image "the shadows come to life." The development in literary translation can be seen by comparing Miles and Pitcher's version to Garnett's version in the text edited for *Anton Chekhov's Short Stories* by Ralph E. Matlaw (1979). Garnett reproduces the Russian syntax too literally, repeating a Russian construction: "there is a string stretched," "there is a big patch of green," "there is a smell." Garnett's "A little green lamp" sounds too cute for the diminutive *lampadka*, whereas Miles and Pitcher's "small green lamp" sounds more like Chekhov. Garnett has retained the "on which" construction and has embellished the concluding line: "There is a smell of cabbage-soup and of the inside of a boot-shop."

Modern perceptions of translation must be kept in historical perspective. It is not Long's fault that a change in English diction makes the description of the green spot sound to the modern ear like "that's a great green spot (you have there on your ceiling)." Moreover, in many instances failings occur regardless of time and our hope that the art improves. This is especially apparent when Chekhov's stylistic devices are central. Chekhov's techniques are used so consistently as to be compelling. We know that certain colors and objects are linked with moods and that shadows and lights set a specific scene. To read Chekhov is to be conditioned—our moods change at his will—and Chekhov's translators are conditioned too. None are so obtuse as to miss a color or a texture. They seldom miss impressionistic functions of Chekhov's clouds, scissors, ashtrays, lamps, icon, and chandeliers. The moods created by Chekhov are so powerful that they come through even when his translators err. There are, however, limits to Chekhov's tolerance, especially regarding the misuse of his devices.

In "A Dreary Story," the professor-narrator following his aged wife up the stairs to comfort his neurotic daughter is aware of the bright spots from his wife's candle dancing over the dark staircase, the trembling of their long shadows, the trip of his feet in his long dressing-gown. His breath catches and he imagines someone is pursuing him, preparing to seize him from behind. At this point he thinks. "'Now I will die here, on this staircase,' I think. Now. . ." This is all he thinks. The words are simple: "now," "here," "on this staircase." There is no need to vary, substitute, or strengthen here. But in *The Bet, and Other Stories*, Koteliansky and Murry have given it as "'I shall die here on the staircase, this second,' I think, 'this second.'" In *Select Tales of Tchehov*, Garnett has conveyed it as "'I shall die on the spot, here on the staircase,' I thought. 'On the spot.'" In *Lady with Lapdog, and Other Stories*, David Magarshack has it as "'Any moment now I shall die here on the stairs. . . . Now! Now!'" In *The Oxford Chekhov*, Ronald Hingley has "'I shall die here and now on these stairs,' I think, 'Now————'" Some translators have emphasized "I shall die" by placing it first in the statement, although the key word "die" should not appear first. The simple words "here" and "now" have been changed to read "this second," "on the spot," "any moment now," or exaggerated into "Now! Now!" The broken syntax has been smoothed, as in Magarshack's "Any moment I shall die here and now on these stairs," and Hingley's "I shall die here and now on these stairs." Each translator, anxious to catch the drama of the scene, has strengthened a thought whose drama is lodged in simplicity and understatement.

Despite this example, literary translation has improved. There are clear indications in translations of Chekhov that translators try to learn from their predecessors. Yarmolinsky and Magarshack each edited Garnett's translations for collections before they began their own translations. Hingley studied all existing translations for his preparation of *The Oxford Chekhov*. His work on the original and translated texts is authoritative. Miles and Pitcher examined Garnett for their edition of Chekhov's early stories and express indebtedness to Hingley for their knowledge of the text.

The character of modern translations can also be shown by comparing the work of Chekhov's translators. Useful here is an examination of Payne's heightened version of "The Student" and Hingley's greater concern for textual fidelity. Where Payne approaches his work as a writer who appreciates Chekhov as a writer, Hingley is a scholar and textologist. Yet Payne respects text and Hingley is sometimes quite imaginative. Where Payne has "the earth herself was in agony" for Chekhov's *samoi prirode zhutko*," Hingley has "striking dread in Nature herself." Where Hingley has simply "he felt famished," Payne has "the student was ferociously hungry." For Chekhov's description of the old widow Vasilisia, "a tall plump old woman," as Hingley faithfully has it, Payne has the overly strong "huge bloated old woman." Where Hingley has "blushed," plainly and correctly, Payne has "flushed scarlet." Hingley sticks to "delicately" for "*delikatno*," but Payne varies it as "refinement." Hingley makes a conscious effort to find the most faithful equivalent, while Payne does not hesitate to reword or to rephrase Chekhov. Hingley's version is not devoid of heightening and embellishment—he turns what Payne has accurately as "deep meaning" into "exalted significance" —but he stays close to Chekhov's expressive means. He has "tall" and "plump" where Payne has "huge" and "bloated," "blushed" instead of "scarlet," "dread" instead of the too strong "agony." Hingley is an authority on Chekhov's texts, and this shows in a few places where Payne has misunderstood Chekhov or erred. The wind does not blow "unreasonably," as Payne has it; rather, it is an "unwelcome" wind (*nekstati*), as Hingley has it both accurately and imaginatively. Payne has caused the younger widow Lukeria to drop the spoons and look "fixedly in the direction of the student," where Hingley, without elaboration, has her simply and correctly "put down the spoons" and "stare at the student." Payne seems not to have realized that when Vasilisia welcomes the student to the campfire, she not only wishes him the good fortune to become rich but also alludes to the peasant superstition that he who startles someone in the darkness will someday become rich.

An even more revealing indication of the character of modern translation is provided by comparing two decidedly different renditions of Chekhov's "The Kiss." Where Payne and Hingley arrive at similarly faithful versions of Chekhov, Dunnigan, a conservative translator, and Miles and Pitcher, who translate by adapting, offer very different work. These two versions of "The Kiss" are both modern translations, but where Miles and Pitcher are modernizers—their syntactic and lexical choices show that they are concerned with audience—Dunnigan has chosen her diction with Chekhov, not the reader, as her orientation. Dunnigan reproduces Chekhov's sentences very closely, for example. When the self-conscious Ryabovich stands watching the dancers at the Von Rabbek estate—this is the story of the young officer whose romantic feelings are awakened when he is accidently kissed by a young woman in a dark room—Dunnigan conveys one key sentence this way: "He was enormously delighted to see a man, in plain sight of everyone, take by the waist a girl with whom he was not acquainted and offer his shoulder for her hand, but he could in no way imagine himself in the position of such a man." The syntax here is good English, not Russian, but the pattern of the original is followed closely—each clause is in the same sequence as the original, each word in each clause is in the same order. Miles and Pitcher, in contrast, move deliberately away from the original syntax to create a more graceful, less austere, and at the same time more efficient sentence for the English reader: "To see a man take a strange girl by the waist in front of everyone and invite her to put her hand on his shoulder appealed to him enormously, but to imagine himself in that man's position was quite beyond him." Syntactic parallelism is operative here: "To see a man take . . . but to imagine himself. . . ." "A girl with whom" has been replaced by a simple phrase: "take a strange girl by the waist." Chekhov's straightforward "offer his shoulder for her hand" has been embellished into "invite her to put her hand on his shoulder."

The instinct of all three translators is sound. Both versions have faithfully repeated Ryabovich's favorite adverb and adjective "enormous," "enormously," as in the sentence just cited and in such exclamations as "'I like your house enormously!'" The lexical choices of the two translations are remarkably similar. But throughout the texts it is evident that Miles and Pitcher prefer to vary, and even to invent and embellish with an eye to modern appeal, while Dunnigan stays close to Chekhov. Thus, where she has "he no longer envied them, but felt sadly moved," they have "he no longer experienced envy, only a feeling of wistful admiration." Where she has the more accurate "beautifully disciplined family," they have "superbly disciplined family," a slight exaggeration. When Lobytko promises to find beer in the middle of the night "and you can call me scoundrel if I don't!" as Dunnigan carefully has it, Miles and Pitcher add an embellishment, "Call me a scoundrel if I come back empty-handed!" For the story's closing sentence Dunnigan has, "For an instant joy flamed in his breast, but he immediately stifled it and went to bed, and in his wrath with his fate, as though wishing to spite it, did not go to the general's." The same sentence in Miles and Pitcher's version reads, "For a brief moment a feeling of joy blazed up in Ryabovich, but he immediately extinguished it, got into bed, and in defiance of his fate, as if wanting to spite it, did not go to the general's." The result is that her faithful recreations of Chekhov are a bit stilted and their versions read better in English. But they have taken liberties with Chekhov to achieve their modernizers' aim.

Despite the differences among Chekhov's translators, they all achieve essentially faithful versions. They are all experienced in the ways of conveying literary works from one language to another, and they use translation devices correctly and effectively. Each of these translators has avoided the failings of the early translators—they know how and when to transliterate realia, they do not mechanically reproduce the original syntax, they have an instinct for Chekhov's differentiations among the speech standards of his characters. None of these translators reveals the slightest tendency to reinterpret or, worse, arrogantly to improve him. It has often been said that Chekhov's modesty and integrity are contagious. If this is so, his modern translators have clearly understood him, for their work is characterized by distinctly Chekhovian modesty and integrity. Perhaps it should not be said that Chekhov is easy to translate; instead, it may be said that his unassuming simplicity provokes determination to be worthy of his style.

Among the older translators of Chekhov, Long, Fell, and Koteliansky failed because they are grammatical slaves without strong literary talent; Garnett is more competent, more skillful, and, given the continued use of her texts in modern editions, more enduring; yet in many ways her version is out of date today. The pioneers are not entirely to blame for their short-comings. Rather, their successors have learned from their mistakes, the art of translation has improved, and literary tastes have changed. Above all, historical change has taken its inexorable toll. Translations are both contemporaneous and temporary. They serve their original in their time and for a time, but only rarely do they become immortal like their original. Among the modern translators, Dunnigan and Hingley are text-oriented, while Payne, Miles, and Pitcher are reader-oriented. Readers of Chekhov have a choice here. They can rely on Dunnigan for careful versions or on Miles and Pitcher for a Chekhov in literate modern English. They can enjoy Chekhov as a fellow writer in America hopes they will enjoy him, or they can turn to Hingley's professional knowledge of textology for an authoritative text. The differences between the generations and among the translators through history are evident. The most decided difference is that modern translators are clearly superior and have a more sophisticated knowledge of the art. They know when to be more literal, when to be more free, and they do not confuse accuracy with fidelity. They understand, whether consciously or unconsciously, that the most artistic translation is a faithful translation.

POETRY

12

THE POET AS TRANSLATOR

████████ Nine poets gathered at the Library of Congress in 1970 to listen to an address by Allen Tate on translating poetry. Two assumptions figured prominently in Tate's address: that only poets can translate poetry and that the poet who translates must have freedom. The assumptions, which can be traced throughout the poets' subsequent discussion, mark the transcript of the event clearly enough to consider them a revelation of what poets value most when they turn to the art of translation. As Tate stated, "I have been saying with some elaboration what we all know: that a translator ought to be a poet himself." This statement was seconded by Louis Untermeyer, who commented, "Only a poet has a right to translate any other poet." Zulfikar Ghose agreed, adding, "I believe that before a poet can be a translator, he's first got to show me that he's a very good poet in the English language. . . . The 20-year old [who translates] is seeking an easy identity with a poet" (Tate 1972:5, 22, 18). William Jay Smith reported that this conviction is widely held in Russia too, noting that the poet Andrey Voznesensky "feels very strongly that only poets should translate poetry. And he quotes Pasternak" (Tate 1972:31).

The translation of poetry, the most difficult practice of translation, provokes the most heated arguments about the very nature of translation. Discussion of poetic translation dominates studies in both the Soviet and American worlds of translation, often in debates over the role of poet as translator. A striking aspect of this discussion is that Soviet and American translators have unearthed the same problems and converged on the same conclusions.

The creation of poetry is one of the most intense expressions of freedom. It is not unusual for poets to demand the same freedom for literary translation that they demand for their original creativity. When Tate declared, "A pragmatic view of the art of translation is, it seems to me, the only useful view" (1972:4), he laid explicit claim to a poet's freedom. With this statement he affirmed an assumption common to poets who translate. Jackson Mathews, referring elsewhere to Valéry's definition of translation as an art of approximation, expressed agreement with Tate when he observed, "To translate a poem whole is to compose another poem. A whole translation will be faithful to the matter, and it will 'approximate the form' of the original; and it will have a life of its own, which is the voice of the translator." In Mathews's view, "in the 'approximation of form'. . . the motive is invention, not imitation" (1966:67, 68). An even stronger demand for freedom was registered by the translator of Japanese literature Donald Keene when he insisted, "The translator is entitled to resort to every legitimate means at his disposal in order to keep the work he is translating immediate and alive." His demand remains strong even when he qualifies it with tongue in cheek by noting, "Rules are not meant for translators of genius. If the reader perusing these lines happens to be such a translator, he may break the rules with impunity" (1971:322).

Insistence on freedom is often coupled with contempt for theory and distrust of rules. This feeling was once proclaimed by Borges's translator Norman Thomas di Giovanni: "To begin with, the whole thing is done by ear; there are no rules" (Borges 1973:110). Poets almost unanimously insist on personal and poetic freedom; in the American world poets who translate take their cue regarding personal and poetic freedom from Ezra Pound, the best-known proponent of the unfettered reinterpretation known as the imitation. "As to the atrocities of my translation," Ezra Pound warned, "all that can be said in excuse is that they are, I hope, for the most part intentional, and committed with the aim of driving the reader's perception further into the original than it would without them have penetrated" (Pound:172). In the Russian world, the poet-translator V. V. Levik, who is considered a model of the Soviet school despite his libertarian views and practice, has recommended that the poet who translates must not allow the original text to become a dictate:

> the poet is left with only one alternative: to set the original aside and in effect forget it. And as material for his subsequent work take not the original, but his own stanza, and taking it as a draft, try to transform it. . . . In so doing a few departures from the original will inevitably appear, but . . . if the verse stanza becomes more powerful and expressive, the gains will be so great that there will be no need to regret the losses. (1959:256)

It is difficult to refute these poets' assumptions. Consider first the notion that only poets can translate other poets. It is not given to many of us to be poets. To those who have tried to translate poetry, it seems there must be an unwritten law that if you cannot create poetry, you will not be able to translate poetry. Poets know this. As far back as the seventeenth-century John Denham wrote,

> Such is our pride, our folly and our fate,
> That only those who cannot write, translate. . . .

There are exceptions to the assumption that only poets can translate poetry. Translators of the Greek and Latin classics have customarily been scholars: Matthew Arnold insisted that translators of classical literature *must* be scholars (1905:36). Although Ghose demanded at the Tate address that translators of poetry prove they are poets in their own language, there are many instances where translators have established status as poets without becoming well known for their own verse. Donald Keene's translations of Japanese poetry come to mind there, and in classical studies we think of Lattimore, Arrowsmith, Carne-Ross, and Fitzgerald. But the best translators of poetry have usually been poets in their own right. Haskell M. Block was correct in saying that, in cases where a sustained commitment to translation "has been the concern of writers of uncommon talent, it has resulted in some of the great translations of world literature" (1981:116). We think here of Baudelaire, Goethe, Auden, and Valéry especially in the Anglo-American and European worlds where, as Block is quick to add, "not very many writers have been so committed to translation as to view the enterprise as a central part of their literary calling." We also think of great poets as great translators in the Russian world where literary translation has always been central to the poet's calling: Pushkin, Lermontov, Bunin, Bryusov, Blok, Pasternak, Akhmatova, Brodsky. D. S. Carne reminds us how closely related are the talent for original poetic work and the ability to translate: "at its highest, a translation comes into existence in the same way as a work of original literature: a man experiences something—in this case, a foreign text—which he has yet to find words for if he is to have any peace" (1961:9).

One problem with judging the quality of a poem in translation, particularly in the American world where standards are so difficult to agree on, is that critics are often uncertain where to draw the line between a good poem and a bad translation. Tate points to Robert Lowell's versions of foreign poets, especially Homer and Baudelaire, as a classic example of this confusion. He notes that Lowell's translations are "brilliant," but comments, "What is wrong with Lowell's fragment of Homer is . . . it is not good Lowell." In Serge Gavronsky's view, however, the contrary is true: "I most violently oppose Lowell's translation that Mr. Tate read yesterday. I find that abhorrent. I find Lowell translating an extraordinarily 'nuanced' poet, Baudelaire, into New England terms. And that does not work; it may be great Lowell, but it's awful Baudelaire" (Tate 1972:5, 21). How often have these formulaic judgments of poetry in translation been encountered? It is a good translation, but a bad poem; it is a bad translation, but a good poem. Criteria of taste in translations of poetry are not established as they are for original poetry, and so we are sometimes left with the suspicion that some translations—especially those known as imitations—hide deficiencies concerning knowledge of the language of the original. This suspicion was stated by Robert Graves when he noted about a highly praised translation by Ezra Pound that "Mr. Pound's translation depends on an almost perfect ignorance of Latin and a guessing at Propertius's sense from the nearest English equivalents" (1965:135).

At issue here are not Lowell's and Pound's reputations as poets, nor the value of the reinterpretations via translation known as the imitation. In reading the transcript of the Tate address and the discussion that followed, it is clear that each poet approached the question of translating poetry from an individual aesthetic orientation. Each poet was concerned with his own ideas about conveying a poem from one language to another—with result rather than with the original poem. The question of the original poet's rights was discussed only secondarily. The question of subordination of oneself to the values of the original poet was mentioned but not explored. Referring to the difficulty of transforming oneself from a poet into a translator, Ghose went so far as to say, "This task is beyond a poet; he just can't do it" (Tate 1972:21).

Nevertheless, poets are sometimes the worst translators. The same gift that makes a poet—an intensely singular, unrepeatable, personal voice—is likely to overcome the original. A distinction has to be made here, therefore. Poets cannot be poet-translators—as opposed to poets who translate—unless they are those rare beings who can overcome their poetic "I" and subordinate their creativity in order to translate another poet. The Soviet Armenian theorist of translation Levon Mkrtchian made a good point about the poetic "I" as it relates to translating poetry:

> Sometimes translators consciously sacrifice accuracy in the name of their "I." There is probably some sort of law in the fact that among strong individuals free translations or reinterpretations are often encountered right along with accurate, adequate translations. In these instances . . . liberties make sense, for we can speak, if not of translation, then of an original work arising on the basis of another language. (1970:37)

There is a place for the exercise of one's own freedom without the restraint of the original text. That place is the libertarian verse genre that Dryden called the imitation, a genre where the motive is not translation but invention. Writing about the two extreme translation gradations, Richard Lattimore has said, "I do not want to write a schoolboy's pony . . . I do not want to take a base of Aeschylus and rewrite it after my own fancy" (1966:48). A crib is not a translation, and the imitation is not a translation. The freedom exercised by Pound and Lowell is not the freedom of a translator; it is the freedom of poets who insist on their own creative freedom and do not abandon their own words to enter the world of another.

What is needed is an appreciation that the motives prompting the imitation and translation proper are quite different. Soviet translators have identified this difference and defined it clearly. It is not at all unusual that a translator creates an original poem through the process of translation, Mkrtchian has pointed out. This occurs "because of departures from the original in the translation, departures called forth not by the translator's capriciousness, but by his creative individuality, by the task he has set for himself: to recreate his own personal experiences by spurning the work of the other author" (1970:36). In other words, the imitation is prompted by an emphasis on individual creativity and the intent to recreate one's own experience in place of what may or may not exist in the original text. To the Soviet translator R. Mustafin there is a clear difference in kind between the imitation and translation proper, and he has traced confusion about this issue to a failure to recognize this difference. "It seems to me that we sometimes still confuse two types of translation," he has noted. "The first is essentially an original work written under the influence (or simply evoked by the subject) of a source in another language. . . . The other type is translation proper, the basic demand of which is an accurate conveyance of the distinctive character . . . of the original" (1965:37).

The issue involves separating translation proper from a kind of poetic activity that should not be called translation. "We have to discriminate," Robert M. Adams has advised, "between a translation that creates, deliberately or otherwise, wholly different effects than its original, and a translation that makes use of different means toward a similar 'ultimate effect.'" (1973:20). Failure to make this distinction—between deliberate departures from the original and those departures necessary to convey faithfully a poem from one language to another—results in unnecessary confusion. Worse, it leaves us with another suspicion, that some efforts at reinterpretation hide a lack of understanding of both language and poetry. The departures from the original that go under the name of free interpretation, John Hollander has warned, "have come to stand for an assertion of commitment to some sort of poetic truth, to a world in which a kind of literary correctness might flourish" (1966:209). Hollander's warning carries substantial weight because he is known to be a translator who demands great freedom for translators. The translation of poetry does require freedom, of course. The language barrier is itself enough to necessitate change, choice, decision—"the use of different means toward a similar 'ultimate effect.'" There is a difference between a poet-translator who accepts that a poetic translation is an approximation, who strives for fidelity while realizing that the ultimate effect can only be "similar," and the poet who is prompted by the original to assert his or her own "poetic truth." But when we read a translation that creates "wholly different effects," we wonder whether the departures are deliberate—a truly original creativity prompted by a poem in another language—or necessitated by an inability to sustain the power of the original.

Such misunderstanding degrades translation proper and demeans the legitimate status of the imitation as original poetic creativity. As Adams has pointed out,

> fidelity is an automatic virtue of translations; and no doubt under many, perhaps most, circumstances, it is. On occasion, it is the only virtue; there are no others. But fidelity may be more of a virtue than a translator dare aspire to. . . .The faithful translator doubtless deserves all the rewards he is bound to get; but infidelity is so widespread and often so deliberate that doubtless it has its rewards too. (1973:17–18)

Other critics agree with Adams. "An error in literary translation is, of course, also perilous to its perpetrator," Zoja Pavlovskis has noted, "yet in this area the quality of the finished product has traditionally carried more weight on the critic's scale than philological exactitude manages to earn. Whether he does it intentionally or inadvertently, a Virgil can afford to misconstrue Theocritus, and an Ezra Pound is allowed to get away with perverse misinterpretation of Propertius." Pavlovskis suggests that "ideally, it takes a poet to translate a poet, but as a corollary of this principle we must necessarily add that considerable latitude, indeed license, must be accorded to such a version if the translator's own originality is to remain unimpaired. The stronger a poet's individuality, the less likelihood that his translation of another's work will be a mirror reflection." Pavlovskis notes that discrimination is necessary: "common sense suggests that there is a point of no return in the process: past it, the re-creation of a work can no longer be called translation but instead becomes another scion in a possibly large grove of books that belong to the same literary tradition" (1981:99–100).

There is also a need to discriminate among literary practices and thereby to refine a definition of translation proper. André Lefevere believes that translation is a kind of interpretation, as interpretation is understood in its largest conceptual framework. As a kind of interpretation, translation must be distinguished not only from the imitation but also from another kind of literary practice that Lefevere defines as the version. That is, in accordance with Lefevere's well-devised schema, *translation*, by which the translator must "render the original author's interpretation of a theme accessible to a different audience," must be separated both from *version*, which "keeps the substance of a source text, but changes its form," and from *imitation*, where the poet "produces . . . a poem of his own, which has only the title and point of departure, if those, in common with the source text" (1975:76; also 1970:75–79).

Lefevere's schema differentiates between translation proper (translation and free translation or version) and imitation (a new poem prompted by another poem). His schema involves literary motivation as well as literary practice (or interpretation), which requires further differentiation. Helpful in distinguishing motivation are Soviet definitions of the poet-translator. The concept of the poet-translator, well established in the Soviet school, is defined with a strong emphasis on artistic freedom and individual personality. The concept assumes that not all poets can be translators, and that not all translators can be poets. The pioneer Soviet translator Ivan Kashkin clarifies this assumption by asking two rhetorical questions: "Is it enough for the creation of a good translation simply to be a conscientious translator?" and "Is it sufficient only to be a poet?" Kashkin addresses these questions by pointing to notoriously bad Russian verse translations by translators who are not poets and to Russian poets who are considered poor translators (1959:113).

In the Soviet school the concept of the poet-translator involves talent and sharp distinctions between the poet's freedom and the translator's freedom. Regarding the often repeated notion of the poet's strong personality, Kashkin notes, "The more talented the translator, the more opportunity he has to display his personal literary talent and fully reveal the talent and distinctive character of the translated author, but at the same time the danger of shunting the author aside and drawing the reader away from the original is all the greater" (1959:129–30). The Soviet definition of the poet-translator does not endorse the surrender of creative individuality. N. M. Lyubimov, known for his skillful translations of Cervantes and Rabelais, has said that a translator's ability to "blend" with an original author "does not mean that he must become his slave. The blend demands search, inventiveness, resourcefulness, it demands reflection, familiarization, empathy. . . . By revealing the creative individuality of the author, the translator reveals his own individuality too, but in a way that does not shunt the author aside. The translator is free to play different roles—upon condition of the fullest possible reincarnation" (1983:88). Likewise, Kashkin has insisted that "without individuality there is no creativity, and without a creative approach there is no truly artistic mastery." There are limits to the translator's freedom, however. Kashkin states that the violation of these limits results in capricious liberties: "But step just slightly over the border" between fidelity and capricious invention, and the translator not only "does not gain his freedom thereby, but falls into capricious interpretation" (1959:119).

The Soviet school makes great demands on poet-translators by placing on them the burden of both their own freedom and law. Poet-translators must lend their talent to the original poet and yet remain themselves, subordinate their individuality without losing it. "There are two quite contradictory qualities that exist together in the soul of the poet-translator," Lev Ozerov has suggested. "He knows how—must know how—to reincarnate himself in the poet he translates. And at the same time he must . . . remain himself" (1959:285). Translators inevitably imprint their own personalities on their work. This is unavoidable, and both its inevitability and its efficacy enter into the Soviet concept of the poet-translator. Mkrtchian has argued that it would be wrong for poet-translators to attempt to efface themselves from their work. But this "does not signify that one must express only oneself in a translation, that one may and must ignore the original. From the correct premise that the creative personality will inescapably reveal itself in a translation, it would be wrong to conclude that *this* is how a translation manifests its power, that the translator must consciously strive toward 'self-expression'" (1970:34).

Concern for the integrity of the original poet and the original text is crucial to the Soviet definition of the poet-translator. The task of the poet-translator is to recreate to the fullest extent possible the original poem, and to do so without transforming it into something else in the name of creative freedom. "The translator's skill," R. Mustafin has said, "is first of all the ability to accurately recreate in another language not simply the words, but everything that lies behind them: the thoughts, and the feelings, and the images, and the colors, and the very inspiration of the work being translated. But to recreate, not reinterpret" (1965:50). Mustafin demands much in these words, and translators often reject the demand. Yet, even though Soviet poet-translators acknowledge the difficulties of such a demand, they recognize, by setting such a high standard, that the poet-translator exercises a freedom that is secondary to the freedom of the original author and the autonomy of the original poem.

Practiced in this way, the translation of poetry becomes a high art demanding as much as the writing of original poetry. Many American poet-translators acknowledge the value of this ideal. "The translator must voluntarily subordinate himself to another person's verbal stance, or verbal attitude," F. Will has said. "He must try to feel his way into that attitude, accurately, in good faith" (1973:78). Jean Paris acknowledges the ideal on the same terms: "The translator has to work in his own language exactly as the poet did in his, putting forth the same effort to organize the same images and to shape similar rhythms. The result may sometimes prove disappointing, but in this regard translation ceases to be a minor genre and becomes equivalent to genuine creation. . . . Thus understood, translation may sometimes be more difficult than poetry itself" (1961:63).

While it is true that poets are the best translators of poetry, the differences between a poet's freedom and a poet-translator's freedom should be recognized. The primary difference is that where original poets are free to follow their own dictates poet-translators must remember that their freedom cannot be dissociated from the rights of the poet they translate. The poet-translator's freedom does not omit creativity, for translation is, as Paris has said, equivalent to genuine creation. But to create while simultaneously following another person's verbal attitude is more demanding than original creativity. "Translation is a two-way process," Ivan Kashkin has said. Consideration of it shows that there is no way to exclude the author of the original. It is not you who have done the writing—so follow him at every stage of his work, if you please. A writer is free to choose the limits of his fancy for himself. . . .And his material is the entire world. The translator is restricted by his choice: the translator's world is defined by the pages of the original, his world is already reflected in the author's mirror. (1959:107)

Literary translation "demands more work than original creativity," the Russian poet-translator Arseny Tarkovsky once declared. "Inspiration is not enough here. I work in both areas, and I assure you it is far easier to write one's own verse than to translate another's" (1973:266). "To translate a poem well," John Nims has said, "is harder than to write a new poem, in which one is always free to change direction. . . .The translator has a responsibility to be as faithful [to the thought of the poem] as the conflicting interests of rhythm and sound permit; certainly he is not free, except in 'imitations,' to follow his own will" (1971:xxiii). E. G. Etkind, in his study *Poeziia i perevod* (Poetry and translation), endorsed this principle when he stated, "The task of the poet-translator is to recreate in another language the poetic content of a work. For him the original is not a 'shunting aside' but a window through which the translator looks out at a world already comprehended . . . by the predecessor-poet" (1963:137).

Fidelity is a key concept of the translation of poetry and a chief value of the poet-translator. Theodore Savory has spoken for this value by noting, "One reason for the advocacy of faithfulness is that the translator has never allowed himself to forget that he is a translator. He is not, he recognizes, the original author, and the work in hand was never his own" (1968:51). Soviet translators strongly emphasize fidelity, defining it antonymically from exactness, accuracy, or precision—that which makes for a pony, a crib, a trot, or a literary work deprived of life by overly direct conveyance. Precision has been banned from literary translation in the Soviet school, and this ban has been succinctly stated by V. V. Levik: "The precision of a translation cannot be the standard of its artistry. . . .The very term 'precision' has become odious to us" (1959:254). Precision suggests a literal copy of the original rather than faithful poetic conveyance, a point that has been made clearly by John Nims:

> a translation aiming at poetic equivalence has little chance of being literal, or "word for word"—although there are always readers who will compare a translation with its original so that they can say "Aha!" triumphantly at any discrepancy. But linguists tell us that word-for-word translation . . . is often impossible. . . . This has always been realized by poet-translators: Horace might have been speaking for all of them when he warned that a faithful interpreter will not translate verbum verbo.

Turning his attention to the question of precision, Nims adds, "The right question to ask about a translation of poetry is not 'Is it faithful?' but 'Does it produce an equivalent effect?' Or perhaps, 'a reasonably equivalent effect?'" (1971:xxiii, xxii).

American translators use the words *accuracy, precision, fidelity, faithfulness,* and *exactness* interchangeably, as can be seen from the foregoing remarks. They do this even though they distinguish between what Nims calls "literal" and "word-for-word" on the one hand and "equivalent effect" on the other. The concepts are understood, although the critical vocabulary is not responsibly established. In the Soviet school the terms *precision* (*tochnost'*) and *fidelity* (*vernost'*) used to be confused but have now been dissociated. Translators in the Soviet school heed an axiom articulated seventy years ago by Chukovsky, who first stated that "'literal precision' often results in a complete distortion of the meaning of the original" (1984:6). The same idea was recently restated by Will with an astute double entendre: ". . . the translation of poetic language is literally impossible" (1973:81). Translators are aware of this problem. Long ago Wilhelm von Humboldt noted, "It could even be contended that the more a translation strives after accuracy, the more deviant it becomes." The problem was stated again by August Schlegel; "literalness is a long way from fidelity. Fidelity means that the same or similar impressions are produced, because these are the essence of the matter" (Lefevere 1977:41, 52). A. Guseynayev articulated the problem as a paradox and expressed the frustration of all poet-translators when he observed, "The translator strains with all his might to reproduce the entire organism, the entire spirit of a poem. And you look: everything is in place, the thought is expressed precisely, the figurative means have not suffered. But the translation does not evoke the delight evoked by the original" (1975:37).

Soviet translators generally agree that the more the translator strives for precision, the more likely a mechanical substitute will be produced. E. G. Etkind believes that literary translation is the art of sacrificing the minor in order to achieve the major. He ascribes such degree of precision to a failure to recognize that the translation of poetry requires priorities. "In the translation of poetry transformations—losses, additions, changes—are unavoidable," he has asserted. "It is natural that the character of these transformations will tell the poet-translator's individuality, his attitude not only toward the text . . . but also toward what stands behind the text, the real world detected by the translator." Etkind deprecates what he considers a futile chase after precision:

> Alas, the pursuit of external verbal precision is the most destructive thing for translated poetry . . . the quest for verbal proximity to the original leads the translator almost inevitably to failure. Behind attempts to achieve maximal verbal precision usually stands a pedantic devotion to the letter of the original, a reluctance to deal with any sacrifices, omissions, or replacements in the recreation of a poetic work in another language. . . . As a rule, without sacrifices, without omissions and replacements, there is no verse translation. It is precisely in a striving for semantic-formal precision that "precision" becomes treason. (1963:75–76, 62–63)

When he refers to transformations, Etkind, like Mustafin, makes a clear distinction between "recreation" and "reinterpretation." His acknowledgment that the translation of poetry requires change should not be taken as license for the unrestrained liberty characteristic of the imitation. Etkind addresses translation, not original creativity, and his advice that the task of the poet-translator is "to recreate the poetic content of the original" is central to his discussion.

We may return to the value of freedom to more fully appreciate the distinction made between precision and fidelity in the Soviet school. Fidelity is essentially a reasonable freedom that represents both respect for the rights of the original poet without denying the legitimacy of the translator's individuality as well as voluntary subordination to the integrity of the original text without excluding the importance of the translator's imagination and talent. Fidelity also implies that a translation of a poem cannot be judged in terms of direct, literal conveyance. The distinction between a precise and a faithful translation is as important as the distinction between an imitation and translation proper.

An important contribution made by Etkind is his insistence that the value of fidelity is predicated on the value of choice and decision. With this position he has arrived at conclusions reached by American and other poet-translators. A literally precise translation seeks perfection, but the translator's art is no more perfect than any other art. The translation of poetry is a process of choice and decision, and of polishing and finishing. "One cannot translate a poem," Nims has said, "but one can try to reconstitute it by taking the thought, the imagery, the rhythm, the sound, the qualities of diction—these and whatever else made up the original—and then attempt to rework as many as possible into a poem in English. Since no translator can manage equally all such data at the same time, with so many conflicting claims to be reconciled, what he has to do is set up a constantly shifting system of priorities." In Nims's view, "something has to give: the translator's fascinating work is made up of decisions, decisions: what to give up in order to gain what? With the all-important *whole* forever in mind: a poem like the original" (1971:xxii). Etkind would agree with Nims: "The art of translating poetry is in large degree the art of sustaining losses and implementing transformations. Without facing up to losses and transformations it is impossible to contend with poetry in another language. And the most important thing for translators of poetry is to know as a certainty in each concrete instance precisely what losses are permitted and in what direction one may transform the text" (1963:68).

Both Nims and Etkind discuss choice and decision in terms of tactics, even in terms of a system of tactics. Nims speaks of reconstituting elements and reconciling conflicting claims by setting priorities. Etkind speaks of permitting transformations and understanding what is acceptable. "Translation, the surmounting of the obstacle," Theodore Savory has said, "is made possible by an equivalence of thought that lies behind its different verbal expressions." He adds, "at every pause the translator makes a choice. . . .His choice is clearly not between alternative yet exact equivalents, but between a number of equivalents, all more or less inexact. Such a choice depends on the personality of the translator, and that it is essentially an aesthetic choice cannot be denied" (1968:13, 26). Where Savory perceives tactics of choice in equivalency, Mathews finds them in invention: "the translator has to invent formal effects in his own language that give a sense of those produced by the original in its own" (1966:68).

Together with the considerations of poetic gift, freedom, fidelity, and choice in translating poetry is the consideration of modesty or humility. Translation is a humbling experience, and as George Steiner has warned, "without modesty, translation will traduce; where modesty is constant, it can, sometimes against its own intent of deference, transfigure" (1975:216). In the worlds *traduce* and *transfigure*, Steiner refers respectively to the unrestrained freedom by which the translator betrays the original work and to the possibility that the modest translator can achieve a miraculous conveyance of a poem from one language to another. Nims alludes to modesty when he advises, "Of course one takes liberties in the interests of any poetic effect, but one should know what liberties he is taking, and with what—and above all should approach a great original with that respect and care that is a kind of humility" (1971:xxxiii). Walter Arndt echoes this statement:

"The translator is . . . a gray eminence deciding what will reach the oliglot public, and in what form; . . . he must be a poet, if not a great one, and one who will put what light he has under a bushel" (1972:xxxii).

Modesty implicates admiration. Paul Selver quotes Max Nordau in regard to this point: "The translator must have character no less than talent. He must possess the noble virtue of ability to admire. He must cultivate modesty, and while clearly aware of his own capacities, be ready to subordinate himself to the workings of an alien spirit" (1966:117). Even in the eighteenth century this translation attribute was deemed necessary. Alexander Fraser Tytler made it a precept in the eighteenth century when he said that the translator "must adopt the very soul of his author, which must speak through his own organs" (1792:114). Nims believes admiration for the poet is one foundation on which a translation must be built: "One should translate only poems he cares very much for; poems he has been living with, more often than not, for many years" (1971:xvii). Steiner goes so far as to say, "An act of translation is an act of love. Where it fails, through immodest or blurred perception, it traduces. Where it succeeds, it incarnates" (1975:271). This conviction is shared by the Russian poet-translator A. Gitovich, who has asserted, "The translator is a man in love. . . . He gives his all unselfishly and without hope of reward to the poet he loves and respects even more than himself" (1970:367).

Translators often speak of admiration and affinity as factors in the decision about what a translator should translate. William Jay Smith commented on the Tate address, "I think that a good translator must always choose only those poets for whom he feels a special affinity" (Tate 1972:25). Chukovsky has said, "Here is the source, it seems to me, of an inviolable law for masters of translation: undertake to translate not just any foreign author you happen to read or who is foisted on you by some editor in a hurry, but only the one you love passionately" (1984:186; also Marshak 1959). Soviet translators often link affinity with both choice of subject and regard for the original text. Levon Mkrtchian has said that "translation begins with selection. And we may judge a writer from what he has chosen to translate." He adds, "The translator cannot be indifferent to the text he translates. It is no accident that writers translate well what is creatively akin to them." Mkrtchian echoes Steiner's assertion that modesty, admiration, love, and affinity are guarantees of fidelity, and he extends these qualities to the process of translation itself: "It is impossible to translate unless one feels creative satisfaction" (1970:23, 25).

Poets make a strong case in arguing that the treasure within a poem lies only in the original poem. A poem is indeed something extraordinarily priceless that cannot be duplicated. But to insist that a translation must repeat an unrepeatable utterance is to make an impossible demand on the art of translation. Translation is not an art of perfection. It is an art of fidelity—choice and decision, sacrifice, transformation, indirection. Poet-translators express unanimity about this point regardless of whether they disagree about terms, as in American letters, or have achieved consistent terminology, as in the Soviet school. Even more remarkably, in their discussions of problems in the translation of poetry, poet-translators clearly follow the gradations of the autonomy spectrum marked out by present-day theorists.

It is clear that poet-translators have tacitly banished both extremes of the spectrum from translation proper, and thereby from translation as art. Libertarian imitation is not translation, and neither is a crib translation. The imitation is banned because it is at worst reinterpretation in which the translators "I" dominates, at its best creation in its own right. Literal translation is banned because it results in a lifeless mechanical copy. Poet-translators accept into translation proper the free, the faithful, and the artistic translation. They grudgingly accept conventional, precise translation. An artistic translation is a successful translation—at once a true translation and an authentic poem in its own right. Conventional translation is a translation achieved with good intentions by individuals without the poetic gift. Artistic translation is indirect and approximate—regardless of whether it recreates the original form and the idea behind and within the words, or whether it substitutes, transforms, reconstitutes the original form in order to achieve what Nims calls "poetic equivalence." Conventional translation is direct and exact, a moribund reproduction of the form and idea of the original that loses the poetry along the way. Poet-translators admire a poetic or artistic translation because it is achieved through the poetic art—it requires creativity, choice, decisions, tactics, intuition. An artistic translation is a consequence of modesty, love, admiration, affinity. These qualities cannot achieve or repeat the original utterance, but they can lead to an approximation that honors the original because it is faithful to the original.

13

THE POET-TRANSLATOR

██████████ Translation is not a perfect art. Form and style in one language are not perfectly equal to form and style in another language. Avril Pyman, a translator of Russian literature and scholar of Alexander Blok, has provided a striking example of this condition by juxtaposing three English translations of one line in Blok's poem "Scythians" (1963:419). It does not require a knowledge of Russian to see how similar Robin Kemball's translation is to the original:

Milliony—vas. Nas—t'my i t'my, i t'my.
Mere millions—you. We teem and teem and teem.

This translation could not seem more direct, precise, accurate. The syntactic structure of the two sentences is almost identical, the meaning is equivalent, the metric pattern is the same, even the verb "teem" is morphologically and phonetically close to the Russian noun *t'my*. But this is not a direct, precise translation. The word "mere," which is not present in Blok's line, is semantically implied by the context; Kemball was right to add it, and his choice is alliteratively fine. Where other translators have simply "You're millions" or "You are millions," Kemball notes that the Russian word order means "you are mere millions (whereas we teem and teem and teem)." All other translators passed over the closeness of the English "teem" and the Russian *t'my* and chose "hosts," "hordes," "multitudes," and even a prolix concoction, "But we sweep an endless flood." In sum, even though Kemball seems to have mechanically copied the line, the version is in fact inventive, imaginative, intuitive—the result not of directness but of talent combined with careful thought. Like all good verse lines, it is so simply rendered that it makes other translators wonder why they failed to think of it.

The poet's gift, poetic freedom, fidelity, choice and decision, and modesty do not represent all aspects of the translation of poetry, but they raise the central questions of the art. Through the translations of Walt Whitman by Konstantin Balmont and Kornei Chukovsky, Russian literature offers an unusually clear model of the difference between the poet who cannot subordinate himself to the rights of the original poet and the poet-translator who respects the integrity of the original poet. As will be seen in this model, Balmont placed his own poetic freedom above his subject's and as a result debauched rather than honored Whitman's work. Chukovsky, in contrast, acquired the knowledge needed to understand his subject's poetry and devoted an entire lifetime to recreating Whitman's *oeuvre*. His motive was to assure that his compatriots would experience the "equivalent" poetic effect in their language that the original poet's readers experienced.

When the advice that a poet-translator should choose only a poet with whom he or she shares an affinity is considered, it would be difficult to find a poet more unlike Whitman than the Symbolist poet Konstantin Balmont. Where Whitman is robust and earthy, a celebrator, Balmont is esoteric and dainty, an aesthete. In opposition to the descriptions boisterous, forthright, and lusty that so often characterize Whitman's poetry, the terms frequently used to describe Balmont's poetic manner are esoteric, exotic, erotic. Where Whitman is simple and direct, Balmont is involved and affected. Where the expansive Whitman's measures are the millions to infinity, Balmont's poetry is personal, his world is internalized, and even his universal other-world abstractions lead regularly back to his lyric "I." Mass appeal eluded Balmont; his intimate verse is in no way similar to Whitman's exuberant singing of the masses in himself. Where Whitman sang of his country, immersing himself in his nation, Balmont spent much of his life abroad and versified faraway places such as Japan, India, Persia, the Crimea and the Caucasus, the France of Verlaine and Baudelaire. Balmont's poetry is not devoid of a celebration of life and joyous praise of nature, but his verses represent what Soviet critics dislike in Symbolism for the lack of relationship to reality and in Decadence for the preoccupation with death and despair. Balmont's version of *Leaves of Grass*, mistranslated as *Shoots of Grass*, appeared first in 1903 and later as a revised edition in 1911; a small selection of his translations appeared in 1922 as *Revolutionary Poetry of Europe and America: Walt Whitman*. The Walt Whitman presented to Russians in these versions is not the Walt Whitman known to readers of American poetry (See Orlov 1969; Patterson 1975).

Chukovsky's translation of *Leaves of Grass* is as close to Whitman as is likely. Kornei Chukovsky shared Whitman's liberalism—he was a spokesman for Russian liberalism before and after 1917—and he was a natural democrat. He acquired the name "the Russian Whitman" early in his career, and he began the introductions to the many editions of his translations stating, "Walt Whitman was the idol of my youth." His first efforts to translate Whitman appeared in 1907 while he was a student at Petersburg Imperial University; the fourth edition of his translations, entitled *The Poetry of Dawning Democracy*, was published in 1923 together with a major study entitled *Walt Whitman and His "Leaves of Grass"*; his revised and polished translations reached a tenth edition in 1944. Chukovsky was a tireless champion of Whitman in Russia in his many capacities as translator, critic, editor, and scholar. He trained Whitman translators and took part in the standard Soviet scholarly editions of Whitman in 1953 and 1955. In 1966, his selections of his favorite translations appeared as a personal memoir-study under the title *My Whitman*, which has been reprinted several times since.

The competition between Chukovsky and Balmont to become Whitman's chief Russian translator is clear. Chukovsky began a campaign against Balmont as a translator of Whitman (and Shelley) in 1903, and he continued until his death almost three decades after Balmont's. He included criticisms of Balmont's translations in his editions of Whitman and in *A High Art*. At first the campaign was considered a joke. Balmont was a supreme authority in Russian poetry then and Whitman an amazing discovery to Russian poets. Chukovsky was a ragged, hungry student, a David who set out to slay one Goliath and save another. By the 1930s Chukovsky had convinced Russian readers of Whitman, and the question of Balmont as a translator of Whitman had become historical.

To Chukovsky, it was deplorable that Whitman became known to Russians in an acutely Symbolist reinterpretation. Balmont's own poetry is marked by extremes of musicality and alliteration. Even to those who have no Russian, his sound effects are obvious: *Vécher. Vzmór'e. Vzdókhi vétra. / Velichávyi vózglas vóln.* Linkages between sound and semantics, phonetic patterns, obtrusive orchestration—these are the features of many volumes of Balmont's verse. Balmont was too prolific as a poet: during his lifetime he published twenty-five collections. No language daunted this poet, no poet was off-limits to him. In 1906, Chukovsky decimated Balmont's translations as false, misleading, and in many instances wrong in an article in the Symbolist journal *Scales*. When the translator Elena Tsvetkovskaya, Balmont's common-law wife, defended Balmont, Chukovsky impudently, even cruelly, decimated both of them. Even at age twenty-four, Chukovsky was a deadly polemicist. He asserted that Balmont understood neither the English language nor the poetry of Whitman and that the poet had turned Whitman into a Russian Symbolist (1906a:43–45; 1906b:52–60). Chukovsky began his campaign against Balmont in 1903 in reviews of *Shoots of Grass*; in 1906 he published critiques of long essays on Whitman written by Balmont in 1904. He resumed the campaign in 1911 and expanded his materials, working them into the 1923 edition of his translation of *Leaves of Grass*. In this edition, Chukovsky documents Balmont's plagiarism of standard English-language assessments of Whitman by such well-known

Whitmanists as Symonds, Burroughs, O'Connor, Bucke, and Traubel (see Leighton 1982).

Chukovsky was correct in stating that Balmont did not know English well and consistently misconstrued words, images, and whole lines. However, the most important point in his assessment of Balmont as a translator was that Balmont could not overcome his poetic "I" and turned all poets into himself. Speaking of Balmont's Shelley in *A High Art*, Chukovsky charged that Balmont disfigured Shelley's poetry and in so doing "marked Shelley's beautiful face" with features of his own personality. "The result is a new face, half Shelley, half Balmont—a face I would call Shellmont" (1984:22–23). Balmont appears incapable of mirroring an original poet in his translations, and the terms Balmontism and Balmontization, invented by Chukovsky, have become standard pejoratives in the Soviet school for capricious treatment of an original poet. Nikolay Zabolotsky has cited Balmont as the chief example of a translator who changes all styles into his own style: "The translator who turns all poets into a single personality is a poor translator. A translator like this is interested not in the poets he translates but in himself. The example of this is Balmont" (1959:252).

Chukovsky did not object to free translation. Rather, he objected to the belief that "only a poet can understand another poet," and he found in Balmont's versions of Whitman everything he disliked about poets who mistake their own poetic sensibilities for poetic sensitivity. To Chukovsky, poets who can overcome their own aesthetic preferences and enter another poet's world are the finest possible poet-translators, but he was not dogmatic about this. He has praised his fellow pioneers Mikhail Lozinsky and Valery Bryusov, who could be deliberately literal in their work, and Samuil Marshak and Boris Pasternak, who were freely creative poet-translators. In Chukovsky's view, "an artistic translation is always in all cases a creative act. . . . Precisely because translation is a matter of art, sweeping rules do not exist. . . . Everything depends on individual circumstances. In the final analysis the fate of a translation is decided by the translator's *talent*, by his intellectual *milieu*, by his *taste*, by his *tact*" (1984:141). To Chukovsky, Balmont's errors and departures were important not in themselves but as symptoms of a worse disease: not only did Balmont disfigure Whitman's ideas, imagery, vocabulary, and syntax, but he also failed to discover Whitman's personality.

As for Chukovsky's own translations of Whitman, they are best represented by his last contribution, *Moi Uitmen* (My Whitman). This translation-study contains Chukovsky's favorite translations as well as essays on Whitman's life, his creative methods, his national-cultural milieu, and his influence on Russian literature. It is a thorough exegesis, including even a brief history of the writing and publication of *Leaves of Grass* and its reception in Russia. As its title indicates, *Moi Uitmen* is a deliberately subjective presentation of Whitman and of Chukovsky's attempt "to resurrect (for myself and a new generation) the Walt Whitman of my youth; that is, to recall . . . only such verses as influenced me most powerfully in that munificent period of my life in which my human intellect was most receptive to poetry" (1966:6).

Much can be learned about choice and decision from Chukovsky. *Moi Uitmen* shows clearly what Chukovsky's affinity with Whitman was—what he especially liked, what he preferred over other possible selections, what he considered his best translations of Whitman. As Chukovsky states, the forty-seven verses selected for this work "are not ordered by generic indicators and are not in chronological succession, but in the same order in which I originally undertook them" (1966:6). Chukovsky's choice is indicated further by his decision to present the longer verses not in their entirety but in accordance with his own judgment of his best versions of parts.

Given Chukovsky's predilection for Whitman's love of freedom and his individuality, it is not surprising to find among the selections "For You, O Democracy!" "Respondez!" excerpts from "Song of the Open Road" and "Children of Adam," and a good portion of "Song of Myself." Believing that "democracy for Whitman is identical to the ocean and the starry sky" (1966:14), Chukovsky appreciated the "Sea-Drift" poems, including "On the Beach at Night" and "The World Below the Brine." He admired Whitman the internationalist and offered as samples of this quality of the later Whitman "To a Foil'd European Revolutionaire," "Europe," and "Spain, 1873–74." Chukovsky liked Whitman's portrayal of the lives and traditions of Native Americans, a penchant revealed by his inclusion of "Squaw," "Osceola," and such parts of "Song of Myself" as the stanzas beginning "Alone far in the wilds and mountains I hunt." Chukovsky grew up in poverty and never forgot his origins. He was a militant liberal and seeker of justice. It is natural, therefore, that he was drawn to Whitman's praises of outcasts, including "You Felons on Trial in Courts" and "To a Common Prostitute." Curiously, *Drum Taps*, the Civil War poems, are absent, with the exception of "O Tan-Faced Prairie Boy." "Memories of President Lincoln" is represented by "When Lilacs Last in the Dooryard Bloom'd" and by "O Captain! My Captain!"—the latter is included because of its popularity. Chukovsky was able to appreciate without exaggerating the most sensual qualities of Whitman's poetry. His selections from "Children of Adam" include "As Adam early in the Morning," "From Pent-Up Aching Rivers," and the fifth stanza of "I Sing the Body Electric." He does not include violent passages of the latter poem and "A Woman Waits for Me." At the same time, the selected excerpts from "Song of Myself," among the most sensual lines of the poem, are so well done that Chukovsky must surely have had an affinity for them.

Chukovsky was one of the pioneers who taught the Soviet school that the translator must know everything. This includes the necessity of analyzing the original author's literary manner in order to find the key that conveys the style into Russian. The poet-translator must develop a strategy, a system of tactics. Regarding the central quality of Whitman's poetry, Chukovsky stated, "His entire power as a writer is to be found in an unusually alive, steadfast feeling . . . for the boundless immensity of the universe." Chukovsky was convinced that no other poet ever felt the infinity of time and space so powerfully as Whitman, and he perceived that "the million is the common denominator of his measure." He knew that Whitman's kosmos is a reflection of his interest in the German Romantic-Idealists— Hegel, Schelling, Kant—and he emphasized the influence on Whitman of the Transcendentalists, particularly Carlyle and Emerson. He stressed the impact of Whitman's interest in the growth of science on his attitude toward Transcendentalism (1966:10–13).

Chukovsky was especially sensitive to the aesthetic implications of Whitman's vision of democracy. Although Chukovsky believed that he had erred in his early translations by treating Whitman almost exclusively as "the singer of future democracy," he continued to emphasize Whitman's demos. He praised the flamboyance and egoism of Whitman's vision and admired its grandeur. He defined for Russian readers the English word *identity* and offered his own articulation of Whitman's concept of the individual: "Whitman does not see, does not feel separate human souls . . . there is not a single—literally not a single—human personality in his poetry." This concept separates Whitman from Russian writers. If even the most sharply drawn Russian literary characters were to appear in his poetry, "it would be impossible to distinguish one from another. . . . There would occur that *depersonalization of personality* which Whitman is unable to hide by broadcasting about a 'personalism' peculiar to American demos." Whitman's celebration of self is of the universal, not the individual man, and "he asserts the spiritual value of human personality as Man with a capital letter" (1966:20, 26, 31). Chukovsky insisted that Whitman's democracy was based on a mystical brotherhood and an equally mystical merging of individual souls into universal humanity—a view he preferred in opposition to Gorky's interpretation of Whitman as a revolutionary.

Chukovsky understood the American tradition of dissent and protest remarkably well (his democratic understanding of the American attitude toward authority distinguishes him from the man he defended at the end of his life, Alexander Solzhenitsyn, and from many other Soviet dissidents). In his understanding Chukovsky distinguishes himself from standard Soviet critics, who fail to perceive Whitman's profoundly American Weltanschauung and do not appreciate the difference between the collective and the individual in Whitman's democracy (see Mendelson 1965). Chukovsky was aware of the contradictions in Whitman's view regarding this matter, but he finds the meaning of Whitman's poetry in Whitman's contradictory yet intuitive attempt to synthesize the concepts of idealism and materialism. Chukovsky quotes D. S. Mirsky's advice to Soviet critics not to impose Russian attitudes toward dissent on American perceptions and not to underestimate "the anti-revolutionary and mystical moments" in such verses as "Song of Myself" (1966:14).

Chukovsky believed that a good poet-translator must be the original author's most severe critic as well as a persevering analyst of style. About his own translations of Whitman he remarked in *A High Art* that "it is very easy to write better, more elegantly, than Whitman, but it is extremely difficult to write just as 'badly' as he," and he reported that it took a lifelong effort to approximate the "vulgarity" of Whitman's poetry (1984:42). With such statements Chukovsky signified his awareness of both the earthy crudeness of Whitman's lexicon and the subtlety of his seemingly uncontrolled lines with their "disorderly enumeration of variegated facts and events." That is, he realized "how painstakingly Whitman worked on the finish of his lines" and emphasizes the line as the most crucial element of Whitman's poetry. The delicate nuances of Whitman's syntax must not be missed; the translator must be aware of the importance of rhythmic and syntactic strands, and he must appreciate their importance to "the careful expression of each thought, each emotion" in the line. Two of the most important determinants of the sustained ebullience of Whitman's poetry are synonymical and antonymical parallelism (1966:39, 41, 42–44).

Chukovsky's tactics of choice and decision are readily apparent in his translations of Whitman. Lexicon and syntax are easily seen in the Russian text:

Uolt Uitmen, Kosmos, syn Mankhettena,
Buinyi, dorodnyi, chuvstvennyi, piushchii, ediashchii, rozhdaiushchii,
Ne slishkom chuvstvitelen, ne stavliu sebia vyshe drugikh
        ili v storone ot drugikh.
I besstydnyi i stydnyi i stydlivy ravno.

Walt Whitman, a kosmos, of Manhattan the son,
Turbulent, fleshy, sensual, eating, drinking and breeding,
No sentimentalist, no stander above men and women
        or apart from them,
No more modest than immodest.

As can be seen, the Russian syntax is almost identical to the original English: line-lengths are similar, the rhythm or blend of meters resembles the English, the listing in the second line of qualities that elaborate the subject (self) or introduce a contrast is preserved, and the intonations (celebration of self) are sustained. The word equivalents, which are earthy and boastful, are precise: "Turbulent, fleshy, sensual, eating and drinking, breeding." Even though the first line yields naturally to fidelity because of the cognates and the felicitous phonetic-morphological similarity between the Russian *syn* and the English "son," Chukovsky has made a choice in regard to the epithet "of Manhattan the son" by translating it as "son of Manhattan." He could very easily have retained the original syntax here, for Russian often achieves an effect identical to English by reversing the order of subject and possessive (*Mankhettena syn*). The last line here is also a significant departure: "No more modest than immodest" is expanded to "Immodest and modest and diffident at once." Chukovsky may have bowed here to a Russian sense of what is poetically correct; his version is more elaborate, but it plays in a manner like Whitman's on semantically and morphologically similar words (*besstydnyi, stydnyi, stydlivyi*).

Regarding the shape of the Russian words, Chukovsky's departure is faithful to the original in both rhythm and alliteration. "No sentimentalist" has been changed to "not too sentimental" (*"chuvstvitelen"*) because the Russian reader would have understood the cognate *ne sentimentalist* to connote the literary trend. In almost every respect, Chukovsky's sense of proportion and his instinct for what to give up and what to preserve enable his Russian lines to make the same impression on the Russian reader as the original lines make on the English reader. One sign of this is that the long string of adjectives and participles in the second line would seem to a Russian, in context with Russian taste, as florid and exotic as if the line were written by Balmont. But a Russian reader of the translation would apprehend the line in an American, not a Russian, context; Chukovsky, having anticipated this mode of perception, has conveyed the full impact of Whitman's "vulgar" boastfulness.

As important as the line, Chukovsky believed, are the musicality and tonality of Whitman's compositional techniques. These qualities are important in Whitman's work because they serve as substitutes for the metrical principles of traditional poetry. In "When Lilacs Last in the Dooryard Bloom'd," which Chukovsky termed "a requiem played on a grandiose organ," tonality and musicality are clearly evident. Chukovsky perceived the alliterative and anaphoric stanzas as "awkward strokes rhythmically depicting sobs" (1966:42) and fully honored these qualities in his translation:

O powerful western fallen star
O shades of night—O moody, tearful night!

O moguchaia upala zvezda!
O teni nochnye! O slioznaia, gorkaia noch'!

Here Chukovsky chooses alliteration and rhythm over syntax and meaning. He drops the modifier "western," for example, and permits himself the word *gorkaia* 'bitter,' in place of "moody" because its deep back vowels and its morphological awkwardness facilitate the tonality and musicality of the lines. Chukovsky's first line—conveyed as "O, a powerful star has fallen"—is not semantically precise, but as poetic epithet and phraseology it is a faithful recreation of the power of the original. Intonation, as indicated by Chukovsky's fidelity to the exclamations and exclamatory "O," are finely rendered, and rhythm reflects the poem's "awkward strokes rhythmically depicting sobs." The conventional reversal of noun and adjective in the epithet "O *teni nochnye*!" is a good representation of "O shades of night."

Chukovsky's standing as a poet-translator is nowhere more evident than when his respect for Whitman's rights, together with his affirmation of his own individuality, is compared to Balmont's violations of original texts. As Etkind has noted, despite Balmont's reputation for free-wheeling, capricious translations, the sensationalist Decadent proved to be a timid, conservative translator of Whitman, while Chukovsky dared to be a radical innovator. What Russians, primarily Futurists, admired about Whitman was his bold casting of lines by syntax rather than traditional metric and strophic constructions. Russian is more receptive to meter and rhyme schemes than English—even today most Russian poetry is written in iambic-tetrameter quatrains. This contrasts sharply with contemporary American and British poetry where meter and rhyme are eschewed in favor of intonation and syntax, where the emphasis is on the poet's own voice rather than the ability to exploit rules of prosody. Certainly Whitman's poetry was a far more radical innovation in Russian poetry than it had been in American poetry.

Chukovsky conveys Whitman's poetry in accord with Whitman's creative persona. Balmont chooses to transform Whitman into a poet of meter and rhyme and conventional strophic articulations. As Etkind has noted, when Balmont undertook to translate Whitman, he was anxious not to "vex Russian readers with long lines of amorphous prose." Balmont apparently concluded that Russian readers of the time would not accept Whitman's poetry as poetry, and so he saw his task as "the introduction of order into Whitman's household—to regularize his rhythms, prune his images, modify his vulgarities, lower his shouts to the level of normal human speech, abbreviate and soften his hyperbole." In direct contrast to this diffidence, "when [Chukovsky] translated Whitman, he strove to reproduce his prosaic qualities and his kosmism, his vulgarity and his chaos, his grandiose exaggerations and his allegorical generalizations." Chukovsky's Whitman shocked Russian readers at first, but in Etkind's opinion, "surprise is a useful reaction to art." Etkind shows that Whitman has now been accepted as a classic of world poetry because Chukovsky did not hesitate to be as innovative as his subject (1963:421–22).

Balmont's method for translating Whitman is clear: his Whitman became a Whitmont. He imposed his "I" on Whitman deliberately. As Etkind has stated, Balmont was uncomfortable with Whitman's radical use of syntactic structures to shape his lines, and because Balmont was in this respect timid, he used unsatisfactory measures. The result is that his translations are neither Whitman nor Balmont, his poetry neither American nor Russian. While Balmont realized that syntax is the basic organizing element, he seems to have felt that syntax alone could not sustain the force of *Leaves of Grass* in Russian. He replaces syntactic devices with simple alternations of long and short lines; or he uses long lines for a few unusual effects in Russian poetry; or he converts long lines into evenly measured lines of normal length. Whitman's rhythms are thereby absent from Balmont's versions, and this strategic error is compounded by Balmont's resort to strictly measured iambs. Because Balmont commits himself in this way to line and meter as his own organizing devices, his lines are alien to the very essence of Whitman. Even worse, he completely misses such syntactic-rhythmic elements as parallelism—the element Chukovsky realized to be so crucial. Balmont's only wise concession to Whitman is that he avoids rhyme. Blank verse was well established in Russian poetry by the early twentieth century, most notably on the authority of Pushkin's *Little Tragedies*, but it had not been used in such a large body of verse. Nevertheless, Balmont seems to have been so awed by this innovation that he also overlooks Whitman's alliteration—a most unusual achievement for a poet notorious for his own sound effects.

Take as an example these lines from *Leaves of Grass*:

On the beach at night alone,
As the old mother sways her to and fro singing her husky song,
As I watch the bright stars shining, I think a thought of the
    clef of the universes and of the future.

Much of the effect of these lines is that Whitman begins with a poetic line, almost a traditionally poetic line, and immediately shifts to prose. The second and third lines are roughly iambic and the phraseology "clef of the universes and of the future" is poetic, a feature underscored through the division of the third line so as to foreground the metaphors. But otherwise these markedly poetic lines serve as a counterpoint to the rough prosaic lines for which Whitman is so well known. Balmont's version of these lines in his 1922 edition of *Revolutionary Poetry* is decidedly unlike the original:

Noch'iu odin na priberezh'i,
Mezh tem kak staraia mat',
Raspevaia khripluiu pesniu,—
Baiukaet chado svoe,
Ia smotriu na blestiashchie iasnye zvezdy.

I dumaiu dumu,—gde kliuch
vselennyx i budushchego.

Whitman's lines have been transformed into careful four-foot measures. The lines, roughly trochaic, are unrhymed, but together with their even lengths they are intentionally poetic where Whitman was prosaic, and their phraseology is standard for Russian verse. Semantically, they are true to the original. The first line is especially faithful to Whitman; "I think a thought" is conveyed with the Russian pleonasm "*I dumaiu dumu.*" "Singing her husky song," "clef of the universes and of the future," "the bright stars shining"—Whitman's phrases are present in Russian. But the form of the translation—lines of standard length, standard quatrain—has almost nothing else in common with the original.

In those instances where Balmont has attempted to reproduce long lines as they are in the original, he is only slightly more successful. Compare Whitman's opening lines for "The Dalliance of the Eagles" with Balmont's translation:

Skirting the river road, (my forenoon walk, my rest)
Skyward in air a sudden muffled sound, the dalliance of the
        eagles

Idia vdol' reki po doroge (eto utrom moi otdyx, progulka),
Ia v vozdukhe, tam, blizhe k nebu, zaglushennyi uslyshal zvuk

Where Whitman introduces "eagles," the poem's key image, at the end of the second line and emphasizes it by breaking the second line, Balmont does not introduce it until the start of the third line. Where Whitman alludes to himself and his witness of the dalliance only briefly and in parentheses at the end of the first line (thereby not intruding on the mating of the eagles), Balmont has personalized the presence by using the pronoun "I" ("*Ia*") at the start of the second line. The dalliance of the eagles is natural, violent, and beautiful in Whitman's poem: "Four beating wings, two beaks, a swirling mass tight grappling. . . . " Balmont's version recreates this striking imagery quite well: *chetyre moguchikh kryla, dva kliuva, stseplenie massy* 'Four powerful wings, two beaks, a coupling of the mass.' Balmont has added a few explicit images of his own. "Amorous contact" has been replaced by the stronger epithet "amorous struggle." Balmont also changes the imagery of the ending. Where Whitman's eagles separate into "diverse flight, / She hers, he his, pursuing," Balmont's male eagle does not pursue. Despite a few departures, the translation is generally faithful and the imagery well done. However, Balmont's long lines do not have the same impact as Whitman's, and not even their striking imagery overcomes a certain lifelessness. Perhaps he was correct to shy away from Whitman's long lines, but when we consider Chukovskys recreations, it is evident that Balmont could not accomplish this conveyance.

Balmont seems incapable of allowing Whitman to speak for himself. In "As Adam Early in the Morning," Whitman states clearly in the last two of his five lines: "Touch me, touch the palm of your hand to my body as I pass, / Be not afraid of my body." Balmont seems to believe that this motif must be spelled out for the Russian reader, because he breaks the simple statement of Whitman's last line into two lines and adds an exclamation point: "Do not fear, not terrifying / is my body!" (". . . *ne strashno / Moe telo*!") Where Whitman is unabashed, Balmont introduces sensationalism. For the most part, however, Balmont does not add to or strengthen *Leaves of Grass*. Rather, he proves timid; he avoids Whitman's most shocking images, and his vaguely iambic lines are limpid. His reproductions of long lines are awkward and without intonations in many instances, perhaps because they simply reproduce the meaning of the original as closely as possible without concern for change of pace, tone, audibility, rhythm. The only recommendation concerning his version of the first two lines of "As Adam Early in the Morning" is that Balmont manages to reproduce correctly what Whitman says in the original—"As Adam early in the morning, / Walking forth from the bower refresh'd with sleep" becomes "Like Adam early in the morning, / I emerge from my nocturnal bower refreshed by my sleep." The life in Whitman's lines is not conveyed, and neither are the rhythms, the levels, or the paces of his voice. Where Whitman is "poetically prosaic," Balmont is dull, awkward, and plain.

The notion of indirectness in translation of poetry, discussed in the preceding chapter, is relevant to a comparison of Chukovsky's Whitman with Balmont's Whitman. Balmont as a translator of poetry presents a clear example of a poet who foists his "I" on another poet and does not permit principles of translation to interfere with his freedom to create. This is the view of Balmont that Chukovsky established in Russia letters. By and large Chukovsky's assessment is valid. But Etkind has shown in addition that Balmont was a timid translator of Whitman. This may be taken even further by stating that Balmont ultimately proved to be not only a tradition-bound translator but also a literalist. Chukovsky ought to stand out as the less imaginative translator, because his recreations of Whitman's lines are amazingly similar, and even identical, in most respects to their originals. As John Nims has commented, "Translations must have their own form and rhythm; but must they have the same form and rhythm as the original?" (1971:xxv). The answer to this question is often no. The transfer of a poem from one language to another and one poetic tradition to another often necessitates change of form.

Chukovsky's translations of Whitman are close and seem even to be direct; Balmont's translations involve changes and therefore might seem to be imaginative. But is it true that Balmont offers the better translations of Whitman's poetry? "The relationship between an original and its translations," Jiří Levý has said, "is the relationship between a work and its *execution in another material*, it being understood that the constant here is the realization in another material not of the unity of the original's form and content, but of the *concretization* of this unity *in the consciousness of the apprehender*, that is, more simply stated, of the sum total impression, the effect on the reader." In Levý's view, it is not possible to reproduce the form of an original mechanically; rather, "one can only reproduce its semantic and aesthetic value for the reader." Levý adds, "It is not possible to preserve in a translation all the original's elements containing its historical and national specifics, but it is certain that one ought to evoke in the reader the impression, the illusion of its historical and national milieu" (1974:129). Translation must not be a direct, literal, mechanical art. It must be imaginative, dynamic, and indirect—in Levý's terms, illusory.

This is where the difference between Chukovsky and Balmont can finally be clarified. One is a poet-translator and one a poet who translates. Despite his notoriously free treatment of foreign poets, Balmont, not Chukovsky, proves to be the literal and direct translator of Whitman. Where he should be imaginative, innovative, inventive, he falls back on conventional Russian forms and, simultaneously, resorts to halfway measures. Balmont must have detected at least some of the essential elements of Whitman's poetry that Chukovsky detected—he was, after all, a poet deeply immersed in world poetic tradition. Surely he did not lack the ingenuity to seek appropriate equivalents. But Balmont nonetheless approached the task of translation head on, mechanically, with no sense for the illusory, the imaginative, the intuitive. There is an even greater irony. For all his reading of, and in fact plagiarism of, existing criticism of Whitman, Balmont seems to have missed or misread *Leaves of Grass* and thereby to have produced a mechanical copy.

Chukovsky, in contrast, has recreated a faithful Whitman. That his lines are so similar to Whitman's does not mean that he translated them directly. His innovation rests on his realization that he could recreate in his language what had never been created in Russian poetry before. Although his recreations are amazingly similar, in form and meaning, to Whitman, they show not only accuracy but also inventiveness. Chukovsky's recreations are a result of indirectness, illusion, intuition, and, at the same time, of an imagination prompted and informed by knowledge, analysis, principle. Chukovsky is, in fine, a poet and a translator in balanced measure. He understood that translation is an art; he knew the difference between his own individuality and Whitman's; and he appreciated that fidelity is not precision. "A translation must be a phenomenon of Russian poetry," A. Gitovich has asserted, and "what is important is that a translation must, as Zabolotsky used to say, be a living organism of Russian poetry" (1970:379). Chukovsky's *Leaves of Grass* is a living organism of Russian poetry. With this achievement Chukovsky pioneered the very concept of the poet-translator in the Soviet school.

14

NABOKOV, ONEGIN, AND OTHERS

████████ *Literalism* is the most despised word in the Soviet school's vocabulary. Translators around the world shun literalism as both a method and a quality, and its place in the autonomy spectrum is tenuous, if not already banned. Poets of the Soviet and American worlds speak of the language of poetry as associative, linking, echoing, allusive. As Walter Arndt, translator of Goethe and Pushkin, has said, allusiveness is an even more delicate quality of poetry than simplicity: "Here a more or less esoteric allusion, or a whole sequence of intramural associations . . . is to be set quivering and tittering in the reader's mind like a mobile" (1972:xli).

Directness, literalism as an approach is rigid. The most demanded quality of literary translation is fidelity. "The whole art of translating from one language into another rests on this basis," Johann Jacob Breitinger stated long before fidelity won its majority of modern converts. He adds, "A translator is required to express the same thoughts and concepts he finds before him . . . with similar emphasis, in other, equivalent signs accepted by, used by, and known to a nation, so that the concept or thought underlying both signs makes the same impression on the reader's feelings" (see Lefevere 1977:163). American poet-translators might not yet have clearly defined the concept of fidelity, but they know intuitively what it is, as poets know intuitively what a mature poetic voice is. Present-day translators and theorists of translation tend to perceive the many approaches to translation along the autonomy spectrum as legitimate; they tend to judge each translation in terms of the choices the translator has made to achieve the result he or she deems appropriate to the task. Translators are also aware that they range through the gradations of translation types in a single translation. Indeed, pragmatism is both an explicit and an implicit quality of fidelity in the discussions and practice of faithful translation. Modern translations tend toward the median point of gradations among translation types when they take the artistic integrity of the original across the language barrier. From the median range translatiors reach in whichever direction is needed to secure literary excellence.

Vladimir Nabokov did not agree with the direction modern theory and practice were taking. As Jane Grayson has shown, Nabokov was not always a convinced literalist and did not develop his "doctrine" of literal translation until late in his career, when he became involved with the task of translating Pushkin's *Eugene Onegin* (1977:13–22). Once he concluded that only an exact, precise, literal "pony" would do justice to Pushkin's novel in verse, however, he propagated his doctrine with increasing conviction. Nabokov believed that a translation should sound like a translation, and this is how he claimed to have translated Lermontov's novel *A Hero of Our Time*. His *Onegin* is the classically precise definition of the literal translation. As Nabokov claimed, the sole aim of a translator should be "to produce with absolute exactitude the whole text, and nothing but the text." In the Commentary to *Onegin*, he wrote that "'literal translation' implies adherence not only to the direct sense of a word or sentence, but to its implied sense; it is a semantically exact interpretation, and not necessarily a lexical one (pertaining to the meaning of a word out of context) or a constructional one (conforming to the grammatical order of the words in the text)."

Nabokov's literal translation is not a perfect translation. It involves serious losses and sacrifices—even "all the elegance, euphony and good taste that the dainty mimic prizes higher than truth." Nabokov believed that what is lost in translation can be restored in a footnote, and he proved he meant this literally when he fitted his translation of *Onegin* into four volumes with two and a half volumes of commentary, a gigantic work of research and scholarship. J. Douglas Clayton, who compared poetic translation in Pushkin and Nabokov, has pointed out that Nabokov defined three types of translation (1983:92–94). *Paraphrastic translation* offers a free version of the original in accordance with the exigencies of form, conventions, and the translator's "ignorance." *Lexical translation* "renders the basic meaning of words (and their order)." *Literal translation* is defined as "rendering, as closely as the associative and syntactical capacities of another language allow, the exact contextual meaning of the original." Nabokov called most translators "paraphrasts," and he asserted repeatedly that only a literal translation is a "true translation." He claimed that it was "mathematically impossible" to reproduce the rhymes *and* the semantics of *Onegin*, and so in his translation Nabokov threw out the rhymes, and thus Pushkin's intricately contrived "Onegin stanza," and concentrated on the iambic-tetrameter lines of the original, their syntax and lexicon, to the exclusion of almost every other quality of Pushkin's great poem. Nabokov did not fear the words *crib* or *trot*, and in the introduction to his translation he states outright that "Pushkin has likened translators to horses changed at the posthouses of civilization. The greatest reward I can think of is that students may use my work as a pony" (Nabokov 1955, 1957a, 1957b, 1958, 1959, 1964b, 1964c, 1965, 1973, esp. 1964a).

In *After Babel*, George Steiner defines Nabokov's literal translation as monadist. The monadist view is contrary to his own hermeneutic perception of the process of translation. "It holds that universal deep structures are either so fathomless to logical and psychological investigation or of an order so abstract as to be well-nigh trivial. . . . The extreme 'monadist' position— we shall find great poets holding it—leads logically to the belief that real translation is impossible. What passes for translation is a convention of approximate analogies, a rough-cast similitude." Specifically rejecting Nabokov's "perfection" argument, Steiner insists, "No human product can be perfect. . . . To dismiss the validity of translation because it is not always possible and never perfect is absurd. What does need clarification . . . is the *degree* of fidelity to be pursued in each case, the tolerance allowed as between different jobs of work." Steiner refutes literalist, monadic, nominalist assertions that translation is impossible: "We *do* speak of the world and to one another. We *do* translate intra-and inter-lingually and have done so since the beginning of human history" (1975:74, 251).

When Nabokov chose literalism as his modus for translating Pushkin's *Onegin*, he knew that his care for the letter ran counter to Pushkin's lifelong attendance to the spirit of everything he translated. He must also have known that the Soviet school developed artistic translation by tracing their concern for the spirit back to Pushkin. In a criticism of Soviet literalists, Evgenya Kalashnikova stated,

> There is literalism and literalism. There have always existed hacktranslators who blindly follow the construction of the original simply because they don't know any better. But never before in the annals of Russian literature had literalism been advanced as a guiding principle. "The spirit rather than the letter"—had been what Pushkin and Belinsky demanded of the translator and in spite of all the differences on questions of detail this had always remained the generally accepted Russian conception of the task of the translator. (1966:11)

Nabokov was not a hack—he knew better than to follow blindly. And Nabokov did not have anything in common with the Soviet literalists. His diapason was too broad for him to conceive of translation as a science, and he never applied the word *scientific* to literary translation because he was too great a scientist and an artist to associate the two so vulgarly as the Soviet literalists did. He certainly did not perceive translation, or any art, in terms of mass production or even of mass appeal. But the fact remains that his literal translation was opposed to everything that Pushkin believed about translation, and to everything the Soviet school took from Pushkin.

Pushkin stated some of his beliefs about translation in an article on Chateaubriand's translation of Milton. Nabokov knew this article well and cited it in his early essay "Pouchkine, ou le vrai et le vraisemblable." In the same article he took from Chateaubriand the term "scholiast" to describe himself, a label he used in contrast with his pejorative term "paraphrast." An obvious parallel that Clayton sees in his comparison of Nabokov and Pushkin is that "the romantic poetic of translation admits . . . of two possibilities, only one of which is the Chateaubriand/Nabokov option. The other, which one might call the 'lofty' path to distinguish it from Nabokov's 'servile' one, is predicated on the genius of the poet-translator. Interestingly, and despite Nabokov's attempts to co-opt him, Pushkin is a proponent of the latter" (1983:99). Pushkin developed the concepts of the poet-translator and the faithful translation in Russian literature. Pushkin was a superb and faithful translator; his immense influence on Russian literature is one reason why the Soviet school, especially its Russian branch, moved swiftly to adopt artistic translation.

Pushkin's *Onegin* presents specific and highly difficult problems for translators. These problems have been exhaustively discussed and analyzed by translators and literary scholars, including Grayson (1977), Clayton (1983, Shaw (1964), Venclova (1965), and Levin (1981). The Anglo-American debate on *Onegin* provoked by Nabokov in 1964 ensured that the problems involved in its translation reached a wide audience of lay readers in this country and abroad. There are eight extant English translations, not counting revised versions or fragments. The novel was first translated by Lieutenant-Colonel Spalding in 1881. Coincident with the anniversary of Pushkin's death, *Onegin* was translated again in three versions by four translators: Babette Deutsch (1936, with the participation of Avrahm Yarmolinsky), Oliver Elton (1937a), and Dorothea Prall Radin and George Z. Patrick (1937b). Walter Arndt translated the novel in 1963, and his version was quickly followed by Nabokov's and Eugene Kayden's translations in 1964. In 1977, Sir Charles Johnston produced the eighth version. Revised editions have appeared of the translations by Nabokov (1975), Deutsch (Modern Library Edition, n.d.), Johnston (1979), and Arndt (1981). Fifteen stanzas of the first chapter of *Onegin* were translated by Reginald Mainwaring Hewitt (1955). An analysis of Nabokov's literalist work can be most effectively accomplished by measuring its revised 1975 version with the two translations most widely read today: the corrected version of Johnston (1979) and Arndt's second edition revised (1981).

The Onegin stanza, what Nabokov in his introduction calls the "basic brick" of Pushkin's elegant Neoclassical structure, relieved by gracefully echoing Romantic themes and motifs, is among the most adroit and tightly organized strophic forms ever devised in any poetic tradition. The unity of the work is achieved by a tense iambic tetrameter line fitted into a stanza that utilizes the three basic articulations of Russian rhyme schemes—three quatrains structured on alternating, contiguous, and enclosing masculine and feminine end rhymes followed by a final masculine couplet. The Onegin stanza is basically a sonnet form used atypically for a narrative verse work in an aBaBccDDeFFeGG rhyme scheme. This form is consistently and powerfully sustained through a total of 389 stanzas and over 5,600 lines in the work's eight completed chapters, two uncompleted chapters, and a miscellany of stanzas not worked into the novel. The work is varied by inter- and intra-strophic enjambment, by a flexible system of stress omissions that create a diversity of inter- and intra-linear rhythms, and by a rapidly shifting pace and tone. The work is further varied by swift and frequent transitions not only in theme and motif but also in narrative character through Pushkin's use of exposition, digression, dialogue, authorial insertions, description of setting, development of charater, and plot.

The great Russian critic Belinsky called *Onegin* "encyclopedic" because of its diversity of subjects, events, modes of narration, allusions, plays on words, tones, and pace. Yet for all its diversity and flexibility, the Onegin stanza sustains the tightly formed, tense, disciplined character of the work. Pushkin's Lithuanian translator, the poet Antanas Venclova, has warned that "the poet who undertakes a translation of *Onegin*, even at the cost of maximal effort, can only dream of reaching the approximate vicinity of the brilliant original." Other languages have the lexicon to contend with Pushkin's novel, but the associations and the meanings of words in their time and place are almost impossible to convey. Pushkin's lexicon is highly associative, but it also manages to be straightforward and simple: "The exactitudinal language . . . is simple and definitively clear throughout, and this obliges the translator to avoid flowery expressions, neologisms, provincialisms. An impression of maximal naturalness—this is what the translator must strive for" (1965:289, 292–94).

J. Thomas Shaw, the translator of Pushkin's letters, states that "Pushkin is a subtle poet, whose effects are not only by the stanza, but by the line." Shaw points out that even though both Russian and English versification are similar in use of syllabo-accentual verse, "the movement of the line is usually quite different . . . in word-accentuation and characteristic word length." Even though Pushkin's diction, syntax, and versification are close to English poetic usage, "the entire poem will not fit into any stanzaic form in which great poetry has been written in our traditions, and duplication of his subtle effects of the movement of the line is impossible in English" (1964:115). The text of *Onegin* is replete with Gallicisms, Slavonicisms, contemporary colloquial language, myriads of realia that require explanation even for native Russians today, allusions, parodies, puns, and an encyclopedic procession of names, literary titles, and references. Pushkin carries on a running dialogue with his reader(s) in the roles of narrator, friend of Onegin, and character in his own novel, so that the narrative mode shifts, and, as Sona Hoisington has shown, the novel has a complex "hierarachy of narratees" (Arndt 1981:lxiii–lxxv).

The style of Nabokov's translation of *Onegin* is not only literal but also, like his own style, artificial, egocentric, and peculiar to his trilingual—Russian, French, and English—consciousness. In Shaw's words,

> Nabokov has long been conducting assaults upon the English language, and they have been largely successful. Perhaps there is no writer who is more a magician with the use of English today than he. But his English is an invented language, one that could not possibly be written by a native . . . . Nabokov's own prose . . . is often pure poetry, but the poetry of his translation of *Onegin* is determinedly and defiantly—one is tempted to say gloriously—not even prose. (1964:118–19)

Arndt, in contrast, is an advocate of faithful translation—what he calls "metrical" translation. In his essay "Translating Faust," Arndt, in agreement with John Nims's defense of formal elements, suggests that "it is beginning to dawn on critics again that rhyme, in both original and translated poetry, is far from being a childish paste-on ornament, a gratuitous upping of the cost of expression, onerous, supererogatory, and, at best, slightly unfair to the plain, honest 'meaning' around it." Arndt rejects the common notion that "the rhyme tyrannizes the meaning"; in his view it is "an inseparable quality of the seamless whole which makes up the poetic artifact, it is part of the 'meaning,' and the 'meaning' is part of it." The translator of poetry must be responsive to "assonance, sonority, rhythm, rhyme, on one hand, and syntax, grammar, phonology, semasiology of the linguistic code, on the other." He or she must constantly make decisions and follow "now rhyme, now reason, now metric, now musical lures along no set course; resisting, manipulating, yielding to, and merging their subtle simultaneous pulls."

To Arndt, modern "free" translation is "Gogolesque quackery naturalized." He quotes the Russian poet Joseph Brodsky's remark that "translation is a search for an equivalent, not for a substitute. . . . Logically, a translator should begin his work with a search for at least a metrical equivalent to the original form." Those who translate freely by using substitutes predicated on their own aesthetic preferences do so because they are usually "themselves poets and their own individuality is dearest of all to them. Their conception of individuality precludes the possibility of sacrifice, which . . . is the primary feature of mature individuality, and also the primary requirement of any (even technical) translation." Arndt continues, "While imitation is an ego trip, translation is service and sacrifice, offering only the rewards of craftsmanship exercised and enthusiasm transmitted." Arndt's translation value is fidelity. Together with his rejection of free translation, he dismisses its opposite extreme, the literal translation: "Which could be more extreme (perhaps second to, perhaps next to, Nabokov's *Onegin*) than Fairley's *Faust*? What could be a more saddening act . . . than this methodical wrecking operation, performed by the ponderous steel ball of a paradoxical 'prose accuracy,' upon the whole splendidly intricate body of Goethe's metric architecture?" Arndt asserts that in all of his translation work, which now includes a significant portion of Pushkin's lyric and narrative verse, he has "striven . . . for a precise or very close reproduction. . . . This cultural and musical fidelity is far from runaway literalness a la Nabokov, which out of worship of the text and antiquarian self-indulgence maims lexicon and syntax of the target language" (1980:356–57, 358, 359, 360, 363).

Sir Charles Johnston is, like Arndt, a poet-translator. With his wife, the former Princess Natasha Bagration, he has translated Turgenev's *A Sportsman's Sketches,* and he is the author of a collection of verse works by Pushkin and Lermontov. Johnston has said little about his translation principles, but his brief "Translator's Note" for his versions of *Onegin* shows that he shares Arndt's preference for the faithful translation. In his note he states his intent "to produce a reasonably accurate rhyming version of Pushkin's work which can at least be read with pleasure and entertainment, and which, ideally, might even be able to stand on its own feet as English" (1979:30). Johnston's version differs from others in that he used Nabokov's translation as an interlinear. His indebtedness to Nabokov is evident in his lexicon, but he shuns his model's ultra-precise equivalents and especially the archaic poetic words taken from the English poetry of Pushkin's time. Where Arndt acknowledges use of his predecessors' translations, Johnston mentions only his use of Nabokov's version and commentary.

Johnston's translation is, as its publishers claim, a new translation. A comparison of Johnston's translation with Arndt's shows how seldom translations of poetry coincide even though basic standards of choice and decision are similar. Here clearly, two different poet-translators with similar standards came up with two different versions of the same work. Even though both men have reproduced the Onegin stanza with similarly sensitive detections and conveyances of alliteration, retention of inter- and intra-stanzaic enjambment, and recreation of tone and intonation in tandem with their rapid shifts and transitions, it would be difficult to find another example of two so different versions of the same work. Such a comparison demonstrates what many faithful translators mean when, as was shown in the previous chapter, they distinguish between the individuality of the original poet and the individuality of the poet-translator. That the personality of the translator will be reflected in the translation is a given; that this reflection is not only unavoidable but also desirable is an aesthetic principle; that the personality of the translator should not be foisted on the original poet is an absolute must. In Arndt's words, "while imitation is an ego trip, translation is service and sacrifice." In Johnston's view, a key translation value is "humility." He believes the translator should "produce a reasonably accurate rhyming version" that provides "pleasure and entertainment" and is poetry in English (1980:30). Perhaps modesty is the reason that even though these translations are different, they are nonetheless similar in two important ways: both are poetry in English and both are reasonably faithful to the original.

As Nabokov warned, a metrical-rhyming version will stint meaning. Although Arndt's translation is superior in some respects, Johnston in others, both men have had to manipulate and sometimes even force syntax into the tight frame of the Onegin stanza. Both translations reflect substitutions as well as sacrifices, and each translator manipulates meaning, lexicon, and syntax in order to meet the demands of the form. There are clumsy lines and rhymes in both translations. Many native speakers of English who know Russian have not been convinced by these translators that we possess a satisfactory translation of *Onegin*. But these are the best translations currently available, and it would be an exceptional translator who could do better. British and American critics are divided on the question of the relative merits of the two translations, but American critics tend to agree that Arndt's translation is generally better (see Leighton 1980:423–24; Bethea 1984:112–14).

A distinct feature of Nabokov's *Onegin* is that it is, as he asserted, exactly in English—semantically, lexically, and syntactically—what Pushkin's original is in Russian. Readers of Nabokov's translation can be confident they are reading a reliable semantic facsimile of the original. This is why his translation can be used to assess the translations of Arndt and Johnston, or conversely, why their translations can be used to demonstrate the literalist, inartistic character of his.

> My uncle has most honest principles:
> when taken ill in earnest,
> he has made one respect him
> and nothing better could invent. (Nabokov)

> Now that he is in grave condition,
> My uncle, decorous old dunce,
> Has won respectful recognition;
> And done the perfect thing for once. (Arndt)

> My uncle—high ideals inspire him;
> but when past joking he fell sick,
> he really forced one to admire him—
> and never played a shrewder trick. (Johnston)

In this well known opening quatrain, Johnston has preserved the linear order, thus coinciding with Nabokov and Pushkin. Reversing the two opening lines, Arndt has taken "My uncle, decorous old dunce"—a parody of a line from a fable by Ivan Krylov—from its crucial first-line position in the novel but has salvaged the opening stanza by creating the rhymes "condition-recognition" and "dunce-once." Johnston, in contrast, has preserved the original syntax but has sacrificed the opportunity for a better rhyme than the duplicatory "inspire him-admire him." He has also chosen not to honor Pushkin's standard device of capital letters for line beginnings—a clear indication of his response to Nabokov, who also begins lines with lowercase letters. Johnston is the more accurate translator here, whereas Arndt has been inventive and imaginative. Nabokov has cast out Pushkin's rhymes and has lost his poet's rollicking style and thus the effect of his lighteared irony toward his hero, which is established at the start with the stanza's concluding couplet: "And think behind a public sigh, / 'Deuce take you, step on it and die!'" (Arndt).

In another instance, in the chrestomatic stanza on winter (5:2), Johnston has surpassed Arndt.

> Winter! The peasant, celebrating,
> in a flat sledge inaugurates the track;
> his naggy, having sensed the snow,
> shambles at something like a trot.
> Plowing up fluffy furrows,
> a fleet kibitka flies:
> the driver sits upon his box
> in sheepskin coat, red-sashed. (Nabokov)

> Winter . . . The peasant, feeling festive,
> Breaks a new trail with sledge and horse;
> Sensing the snow, his nag is restive
> And manages a trot of sorts;
> Here passes, powdery furrows tracing,
> A spirited kibitka, racing,
> The coachman on his box a flash
> Of sheepskin coat and crimson sash. (Arndt)

> Winter! . . . The countryman, enchanted,
> breaks a new passage with his sleigh;
> his nag has smelt the snow, and planted
> a shambling hoof along the way;
> a saucy kibitka is slicing
> its furrow through the powdery icing;
> the driver sits and cuts a dash
> in sheepskin coat with scarlet sash. (Johnston)

In this instance both Arndt and Johnston have succeeded in recreating Pushkin's lines as they are in the original. But where Johnston has made the horse seem to shamble reluctantly (or barely trot) when he is actually restive, Nabokov and Arndt have caught the image: the horse wants to trot spiritedly but is unable to do so because of the deep snow. The translators have also coincided in their choice of the rhyme "way-sleigh," and they have wisely joined Nabokov in transcribing the realia "kibitka."

In his 1963 version, Arndt missed the restive horse, too, and for some reason he created more than one kibitka where the original image has a single horse, sleigh, and driver. In this version Arndt has strained for rhyme by using the American expression "hell-for-leather," and in both versions he neglects the brisk opening exclamation "Winter!" Johnston has best recreated the imagery and the lively expressiveness of the scene. The peasant is not "enchanted" in the original, but the concoction is in keeping with Pushkin's assumption that peasants can be enchanted by winter too. Johnston's translation has been praised for just this stanza. He has done especially well for those stanzas of *Onegin* that convey the passing of the seasons and the character of Russian nature. "Enchanted," "saucy kibitka," "a shambling hoof along the way," "powdery icing," "cuts a dash . . . with scarlet sash"—some of these images and phrases are not equivalent, but they are as lively and expressive as Pushkin's original. Keeping in mind that the brilliance of Pushkin's rhymes is to be found not in new inventions but in diversity of applications of conventional rhymes, Johnston's rhymes are especially good here: "enchanted-planted," "sleigh-way," "slicing-icing," "dash-sash." Nabokov also has some excellent conveyances. "Inaugurate the track" is perfect for Pushkin, and "Plowing up fluffy furrows" is not only a more accurate image than Arndt's "powdery furrows tracing" and Johnston's "slicing / its furrow through the powdery icing" but also a fine phrase. But "naggy" is pure Nabokov, and "a bold kibitka flies" is trite for Pushkin's poetic phrasing. Johnston's "saucy kibitka" is a fine translation for Pushkin even though the line does not scan.

Nabokov's type of translation is radically different from Arndt's and Johnston's type. Juxtapositions of Arndt's and Johnston's faithful versions show more about the character of Nabokov's literalism than any direct consideration could. Furthermore, analysis shows how flexible the concept of fidelity can and should be, how closely two different faithful translators can come to both the style and the meaning of an original text with very few points of similarity in actual wording and phrasing.

Nabokov was right when he said that achievement of both rhyme and meaning is impossible. The weakness of both Arndt and Johnston is that in order to construct the rhymes in their strictly disciplined scheme, they have had to stint meaning and cramp style. Johnston's concern for preserving the formal essentials of the Onegin stanza has obliged him to resort to contortions and shifts of word stress in order to make the meter fit or to make a rhyme. At the same time, many of his lines do not scan, and it is these lines that often interrupt the flow of the text.

Throughout the text Johnston seems to have been constrained by the need to find a rhyme. Among his most obtrusive inventions is the transformation of the *Russian Academy Dictionary* into something quite peculiar: "though years ago I used to look / at the Academic Diction-Book." He similarly transforms Petersburg's Summer Garden: "a mild rebuke was his worst mark, / and then a stroll in Letny Park." The problem is admittedly difficult, for these rhymes are important concluding couplets that demand masculine line endings. Arndt replaced the word "Dictionary" with "Academic Lexicon" and like Johnston translated the word "Garden" with "Park." In another instance, Johnston turned the ubiquitous Petersburg "*vasisdas*" into a "serving trap," whereas Arndt has more accurately "serving hatch." In one instance where two French words are rhymed, but the stanza demands feminine rhymes, the French words are anglicized: "to all the most adored *actrices*, / this denizen of the *coulisses*." In the very next stanza the stress on "*coulisse*" is shifted for the sake of scansion ("there, where the *coulisse* entrance went"). The surname Larin is Frenchified with the stress on the last syllable in some places and kept Russian by stressing the first syllable in others.

There are enough lines that do not scan in Johnston's translation to cite them at random throughout the text. Presumably, it is permissible to sacrifice meter occasionally for the sake of rhythm and syntax; this seems to be the reason for Johnston's many metrically disrupted but rhythmically smooth lines. But such lines often sound awkward: "stumblingly call to mind he did / two verses of the Aeneid," "far, far from Italy, his adored," "in silence all day she'd remain / ensconced beside the window-pane." Not all the disrupted lines are bad, and many are quite good. Even though initial line inversions are decidedly rare in Russian Romantic poetry, this device has resulted in some of Johnston's finest lines: "startling the ingenuous with a jest," "frightening with all despair's disguises," "tell me, our neighbors, are they thriving?" "Winter! . . . The countryman, enchanted."

Arndt's weakness in translating Pushkin is similar to Johnston's. He has had to twist and turn to meet the demands of the Onegin stanza, but his shortcomings in this are fundamentally different. His lines scan better than Johnston's, his stress on names and on French words are consistent, and he does not resort to inversions, anachruses, or hypersyllabicity. But he pays for this formal precision with sometimes awkward phrases and syntax. Consequences of such a determined effort to honor so many different requirements of meter and syntax can be found throughout Arndt's translation, but they can best be illustrated at the most strategic point of the Onegin stanza, the concluding couplets, some of which are markedly strained: "Of moms and aunts who sit up late, / And jovial husbands hard to hate?" "Accept my confession now, / And to your judgment I will bow," "Bright gowns with somber dress suits lined, / Like pictures in black frames confined."

The all-important lexicon of *Onegin* requires special attention in an assessment of these three translations. It has already been noted that Pushkin used the language of his time to create his novel in verse; this means that he used not only current spoken Russian but also Gallicisms and Slavonicisms. Nabokov drew attention to this key feature of the work and to his own determination to convey the French character of Pushkin's Russian (see, for example, "The Servile Path," 1966). Arndt and Johnston also give great weight to this aspect of lexicon, and they join Nabokov in using French words and French expressions in English. They do not agree, however, with Nabokov in the kind of English he chose to reproduce *Onegin* as a diachronic verse document. Johnston, who uses Nabokov's lexicon extensively, deliberately avoids the rare and archaic poetic words that mark Nabokov's translation and that have been severely criticized by reviewers: "lo," "anon," "hither," "thither," "precognizing," "prevene," "larmoyant," "meseems," "never-haps," "divinistre," "cornute," "juventude," "rememorating," "sapajous," and "agrestic," among others. Nabokov's translation is a taxonomical translation, and while the master's knowledge of dictionaries is what makes his own style one of the most powerful in the English language, his use of such words has made his *Onegin* something of an oddity.

Johnston, whose language perception is British, has successfully overcome a common failing of British translators through his avoidance of British expressions. One exception is the realia "master of his college," which is not appropriate as a characterization of Onegin's French Neoclassical education. Johnston's arbitrary shifts between English and French pronunciation of French words for the sake of rhyme and meter should be faulted, but his diplomat's command of French cannot be doubted. Arndt's language perception is German and English, but he has a few Americanisms: "Step on it," in the sense of "hurry up," from his version of the opening stanza, stands out as inappropriate. But the lexicon of these two translators does not disrupt the reading as often as Nabokov's lexicon does.

What *is* a literal or literalist translation? To Nabokov literalism means semantics; to most theorists literalism means formalism—style as well as form. But Nabokov's insistence on "meaning, above all meaning" is carried over into his conveyance of Pushkin's style—to the point that he creates an unnatural English language by forcing Russian grammar onto English. Arndt's and Johnston's careful reconstructions of the Onegin stanza also seem literal at times. Each has had to distort English poetic language in order to meet the terrible demands of rhyme, rhyme scheme, enjambment, and scansion. Their intent is formal fidelity, but some of their manipulations reach toward a formal literalism that does not differ greatly from Nabokov's semantic literalism. Whatever their shortcomings or merits, Arndt and Johnston have not, like Nabokov, invented their own peculiar language of translation; they have not, like Nabokov, imposed Russian syntax on English. But when they chose to recreate the structure of the Onegin stanza, they accepted the necessity to resort to linguistic maneuverings. Many of these manipulations result in artificial poetic phrasing that often resembles Nabokov's too Russian syntax. Among Arndt's less graceful conveyances are lines such as "Then of their touch how I was aching / With my own lips to be partaking!" "Constant inconstancy turns dreary; / Of friends and friendships he grew weary," "With this disease he was infected; / He never, thank the Lord, projected," and

> On their delights I shall be gloating
> At will; with a Venetian girl,
> Her tongue now silent, now apurl,
> In secret gondola be floating;

With less attention to Pushkin's perfect iambs and less fidelity to the demanding rhyme scheme, the result could have been smoother rhythms and more natural English verse diction. But Arndt's consistent formal fidelity to the Onegin stanza does not permit these liberties. Johnston takes more liberties, using inversions, and he often sacrifices scansion in favor of natural verse rhythms. But his formal fidelity to the rhyme scheme also results in awkward lines:

> "Let others learn from his example!
> But god, how deadly dull to sample
> sickroom attendance night and day
> and never stir a foot away!
> And the sly baseness, fit to throttle,
> of entertaining the half-dead:
> one smoothes the pillows down in bed,
> and glumly serves the medicine bottle,
> and sighs, and asks oneself all through:
> "When will the devil come for you?"

"Sample-example" is not a good rhyme, and it is difficult to accept the phrase "to sample sickroom attendance." The phrases "and the sly baseness" and "of entertaining the half-dead" place "the" in stress position twice in close proximity (the reader is tempted to stress them because their positioning so strongly marks them). The word "down" has been added for the sake of scansion; "all through" in the phrase "and asks oneself all through" has been added for the sake of scansion and to make the rhyme "through-you." All the failings within the first stanza can be traced to the need to meet Pushkin's demanding iambic tetrameter line and even more demanding rhyme scheme. Arndt's and Johnston's manipulations of wording match Nabokov's manipulations of the English language in order to convey literally Russian syntax: "him who has felt disturbs / the ghost of irrecoverable days," "him does the snake of memories, / him does repentance gnaw," "to the dead man from every side / came driving foes and friends," "For two days new to him / seemed the secluded fields."

Nevertheless, where Arndt's and Johnston's failures are the result of courage to try their best, and their awkward phrasings do not characterize their work as a whole, Nabokov's literal reproductions of syntax are deliberate and wholesale, to the point that he aplogizes for inadvertently poetic lines. No doubt Nabokov's translation was the easier task. Conceivably, some of Pushkin's other works could be modernized. His *Little Tragedies* and *Boris Godunor*, which are written in blank verse with longer iambic pentameter lines, offer flexibility to translators. But *Eugene Onegin* would not be *Eugene Onegin* without the strict rhyme scheme and tight iambic tetrameter lines of the Onegin stanza. The wonder is not that Arndt and Johnston undertook to preserve consistently the Onegin stanza but that they succeeded in translating all of *Eugene Onegin* so well. They translated sometimes awkwardly, sometimes brilliantly, but overall as well as this difficult to translate masterpiece can possibly be translated. As for the original *Eugene Onegin*, there it stands in all its daunting complexity, waiting like all great works to be translated again, and perhaps even better, by and for a new generation.

PROBLEMS

15

ON LITERAL TRANSLATION

Translators regularly confront problems from which there is no escape. Translators and translation theorists discuss them often, and approach them from many methodological directions. The terms for these problems have been encountered throughout this study, and their effects in practice have been explored: equivalency and equivalentation, method and gradation, function and process, concept and terminology, contemporaneity and changing taste, national preference and transfer of value. The most remarkable contribution of the new field known as translation studies is that modern theorists have offered not only new knowledge but also coherent new solutions to old problems. Ideas about translation have been converging on a worldwide basis. This unprecedented transnational development has led to, among other contributions discussed in this study, practical new descriptions of the translation process and methodologically sound gradation or spectrum theory. Among the most daunting problems are literalism, colloquial speech and realia. These problems have not been solved in this study, nor can they be, for they are so vexing that they might very well never be solved or will not be satisfactorily solved. Precisely for this reason they need special attention: the simple fact that they resist solution shows that they promise continued frustration to translators and pose dangers to attempts to deal with them. Soviet translators have had no better luck dealing with these problems than others, but they have discussed them in ways that are not generally typical of other worlds of translation. An examination of their debates therefore offers useful new knowledge to translators. When examined in context with attempts to deal with these problems in the new field of translation studies, they show at the very least how *not* to deal with them. By so doing, they also show the way to possible solutions to particular aspects of the problems.

The Soviet school's obsession with literalism, *bukvalizm*, makes it a problem of the highest priority with which to begin this section of this study.

Jiří Levý, who believed that "the problem of faithful reproduction is the basic problem of translation theory and practice," has pointed out that the struggle between two opposite extremes of translation, the adaptive Neoclassical theory and the conditional Romantic theory, "between free and precise methods of translation," extends through the entire history of discussions of literary translation "and is the moving force of progress in this area." In his view, "this problem of contradiction has not yet been overcome," even though both extremes have been so widely rejected in favor of faithful translation (1974:119). Seemingly, this "problem of contradiction" was resolved when the literalists were banished from the Soviet school. In the late 1960s and early 1970s, literalism was revived, and the ensuing campaign to subdue it "once and for all" raised a number of fundamental questions about translation. Occurring as it did at the same time Vladimir Nabokov's translation of *Eugene Onegin* touched off Western furor over literalism, the Soviet debate can be seen in context with international concern over the problem.

Jiří Levý was correct in his assessment that the question of literalism is almost always conjoined with the question of free translation. The incestuous relationship between these two sides of the problem has been seen in the modern development of spectrum theory. Its age-old vitality can be appreciated by a reminder that Virgil, Dante, St. Jerome, Martin Luther, Pope, and Dryden all contended with literalism as the polar opposite of free translation. Writing in the nineteenth century Jakob Grimm commented,

> We translate faithfully, because we allow ourselves to incorporate all the specific traits of the foreign language through osmosis and because we decide to imitate it, but we translate too faithfully, because the forms and the substances of words in two languages can never totally cover each other and one loses what the other gains. Whereas free translations, therefore, only aspire to attain the thought and give up the beauty of the dress, strict translations pedantically strain themselves to weave a copy of the dress, and fall short of the source text whose form and content naturally and spontaneously agree. (See Lefevere 1977:95)

Arthur Waley was often criticized for translating Chinese and Japanese classics too freely, and his admirers inevitably raise the question of literalism when they defend his translations. "If he [Waley] were translating scientific texts or political treatises, such a charge might be justified," Ivan Morris has pointed out. "But it decidedly does not apply to works like *The Pillow Book, The Tale of Genji* or *The Ainu Epic*, for here the main value is literary, and any pedantically 'accurate' translation will vitiate their character in a far more damaging way—by making them unreadable" (1970:74–75).

The same conjoining of literal and free translations characterizes Soviet concern with the problems of literalism. Pavel Antokolsky clarified the relationship between free and literal translation by likening translation to a troika. At the shaft bow is the horse of the translator's talent, on the left is the capricious horse of "concoction," on the right is the short-sighted horse of literalism. As Antokolsky states, "Concoctions and literalism. Literalism and concoctions. These are the two most widespread and harmful deviations in translation practice. Which is more harmful? It stands to reason that it is the one which is ahead at any given moment of the battle between them." Concoctions are easy to recognize because they are obvious lies. Literalism is more difficult to recognize, but it reveals itself when "the demand of reasonable fidelity develop into literalist niggardliness" (Antokolsky et al 1955:22–23).

Among the literalist and scientific translators of the 1930s whose work led to the Soviet school's rejection of literalism are Evgeny Lann and A. V. Krivtsova, translators of Dickens's *Oliver Twist*; V. D. Merkureva, much criticized for her translations of Shelley; G. A. Shengeli, known for his scientific version of Byron's *Don Juan*; Anna Radlova, whose equiform translations of Shakespeare were performed by Stalinist fiat on the Soviet stage though they were discredited at the Moscow Shakespeare Society by Chukovsky and others; and the Futurist and Constructivist poet I. A. Aksyonov, translator of Anatole France. A. A. Smirnov, whose definition of the adequate translation has been shown to be so important, championed Radlova's scientific translations as a truly revolutionary breakthrough in the art of translation, and Evgenya Kalashnikova, as already quoted, has noted that the scientific, formalist, and literalist methods of translation were perceived as a key to the mass production of translations. Among the pioneers, Valery Bryusov was a literalist when he began to translate *The Aeneid*, and even though M. L. Lozinsky's many translations are still widely admired in the Russian world, critics have rejected some of his literalist efforts, particularly his translations of *Tartuffe* and *Hamlet*.

The debate over literalism began in 1960 when discussions of Boris Pasternak's intentionally free translation of *Hamlet* drew attention to the previous translations of Lozinsky and Anna Radlova. The question was put to full debate in 1971 and 1972 when M. L. Gasparov wrote a strong defense of Bryusov's literal version of *The Aeneid*.

Hamlet was one of the first foreign works translated into Russian in the eighteenth century and has been translated over thirty times (Levin 1968). Russian translators began to consider the need for yet another translation in the 1960s, and to this end Yu. Garvuk, the Belorussian translator of Shakespeare, reviewed the three best known modern versions. He repeated previous criticisms of Radlova's translation, namely, that it was marred by her reliance on the scientific method. As for Pasternak's *Hamlet*, Garvuk conceded that it is the most artistic and in many places the most faithful version, but "it is not a fully Shakespearian *Hamlet*. The image of the Prince of Denmark has grown a beard of so many diverse and contradictory musings that it is not all easy to see his real 'Shakespearian' face" (1968:129–30).

Pasternak's version is more Pasternak than Shakespeare. Where Radlova's version was considered too scientific and Pasternak's too free, Lozinsky's was criticized for its formal and technical literalism. "Lozinsky's most insidious and dangerous enemy in his work was equilinearity, " Garvuk believed. His consistent line-for-line reproductions of *Hamlet* obliged him to force words without regard for natural syntax and diction. As a result, "stage practice has shown that the *Hamlet* staged in theaters in Lozinsky's translation is apprehended with difficulty by even the most well informed spectator. The sense of many words simply cannot be caught." The translation is artificial, contrived, unnatural. In addition, Garvuk stated, "for the sake of equilinearity M. Lozinsky often violates syntactic norms of Russian speech, abbreviates words, and, particularly often, casts out auxiliary words which do not bear a direct semantic burden but facilitate the correctness, naturalness, euphony, and intelligibility of phrases." In his eagerness to produce a direct, literal version of Shakespeare's play, Garvuk continued, Lozinsky reveals "a passion for archaic, little known, bookish words and tropes. These words pollute his entire translation" (1968:124–26).

Garvuk's opinion of these three translations is in accord with the general Russian assessment. He also repeated serious criticism of Radlova's use of expressions, which were deemed inappropriate on the Soviet stage. In effect, she "cast Shakespeare down from Olympus" (1968:127–28). In Chukovsky's view, however, Radlova's *Hamlet* is vulgar not because of words but because of the scientific method, a charge he extended to Lozinsky's version too. In Radlova's case, the method caused her to force syntax into the restricting confines of equilinearity and equirhythmics (1984:159–77). Her translations do not read well on the stage because they are marred by cacophony—Chukovsky cites "*kakkassio*" ("like Cassio") as one of many proofs of bad diction. Such crudities mark another shortcoming of Lozinsky's *Hamlet*, which has tortured diction-conscious actors. Both translators have provided Russians with precise, line-by-line, word-for-word literal texts of Shakespeare, but their methods obliged them to cast out so many "little" words and epithets, that the texts are not sufficiently reliable for use by students and scholars who want to familiarize themselves with the real Shakespeare.

Garvuk is right that Pasternak's version of *Hamlet* errs on the side of art. Pasternak's is a major poet's version of Shakespeare's masterpiece in which Hamlet is made more humane. His version elaborates Hamlet's musings and in many cases adds to them (recall Etkind's remark that Pasternak found in Shakespeare a vehicle for the expression of his own musings in Stalin's time). Garvuk does not mention, however, that Pasternak's *Hamlet* is not only a beautifully poetic work but also a fine stage version. Used for the script of the film, Pasternak's version is still the favorite of actors and directors. Russians love it because they understand that Pasternak offered them a humane *Hamlet* profoundly reinterpreted to express their anxieties during the Stalinist terror, a time when Russians desired this quality above all others. (Garvuk does not mention that Stalin personally banned the version for just this reason; Chukovsky hints at it.) As a result, Pasternak's translation is usually immune from the criticism that is standard for departures from the canons of artistic translation.

It should also be said that Lozinsky is considered one of the idols of the Soviet school despite his faith in scientific translation. Chukovsky criticizes his version of *Hamlet* but expresses admiration for other translations. In Antokolsky's view, Lozinsky compares well to Pasternak as a translator because both men possess the remarkable talent of "reincarnation." A reading of Lozinsky's translations of Corneille's *Le Cid* and Dante's "divine poem" shows that Lozinsky and Pasternak are very different poets. Pasternak seeks poetic fidelity as a translator where Lozinsky seeks language fidelity, but Pasternak's translations of *Hamlet, Faust*, and the Georgian poets Baratashvili and Tabidze show that he scrupulously respected foreign poetry (1964:6–8).

Where Lozinsky's critics were concerned with recommending a new *Hamlet*, Bryusov's critics directly debated the question of literalism at length and in detail. And where previously literalist translations had been rejected, literalism now found a champion. The debate began when M. L Gasparov analyzed published versions and unpublished drafts of Bryusov's translation of *The Aeneid*, an approach he believed enabled him to "bridge the gap" between a published paraphrased translation done in Bryusov's youth and a literal translation he published and pronounced canonical twenty years later. Bryusov's drafts—five versions of the beginning of Book 2, Jason's story of the destruction of Troy—permitted Gasparov "to . . . trace Bryusov's 'road to literalism.'" He found that the drafts correspond to three stages of work, and by analyzing Bryusov's revisions in chronological sequence, he found that changes could be grouped into six categories of refinement: 1) paraphrases, 2) images (tropes), 3) lexical semantics, 4) morphology, 5) word order, and 6) stress. The three stages of Bryusov's work moved from the published paraphrase version to a previously unknown and unpublished verse translation to the final approved literal version with two uncompleted drafts intervening. Because Bryusov rejected his verse translation, there must be good reason why he preferred his literal version, which Gasparov called "an artistic interlinear." Gasparov argued against those who scorn Bryusov's *Aeneid* and use it as a surrogate for attacks on the "petty translators" of the literalist school of the 1930s: "But it seems that until now no one has thought to ask: how did it happen that a major poet, an experienced translator, the author of exemplary translations of Verhaeren, the French Symbolists, the Armenian poets, suddenly in this particular instance, in a translation of his favorite Virgil on whom he labored many years, missed his aim so badly?" (1971:92–93, 97–98, 90–91). To this it might be added, How did it happen that Russia's great Symbolist, a poet who was notorious for his insistence on personal and poetic freedom, produced one of the most slavish literal translations in the Russian world?

Gasparov saw "a complete gradation of 'degrees of literalism'" in the several "variants" of *The Aeneid*, Book 2, opening.

> At the one pole is a translation that strives to convey the original word for word. . . . Such, for example, are translations of the Holy Writ into all languages. . . . At the other pole is a translation that strives to convey the original on the scale of the work as a whole—a complete lyric poem, say: the conveyance of the "impression," that is, above all the emotional and ideological content of the original independently of the conveyance of its images, and even less of its stylistic figures and individual words; one may imagine here a "translation" in which not a single word of the original is conveyed precisely, but the general emotional "impression" is preserved.

And here Gasparov offered several useful distinctions between free and literal translation. Free translation strives to ensure that the reader does not realize it is a translation; literal translation strives to ensure that the reader is constantly aware he is reading a translation. "The free translation strives to bring the original to the reader and therefore strengthens the style of the original; the literalist translation strives to bring the reader to the original and therefore strengthens the reader's stylistic habits and tastes." Where free translation "strives to broaden the circle of reader knowledge of foreign literatures," the literalist translation "strives to broaden the circle of writers' abilities as regards artistic devices." The free translation is for "literary users," the literalist for "literary producers" (1971:101–3). Stated otherwise, free translation is oriented to the reader, literal translation to the text.

"The translation program of the young Bryusov was a program of 'the golden mean,'" Gasparov noted. "The program of the later Bryusov was a program of 'literalism' . . . a struggle to ensure that the translation would indicate not only every phrase or every line in correspondence to the original but also every word and every grammatical form in correspondence to the original." According to Gasparov, Bryusov's *Aeneid* even duplicates the Latin syntax and, wherever possible, the lexicon, imagery, and alliteration of the original. If the result sounds alien, provocative, this was exactly what Bryusov wanted. Gasparov quoted Bryusov in his consideration of translation as a program of "small quotation," stating that a translation is a quotation of both a foreign literary work and another culture. In addition, Gasparov believed, a long verse work should be translated as closely as a lyric poem. Gasparov asserted that Bryusov was right to discard his version of "the golden mean" and allow only his paraphrase and literal translations to be published, because only a free translation and a literalist translation, side by side, make up true translation.

Different readers need different types of translation. Some need to see and hear how Horace differs from Pushkin, so they require a free translation. Others, however, need to see and hear the difference between Horace and Sappho, and only a precise, exact, and literal translation can convey this difference to them. Cultural communication requires both an "expansion in breadth" and an "expansion in depth." Expansion in breadth is a "transference" of culture at a surface level, in its most simple and elementary manifestations. Expansion in depth goes beneath the surface and is more complex, more creative. Only a literal translation can convey a foreign culture into one's own society with requisite complexity. Therefore, in Gasparov's view, "literalism is not a dirty word, but a scientific concept. A tendency to literalism is not an unhealthy phenomenon, but a legitimate element in the structure of literature in translation. There are no golden means and no canonical translations 'for everyone'" (1972:103, 106–8, 111, 109, 112).

Gasparov's article in *Craft of Translation 1971* is an unwavering defense of literalism. In the next issue of *Craft of Translation*, A. Starostin, F. Petrovsky, V. V. Koptilov, and Levon Mkrtchian objected to Gasparov's division of translations into free and literal. In the opinion of Starostin, "the author . . . obscures the question of the merits of V. Ya. Bryusov's translation when he divides all translations into a dichotomy of 'free' and 'literalist.' This division permits the author to generally demur from an examination of the question of the adequacy and inadequacy of translations, their fidelity and infidelity." By confining his argument to these two types of translation, Starostin wrote, Gasparov was able to define the literalist translation as adequate, the free translation as inadequate (1973:269).

Petrovsky perceived this strategy, too, but he chose to attack Bryusov's literalist version of the *Aeneid* instead. In Petrovsky's view, Bryusov found the merit of Virgil's poem not in its content or plot but in its form, and "he set himself the task of conveying its form as carefully as possible." According to Petrovsky, Bryusov refined Virgil's images, semantics, morphology, word order, and alliteration, but in so doing he forgot Pushkin's admonition that "every language has its own tropes, its own conventional rhetorical figures of speech, its own peculiar expressions that cannot be

translated into another language with identical words." As Petrovsky reminded his readers, no translator should forget that the translator cannot
use perfect equivalents and is therefore "obligated to find in the means of
his own language words, tropes, and images that are closely correspondent"
to those of the original. Bryusov did forget this, and as a result, his translation is filled with transcriptions of Latin words that hinder the reader:
"*lutserny,*" "*pugiony,*" "*krinalii,*" "*tsintsinny.*" Bryusov forgot the rules
of Russian usage, and his literalism led him to absurdities. Worst of all,
he forgot his own advice: "We presume that a translator commands his
own language to perfection and generally possesses the giftedness of a writer
or poet, without which, it stands to reason, no knowledge and no effort
will help him to create a worthy translation." And, finally, "a literalist translation not only does not bring us to the original, but, on the contrary,
simply distorts it. Consequently only that translator who . . . distorts nothing and strives to recreate the very essence of the original, can convey the
original." (1973:254–56).

To Koptilov, Gasparov was wrong about translation as an "expansion
in breadth" and an "expansion in depth." Where Gasparov argued that
free and literal translations alternate with each other through literary history, Koptilov pointed out that the "free translator" was a contemporary
of the literalist Bryusov, just as Lozinsky and Lann were contemporaries
of Pasternak and Marshak. Free and literal translations do not alternate
through the history of literature; rather they coexist in time as different
approaches to translation and as contradictory demands facing every translator of every work at every stage of the translation process. Taken together,
"they are an exaggeration carried to the point of absurdity of two basic
demands made on all translations: the *precision* of its correspondence to
the original and the *naturalness* of its existence as a work of art." One
approach leads to a mechanical copy of the original, while the other results
in arbitrary reinterpretation. "Attempts to find a 'middle way' in translation
are not new, but they must not be made to depend on an eclectic blend
of extremes, on a palsied swing from literalism to liberties and back." The
process of translation cannot be a blend of extremes; it must be one of
thorough analysis of the original. The translator must attend both the idea
or content and the imagery or style of the original. A translation cannot
be a mechanical copy of every sound and every word. Koptilov concluded
that "the decisive majority of readers needs a translation that combines
fidelity in conveyance of content with a full-valued recreation of the artistic
form of the original, and neither the free translation nor the literalist translation are up to this task" (1973:257–61).

In the view of Mkrtchian, the idea of drawing the reader to the original
is initially attractive. But when one examines the examples Gasparov took

from Bryusov's literal translation, it becomes obvious that, as has been long known, "it is impossible to recreate . . . the perfection of a Latin original in Russian through the medium of Latin syntax. . . . Translations must be accomplished by the means of the language of the translation." Bryusov's *Aeneid* does not "draw" the reader to Virgil, it "drags" him there. Mkrtchian admired Gasparov's reconstruction of Bryusov's drafts and agreed that this indeed was how Bryusov worked. But in the end, Bryusov's literalist approach betrayed him. Mkrtchian's own analysis convinced him that "the translation does not bring us to the meaning of the original . . . it is literal where there is no need to be literal" and "it is free where it would have been better to be literal." Mkrtchian thus agreed with Starostin, Petrovsky, Koptilov, and those who previously criticized Bryusov's translation. "It is needed neither by lay readers nor specialists. True, it is of interest to historians of literature and especially those concerned with the history of translation. But only to them" (1973:263–65, 270, 272, 274).

Gasparov's opponents were clearly interested in two questions raised by his unexpected defense of literalism: they were anxious that literalism not be revived, and they reaffirmed the aesthetics of adequate, full-valued translation. Mkrtchian was impressed by Gasparov's systematic analysis of Bryusov's "way to literalism," and all four debaters paid attention to such questions as translation gradation, syntax and semantics, small versus long genres, and Bryusov's own principles of translation. The question of literalism was raised above irrelevance, because the debate dealt with essential factors of the process of translation. Nevertheless, given Gasparov's schematic forthrightness in demonstrating the degrees of Bryusov's journey to literalism, it is curious that his opponents did not take the opportunity to elaborate the problem of gradation, especially since Gasparov's distinctions between free and literal translation as method rather than process are the most vulnerable point of his argument. Starostin correctly assessed that Gasparov's focus on the two extreme poles of gradation caused him to avoid other types of translation, and Koptilov effectively demonstrated that the free and literal approaches are not historically alternating types of translation but two demands that every translator must contend with at every moment of the translation process. The weakest point of Gasparov's argument is that he used free translation as a foil for his defense of literalism; his opponents' weak point is that in their anxiety to reaffirm artistic translation, they barely touched on the problem of gradation as it relates to process.

The cause of this failure to explore more fully a theoretical question is undoubtedly the undying Soviet enmity toward the literalists. The problem of literalism will always be with us, and no doubt we need to understand it better. But Soviet discussions of literalist sins are obsessive, and the ability of Soviet translators to put problems behind them has in this instance failed.

Apparently, it is one thing to advocate the expulsion of literal translation from the spectrum and hope its garrulous foes will be appeased by the good sense of this solution; it is quite another to define its legitimate place.

Where, for example, does literal translation belong? What is its use? What function does it perform? This question was partially answered by Gasparov, even though his argument was rejected by Mkrtchian. There is a place for literal translation, and that place can be found in Gasparov's advice that literal translations are intended for "literary producers." Literal translation is the preferred method of scholars, and even if they do not specify it, they vote for it when they quote literary works to illustrate a point.

No literary translator would advocate the literal translations of poetry by scholars to facilitate their discussions of foreign poetry for their English-speaking audience. But these word-by-word, line-by-line reproductions, given parallel to their original texts, perform a respectable *literary* function. A recent example of this is offered by David Bethea's literal translations of verse excerpts for his study of Vladislav Khodasevich (1984). For the reader without Russian, these exact, line-by-line, word-for-word texts give access to the meaning of the poetry under discussion, while their formal values are elaborated in subsequent discussion. For the scholar who reads Russian, the translations also meet important needs. Khodasevich is not a poet commonly taught and known to scholars of Russian poetry. Bethea's translations are devoid of rhyme; they only vaguely correspond to the meter of the original; the associations of the English words do not approximate the connotations and nuances of this erudite poet, profoundly steeped in the poetic traditions of his native language. But the lexicon is precise and accurate, the linear structure and stanzaic articulation are honored, and the exact meaning of the poem in its parts and its whole are conveyed.

For the reader of Russian these texts are reliably and imaginatively interpretive. They provide meanings only a specialist on Khodasevich is likely to know and refine subsequent discussion with marked authority. A faithful translation could not meet this need, and the need could certainly not have been met by a free translation. A literal translation can serve a literary need and provide a valid tool for critical exegesis. This is indicated further by a curious turnabout among scholars of Russian literature. Pushkinists in the English-speaking world abhor Nabokov's translation of *Eugene Onegin* and prefer the faithful translations of Walter Arndt or Sir Charles Johnston. But the text that most readily facilitates *literate* analysis through an exact, word-for-word copy is Nabokov's *literalist* version.

16

ON COLLOQUIAL SPEECH

■■■■■■ Soviet and American translators seem to agree that a satisfactory solution to the problem of translating colloquial speech has not yet been found. On the one hand, many translators believe that the problem of colloquial speech has no solution and that translators should not attempt to translate slang, jargon, dialects. On the other hand, some of the most highly admired translators in the Soviet school are those who have attempted to convey colloquial speech. As has been shown in an analysis of Nina Daruzes's *Huckleberry Finn* and Natalya Volzhina's *Grapes of Wrath*, the two basic approaches to colloquial speech are bold and careful conveyance.

Colloquial speech is one of those problems in translation that persists. In the 1960s Soviet translators and linguists debated the problem on the All-Union level. Not surprisingly, an agreement was never reached. Nevertheless, the problem was explored in useful ways, and recommendations were offered. At the very least, translators identified what should *not* be done to convey colloquial speech.

Any discussion of translating colloquial speech has to begin with a phenomenon translators call equivalence, equivalency, or equivalentation. The concept recurs as often in the literature of the Soviet school of translation as in the literature produced by American and other translators. The concept signifies equivalent effect—the question of a faithful, rather than a direct, literal conveyance—but is used most often to refer to the notion that one word in one language ought logically to have a single equivalent word in another language, and to the untruth of this expectation. For example, *chien, der Hund*, and Russian *sobaka* would seem to be exact equivalents of "dog." Because the majority of words in all languages designate common objects, there ought not to be a problem in conveying most words from one language to another. This is not so, of course. Robert Graves has remarked that "*ein Stückchen Brot, un morceau de pain, un trozito de pan,* are all similarly rendered in English as 'a morsel of bread'. But the altogether different sounds of these words convey immense variations in shape, colour, size, weight and taste of the breadstuff to which they refer, and in the eater's attitude to them" (1965:138–39; see also Payne 1971:364). Vera Stanevich makes the same point when she argues that if one takes the simple French phrase "*la nuit etait sombre*," one finds that it means not only "the night is dark," but also "black," "gloomy," "impenetrable," "dismal," "pitch dark," "somber," and many other possible things (1959:55). Theodore Savory has said that "the idea that lies behind the nature of a dictionary of the X=Y type is essentially fallacious. . . . The notion that for every word in any one language there is another word accurately equivalent to it in every other language is not in accordance with experience" (1968:14; also Lefevere 1975:28). So also with the word *dog*. There are apt to be semantic, cultural, and experiential differences between what the word *dog* means to an American child and what its equivalent means to a Japanese business-man contemplating a dish of sukiyaki.

Translation is not a perfect art. It is, as John Nims and E. G. Etkind have said, an indirect art of sacrifice, gains and losses, choice and decision. It requires painful decisions. Walter Arndt asks, "What shall we betray, the irradiated simplicity of the original, or the zest and shock of our own words?" (1972:xxxix). Equivalency is the source of some of the strongest expressions of despair over literary translation. George Steiner, who is hardly a pessimist about translation, has declared

> No two languages mesh perfectly, no two languages . . . set the world in the same order. . . . There are no total translations: because languages differ, because each language represents a complex, historically and collectively determined ag-gregate of values, proceedings of social conduct, conjectures on life. There can be no exhaustive transfer from language A to language B, no meshing of nets so precise that there is identity of conceptual content, unison of undertone, abso-lute symmetry of aural and visual association. (1968:49)

In these statements we again encounter the question of untranslatability. Juliane House, in her examination of the question, has identified four limits. "Translatability is limited whenever the form of a linguistic unit takes on special importance," that is, in Nida and Taber's formula, whenever "the form is an essential element of the message." Translatability is also limited in instances of "metalanguage," when language is used to discuss itself and when language is its own object, not a medium. Translatability is limited when "language is used differently from its communicative functions," in plays of language, puns, and so forth. And, finally, translatability is limited when language is perceived as something more than itself, as extralinguistic

—for example, social, economic, or political phenomena that cannot be considered apart from their own peculiar environment (1973:166–67).

Soviet translators, no less aware of the difficulties of equivalency, perceive the same relationship between equivalency and the question of untranslatability. But again they are more optimistic about possible solutions, or at least ameliorations. And though they also experience serious doubt regarding ultimate translatability, they have been emphatic about putting the problem in its place. V. Koptilov has even insisted that the language barrier can be completely overcome by persistent work: "The virtuoso translator does not know the word 'untranslatable.' And that which has at times been termed an untranslatable play on words or consonance he reproduces skillfully with the help of a different verbal material which he organizes 'in the image and likeness' of the original" (1971:164).

Still, colloquial speech continues to daunt even the most optimistic Soviet translators. There is unanimous agreement in the Soviet school that no translator has yet found a satisfactory solution to the problem. All translators must sympathize with Russian translators who have had to contend with the following examples of style from two English-language classics, *Huck Finn* and "Auld Lang Syne":

"Why, yes, dat's so; I-I'd done forgot it. A harem's a bo'd'n-house, I reck'n. Mos' likely dey has rackety times in de nussery. En I reck'n de wives quarrels considable; en dat 'creases de racket. Yit dey say Sollermun des wises' man dat ever live'."

And there's a hand, my trusty fiere,
    And gie's a hand o'thine;
And we'll tak a right guid-willie waught
    For auld lang syne.

Russian translators subsume the various manifestations of this kind of style under the term *prostorechie* 'colloquial speech,' by which they signify the vulgate, substandard, nonliterary forms and phraseology of spoken language. The term has been poorly defined by both translators and linguists in the Soviet Union. It covers every verbal manifestation of irregular speech, including slang, argot, jargon, dialects, vulgarisms, the vernacular, curse words. *Prostorechie* often refers to the popular language of the people, but more carefully used it designates the departures from the norms of spoken or literary language that are the peculiar and unique quality of any given language. Colloquial language is a phenomenon of time, place, social class, level of education, cultural condition, and individual speech. It is the most extreme form of a language that presents the most challenge to the concept of equivalency.

How could any translator hope to contend with the dated and localized language of Robert Burns: "Wee, sleekit, cow'rin', tim'rous beastie, / O what a panic's in thy breastie!" How could anyone except an American approximately fifty years old ever hope to catch the nuances of a mild, yet particularly dated and placed bit of colloquial speech like Holden Caulfield's reply to old Phoebe: "I mean, they're all right if they go around saving innocent guys' lives all the time, and like that, but you don't *do* that kind of stuff if your a lawyer. All you do is make a lot of dough and play golf and play bridge and buy cars and drink Martinis and look like a hot-shot." Many translators answer these rhetorical questions arguing that no one can possibly convey such rich kinds of language to readers, for colloquial speech is the most native, the most peculiar, the most untranslatable property of any language. No matter how close two languages might be, no matter what their linguistic and cultural affinities, one language does not possess the lexical means for taking possession of the distinctive colloquial properties of the other.

Speaking about the problem of equivalency posed by colloquial speech, Viktor Khinkis, a very good translator of John Updike and William Faulkner, has said, "The question of the use of colloquial speech in an artistic translation (and equally about the harm it can cause) arises constantly in both the practice of every translator and in almost all conversations and discussions" (1965:132). The problem of translating colloquial speech has been frequently discussed in the Soviet school, particularly given the high ideals and far-reaching demands of the school. Every translator knows the problem. The entire force of a literary work can be destroyed by mistranslating a single word or expression. American literary legend has it that an unknown young writer named William Faulkner once withdrew a novel from consideration for publication because an editor wanted to change a few marks of punctuation. Tolstoy believed that in his opening of *War and Peace*, every single word, in their given order, with every echo among the carefully placed French and Russian words was important. No wonder that even in the Soviet school, where attention to the slightest nuance is considered an absolute, some of the most conscientious translators have refused to attempt to convey colloquial speech.

This refusal to deal with the seemingly impossible was severely criticized in the early 1960s by S. M. Petrov, whose remarks in a paper read at a translators' conference and later published in *Craft of Translation* set off a sharp controversy over the question of translating colloquial speech. According to Petrov, a mark of the Soviet school from its inception was the translators' attempts to translate poetry in all its impossible demands of meter, rhyme, stanza, and syntax; even when faced with difficult words and plays on words, translators did not hesitate "to invent neologisms and find substitutes for puns and folk sayings." But when confronted with "colloquial speech, the broadest, most native colloquial speech, and particularly archaic and rural coloration," the same boldly inventive translators become so stricken with terror that "they are ready to declare such lexicon totally taboo." Soviet translators have failed to deal with colloquial speech, Petrov charged, and worse yet, their justifications of their refusal amount only to so many rationalizations (1963:73).

According to Petrov, translators make essentially five arguments against attempts to recreate colloquial speech. They claim that Soviet readers do not like "dialectisms and vulgarisms"; attempts to recreate colloquial speech have traditionally resulted in Russification of foreign works; any extensive use of the colloquial speech of their language as a vehicle for recreating foreign colloquial speech will result in a distortion of the national color of the original; they do not know how to recreate colloquial speech; and knowledge of Russian colloquial speech is not sufficiently developed for translators to use it to deal with foreign colloquial speech (1963:76–78).

Petrov's paper was strongly attacked by his opponents. It was pointed out that he failed to define clearly the distinction between literary norm and the use of colloquial speech in literary works, that his definition of the phenomenon was too broad and should not include jargon and dialectisms, which are another kind of speech, and that the phenomenon of colloquial speech does not even exist (Bekker 1963:488–89). The criticisms are largely true, since Petrov's definition of colloquial speech is rather broad. "Under the term colloquial speech," he said, "I unite *conditionally* any departures from the strictly literary norm of language right down to dialects and jargon." Colloquial speech can be divided into its "principal manifestations": common, everyday spoken speech that has become acceptable in literary language; expressions of the "language of the people" that have entered into the literary language; urban nonliterary speech; rural nonliterary speech; jargon, including professionalisms that depart from the literary norm; dialects; and vulgarisms, including curse words. These kinds of colloquial speech are difficult to translate, Petrov admitted, but here as elsewhere the integrity of the original text must be the final dictate: "Colloquial speech must be used in the translation in approximately the same measure that it was by the original author" and in accordance with "the artistic function it fulfills" (1963:71–72, 79–80).

Petrov's definition of colloquial speech is clearly too broad and vague. He touched on a chief reason for this shortcoming when he noted that colloquial speech has not been properly studied in Soviet letters. It is probable that the phenomenon has not been given proper attention because colloquial speech includes vulgarisms, curse words, dirty words—all of which have been taboo in the Soviet Union. Vulgarisms are not included in Russian dictionaries. There are few slang dictionaries in circulation in the Soviet Union—a rare but still authoritative dictionary of slang was compiled for the tsarist police in the late nineteenth century—and those that are circulated among police organizations today are decidedly innocuous. A dictionary of "substandard Russian" compiled by the Leningrad writer and lexicographer Kiril Uspensky (Kostsinsky) in a labor camp, expanded to over thirty-five thousand classified and analyzed items, was not considered publishable in the Soviet Union and is now being completed in the United States. The most significant Russian work in lexicography since the compilation of the first *Analytic Dictionary of the Great Russian Language* in the 1840s by Vladimir Dahl will be published in American, not Russian, letters. "Dirty words" were a controversial aspect of Petrov's paper. Indeed, the word *prostorechie* was a code word for "dirty words" in the debate, and the dependence on euphemism is partly responsible for the failure to define terms properly.

Nevertheless, Petrov did take a strong position on a controversial question and forcefully rebut each of his specified objections to attempts to translate colloquial speech. It is not true, he asserted, that Russian readers dislike colloquial speech in literary works. On the contrary, such Russian masters of colloquial speech as N. S. Leskov, A. N. Ostrovsky, Vladimir Mayakovsky, and Mikhail Sholokhov are among the most popular classical writers. As for the contempt for the traditional Russian translators who used Russian colloquial speech to Russify foreign works, Petrov suggested that the shortcomings of some translators should not serve as examples to all translators and argued that the shortcomings are certainly not convincing proof against the efficacy of the *principle* of translating colloquial speech. By the same token, a recreation of colloquial speech does not necessarily signify that the national color of foreign works will be distorted. Lozinsky, among others, has shown that Russian colloquial speech can be used successfully to represent foreign equivalents. And, finally, simply because many translators profess not to know how to convey colloquial speech does not mean they should not be expected to learn, and simply because knowledge of the phenomenon is unattended in Soviet letters does not mean Soviet translators and linguists should not begin compiling dictionaries and studying the phenomenon (1963:76–78).

More than two decades after Petrov's attempt to define colloquial speech, Soviet translators have yet to face this problem. The Soviet school seems to be divided between those who believe they should attempt to convey what is, after all, a literary fact of life and those who believe that any attempt is certain to fail. As a rule, translators have tended to judge each attempt individually. Soviet critics are able to identify translators who have failed at this task and translators who have enjoyed remarkable success in solving the problem in specific instances. Successful attempts are usually ascribed to the individual translator's talent. As Viktor Khinkis put it,

Everyone acknowledges that it is necessary to strive to introduce colloquial speech in the same degree that it is used by the author of the original. It is perfectly clear that it is impossible to give a recipe for every occasion in life. In every concrete instance the question is resolved by the translator's taste, conscience, and sense, as also by his editor's. Colloquial speech should not be shunned, of course. Colloquial speech can enrich a translation, and it can inflict irreparable damage on it. (1965:132–33)

Despite the reluctance to confront colloquial speech, several methods for dealing with it have been discussed, applied, and either rejected or partly approved. One of the most well-known methods concerning dialects has been to substitute a dialect of the language of translation judged to be equivalent in terms of time, place, and cultural-historical associations to the dialect of the original. This was a favorite method of the Soviet literalists in the 1930s, and it was used in early Anglo-American translations of Dostoyevsky, Tolstoy, Chekhov, and Gorky. Even as recently as the 1970s, F. Will stated, "The translation of such language must be into comparably local forms of the language of translation" (1973:84). Nevertheless, Will immediately admitted, "These local forms, as we know, become rapidly outdated, for all their temporary vitality." The majority of modern translators agree that the dialect-for-dialect method has proved to be the worst solution to the problem simply because dialects do not have equivalents in terms of time, place, and cultural-historical associations in other languages. We are all familiar with those first British and American translations of Russian classics in which Chekhov's clerks speak with a Cockney accent and Gorky's worker-heroes sound as if they had just walked out of a Birmingham ironworks. Similarly, the nineteenth-century Russian translator Irinarkh Vvedensky forced Dickens's characters to speak in the Russian dialects of Petersburg civil servants and Moscow grain merchants.

The translation of dialect using dialect does not work. The Russian Siberian experience has sometimes been compared to the settling of the American West in the general outlines of two national experiences, but when the comparison involves colloquial speech, it would be foolish to oblige Vladimir Korolenko's Siberian tramp-convicts to say, "Howdy, podner." Simply stated, there are few similarities of mutual experience touched on by the colloquial speech of two different languages. George Steiner has stated, "Different castes, different strata of society use a different idiom," and this holds true both within a single culture and across distant national boundaries. Steiner devotes considerable attention to this condition in *After Babel* (1975:31ff.), and Khinkis has stated succinctly that "colloquial speech . . . is inseparably linked with the distinctive qualities of an environment, and the environments of different peoples (even of such peoples as close as the Russians and Ukrainians) are in many ways distinct" (1965:134).

Another method devised for the conveyance of colloquial speech is to be found in the term *blandscript* (*gladkopis'*). In their use of blandscript, translators suggest that colloquial speech cannot be conveyed into another language and that the attempt should not even be made. Translators resorting to blandscript replace colloquial speech with normal human speech, with little or no attempt to indicate that the language of the original is composed of departures from the norm, no matter how sharp such departures may be. Chukovsky devotes considerable attention to blandscript in *A High Art*, and he quotes the poet Nikolay Zabolotsky's observation that "blandscript is our personal enemy. Blandscript bespeaks an indifference of the heart and a disdain for the reader" (1959:252). Chukovsky conceded that there is no satisfactory solution to the problem of conveying colloquial speech, but he insisted that the phenomenon must somehow be confronted. Although blandscript is at least an honest confession of an inability to deal with a difficult problem, Chukovsky concluded that in the final analysis blandscript bespeaks a disrespect for language and a lack of professional care. Translators cannot be excused from the task presented by their chosen text; they must do the best they can with it (1984:122, 126–27, 130–31, 220–21). Petrov agreed, pointing out that "it is very risky to match colloquial speech, especially vulgar speech, with a neutral lexicon and even more with bland syntax" (1963:87).

Two other methods that have been used by Soviet translators are the so-called protocol or distillation translation and the signal translation. Using the protocol translation, translators simply explain what is happening: a character did this and then went there and said that. An obvious result of this device is that a single word or phrase can be transformed into laboriously prolix syntax. The translator who uses this device seems to assume that readers cannot divine for themselves the meaning of an unusual native expression, or cannot even appreciate the distinctive peculiarities of another culture. An example of this translation method has been cited by Chukovsky, who pointed out that a particularly poignant and readily understandable expression used in Solzhenitsyn's *One Day*, "If he didn't sign, a wooden jacket for him," was explained out by Solzhenitsyn's six translators as, variously: "Shukhov had it all figured out. If he didn't sign, he'd be shot." "If he didn't sign, he was as good as buried," and "If he did not sign, he was dead." Only Thomas P. Whitney chose not to explain the obvious here, allowing the original Russian expression—a long honored peasant colloquialism—to stand for itself (1984:120–21). The protocol or distillation translation betrays the translator's desire to accommodate readers' tastes. But, as Petrov has suggested, "one must carefully and conscientiously translate a foreign-language work . . . without distilling it for just anybody's taste" (1963:95).

The signal translation is an attempt to let the reader of the translation know that the language is unusual, even though the translator is reluctant to attempt to recreate its full flavor. The method is best known in Samuil Marshak's translations of Robert Burns. Realizing that any attempt to reproduce systematically the eighteenth-century vernacular of Burns's Scottish farmers would lead him into a morass of eccentric Russian colloquial speech, Marshak chose to "signal" his Russian readers that Burns's language is strange, outdated, and marvelously rich in syntax and lexicon by using a careful blend of eighteenth-century Russian archaisms, words of Old Slavic origin, and Russian folk expressions. The challenge in this instance was to avoid inventing a preposterous new Russian language, and not to develop an obtrusive new style. In this endeavor Marshak was assisted by his own great talent as a poet; the success of his method can be traced also to his vast knowledge of Russian and other folklores. Rather than attempt to recreate an impossible lexical item in Russian, which lacks resources for "auld," "lang," and "syne," Marshak chose to convey the refrain in different ways, using a different Russian folk expression for each conveyance (see Kashkin 1959:116–17). Through this technique, Marshak was able to convey the different meanings of the phrases and signal his readers that the original language is a departure from the norm. As for such dialect forms as "fiere," "gie's," and "guid-willie waught," Marshak did not even attempt a conveyance; instead, he used folk and archaic Russian as modest substitutes in moderation, as a signal.

No Soviet translator claims to have solved the problem of conveying colloquial speech, but several pragmatic rules have been drawn from confrontations with the problem. The first rule is that the translator should be sensible and compromise imaginatively, as elsewhere in literary translation. L. G. Kelly has stated, "There are three broad criteria on which relevance of style is judged: that style conforms to matter, that style is selected to suit readership, that style reflects author. Translators adopt two approaches to the style of the original: they either imitate it through extended formal equivalence, or they use a target-language style deemed functionally equivalent." In Kelly's view, "there are three ways of seeking lexical equivalence: one can attempt to translate completely literally; one can attempt consistent dynamic equivalence; or one can mix the two at need" (1979:179, 134).

When Petrov ridiculed the dialect-for-dialect method, he pointed out that a better approach to the problem of dialects is to "employ lexicon and forms that are not tied to any single dialect, but instead can be felt as some kind of dialectical speech in general" (1963:81). Petrov does not mean that the translator should invent a dialect for a dialect. Rather, the translator should avoid the unpleasant impression made on readers by the use of a clearly recognizable native dialect: Solzhenitsyn's Ivan Denisovich should not be made to sound like a Chicago gangster. The translator should seek neutral ground between the extremes of blandscript and the use of dialect for dialect.

Speaking particularly about translating slang, Jorge Luis Borges insisted, "If you're working on something written in Buenos Aires slang and try to translate it into, let us say, the slang used by hoodlums in the United States, you've got something quite different." Borges's collaborator-translator Norman Thomas di Giovanni, commenting on one of their failed attempts to do just this, stated, "Several reviewers thought it sounded like a combination of Damon Runyan and cowboy slang. I'm planning to tone the slang down" (Borges 1973:112–13).

Concerning the problem of equivalency, Vera Stanevich has offered much the same advice as Petrov. She argues that the translator should be sensitive about word-usage and employ words and word associations carefully:

> The translator must control lexicon and word-usage the way a violinist controls precise sounds. But this precision is needed not for the external coincidence of the words of two different language systems, but for internal freedom and precision. The logic of language is realized not only in grammatical and syntactic changes and links, but also in a correct usage of words, for which the translator must know the word-usage of both languages that he works with. We signify by word-usage . . . the potential capacity of the word in its dependence on content *to enter into conjunction with other words.* (1959:55–56; emphasis in the original)

The translator must be aware that when a word, especially a colloquialism, is taken out of its native context, where it may very well have served an excellent artistic effect, it can seem preposterous. A new language environment for such a word may be inappropriate. To Kelly this would seem to suggest that the translator must find an effective compromise toward a literary conveyance of style. To Petrov it seems to mean that the translator must be inventive and avoid strong identification with any pronounced language stratum. To Stanevich it means that the translator need not be bound to a single word but may instead seek to convey a word by joining it to other words that will enable it to stand for its contentual meanings and associations in the original. Speaking of archaisms, Khinkis has warned that an overly strong and direct conveyance of a style can be a hindrance rather than a help: "a strengthened archaization, just like abuse of colloquial speech and dialectisms, makes the text vague, hinders understanding of it." In the end

> the use of colloquial speech demands caution. Colloquial speech is a weapon that cuts both ways so sharply that in those instances where it is impossible to find a fully adequate equivalent it is sometimes better to make the text a bit less colloquial than to overdo it. . . . And one should always be leery. . . . Because they understand this, our best translators use common folk speech, and dialectisms, and jargon appropriately and in moderation. (1965:133)

Soviet translators agree that whatever the importance of method and theory to literary translation, there are still no final answers to the problem of translating colloquial speech. Theory and method are necessary, but in the end translators must rely on their own instinct and judgment. "All attempts at a principled solution to this problem are filled with contradictions," the Ukrainian theorist and translator Oleksy Kundzich has stated. Translators do not yet have a theoretical basis for the problem, and the problem does not lend itself to theoretical analysis. "All judgments rest on an inner conviction, on intuition, on examples taken from creative practice" (1968:229). In their search for principles for the conveyance of jargon and slang, translators must not forget that translation is a creative act, and personal talent is just as important to the successful conveyance of colloquial speech as mastery of other language resources. As Kundzich has pointed out elsewhere, "the possibility of assimilating the spiritual treasures of another people . . . is not limited to available language resources . . . every language bears within itself, in addition to language resources, potential possibilities which are regularly uncovered through the creative efforts of writers of original and translated works. Consequently, only creativity develops a literary language" (1959: 8–9).

Still another concept stressed in Soviet discussions of colloquial speech is the sensible idea that translators should look beyond the resources of language to cultural context. Cultural potentials are particularly important in the Soviet school, of course, and it is understandable that colloquial speech is perceived in context with "national realia." A. Andres has noted, "The capacity to see a translated work in its literary-historical retrospect is one of the characteristic and most fruitful . . . trends of the Soviet school of translation" (1965:129). The national-cultural context of colloquial speech is an indispensable aspect of its conveyance, and an aspect central to the problem of equivalency. In stressing the importance of word-usage, Stanevich complained, "Translators . . . are prone to forget that word-usage is tied to national realia and the history of a people. . . . inaccurate word usage leads to inaccurate expression of the author's thought, to confusion. Word usage is inseparable from the history of a people, from the life of a word in its language, from, so to speak, the biography of a word, its birth, maturation, old age" (1959:58, 56). Word usage is perceived in the Soviet school as both avoidance of an unwarranted "nationalization" of foreign works and the necessity of adapting the same works into the new national environment while consistently preserving their original national character. Nationalization is an inevitable result of the dialect-for-dialect method: a dialect is so unique to its given language that any foreign text can easily be Russified or Americanized. When using the resources of their own language to convey foreign colloquial speech, translators must take care to preserve the original national features intact. Such care can be rewarding, for languages can be used in ways that enable them to complement one another, and thus enrich the language in a translated text.

The translator's own language can be a rich source of both lexical and cultural values for the enhancement of the work being translated. N. M. Lyubimov has spoken strongly on behalf of this possibility: "Those who translate into Russian must read Russian writers in every spare moment . . . they must read with pencil in hand, they must gather their honey from different flowers like a bee. This will remarkably broaden the translator's vocabulary diapason and it will help him to bring the verbal wealth of the original to the Russian reader" (1983:9). Conversely, the language of the original can be a rich source of new expressions for the translator's language. Speaking in defense of Petrov's paper, E. G. Etkind pointed to the need to "open the sluice-gates" between two languages and allow them to enrich each other (Bekker 1963:490). Speaking of the importance of communicating cultural value, Steiner has gone so far as to say that languages can not only enrich each other but also facilitate understanding among human beings at the deepest, most universal levels: "The translator enriches his tongue by allowing the source language to penetrate and modify it. But he does far more: he extends his native idiom toward the hidden absolute of meaning" (1975:65).

In the American world, the problem of colloquial speech has been left largely to lexicologists and lexicographers. Those translators who have attended to the problem usually keep their comments brief, and they almost unanimously recommend that the translator should not attempt to translate dialects or other extreme departures from the literary norm. Donald Keene expressed this attitude when he stated, "Another problem faced by the translator seeking vividity is the advisability of using language which is either datable (slang) or restricted as a dialect. . . . Dialects should be rejected, except in very unusual cases" (1971:328). One reason for this difference in attitudes is the radical difference between Russian and American literary taste. Where dialects are highly valued by Russians—there is an entire school of modern Russian village prose writers devoted to the cultivation of colloquial speech—dialects are currently considered silly in American literature. The village prose writers are valued because they expertly employ regional dialects. In American culture, in contrast, audiences consider most colloquialism as overused, trivialized expressions. Westerns, for example, both novels and movies, no longer feature such colloquialisms as "Howdy, podner." Russians value dialects so dearly that they could not begin to appreciate this very different cultural attitude.

The problem of conveying colloquial speech is vexing. After the most promising and the most obviously wrong methods have been analyzed and a few prohibitions articulated, Soviet translators have not been able to lay claim to convincing solutions. Soviet translators are divided between those who, like Keene, reject attempts to convey colloquial speech and those who agree with Petrov and Khinkis that the translator is obliged to contend with the phenomenon. In the end, the state of the art of literary translation as it pertains to colloquial speech can be reduced to two tentative conclusions. First, any attempt to convey colloquial speech in its entirety, systematically, is doomed to failure and to absurdity. Second, to their chagrin, the only key that Soviet translators have found to the conveyance of colloquial speech is the translator—the translator's taste, tact, instinct, talent, judgment, and, especially, the translator's moderation.

ON REALIA

Realia constitute a special problem of translation that is pervasive in discussions of the art. The problem has been touched on in reference to the relationships among translation, communication, and culture; the world *realia* occurs frequently in the chapter of this study on conveying colloquial speech and the chapter on colloquial speech as a translation problem. A. V. Fedorov alludes to the links between realia and cultural communication in his warning that conveyances of national character should not be too closely tied to national realia; the close relationship of realia to colloquial speech is indicated by Vera Stanevich's reminder that usage of colloquialisms "is tied to national realia and the history of a people."

We have already seen that Soviet translators and theorists of translation are somewhat vague about the specifics of conveying distinctive national character and that their solutions to the problem of conveying colloquial speech are not fully satisfactory. One reason for this, it might be suggested, is to be found in an observation made by Roger Roothaer that translation theorists fail to discriminate between realia as a problem of linguistics and realia as a problem of culture (1978:131). Soviet translation theorists, who, with the exception of Fedorov, are generally weak on linguistics, do in fact become more specific when they shift discussions of distinctive national character from language to culture—that is, when they treat lexical constraints as a problem of realia. Realia, says L. N. Sobolev, "are those words of a national environment that do not exist in other languages because these objects and phenomena do not exist in other countries" (1955:290). Realia, agree the Bulgarian translators Sergey Vlakhov and Sider Florin in an address to their Soviet colleagues, are "those words (and word-conjunctions) of a native language which represent the names of objects, concepts, phenomena characteristic of a geographical environment, culture, material existence, or distinctive socio-historical features of a people, nation, country, tribe, and function thereby as bearers of national, local, or historical color; precise equivalents of these words do not exist in other languages" (1970:438).

Taken as words, realia constitute a problem of linguistics; as objects, concepts, or phenomena, they become a cultural problem of conveying distinctive national character. Because certain objects, concepts, or phenomena are distinctive to a given national culture, the words that designate them are said to exist only in the language of that nation. Realia thus present an especially acute problem of translation as communication. Sobolev goes so far as to say that realia are untranslatable by definition and must be transliterated. However, M. J. de K. Holman, who bases a study of English translations of Tolstoy's novel *Resurrection* on Sobolev and Vlakhov and Florin, says that this categorical view cannot be accepted in practice: the translator must decide when to transliterate and when to translate. The more distant two cultures are and the more general the audience, the more readily the translator will translate; the closer the cultures and the more specialized the audience, the more often the translator will choose to transliterate. If the choice is to translate, the translator must then decide whether to use a calque, or to adapt, to approximate, or to describe (1983:127).

The Soviet theorist L. Mikulina believes that realia must be translated whenever possible. She places the problem in its broader context—in its relation to cultural communication—by identifying realia as one aspect of what she calls specific national-cultural character. She includes under this heading such phenomena as idioms and "nationally, culturally unique" images, similes, metaphors, and epithets. Tracing her work to recent developments in the fields of information theory and speech behavior rather than to discussions of distinctive national character, Mikulina has examined a mass of materials derived from Soviet translations of Russian literature into English. She concludes from these data that realia are a problem of equivalency, untranslatability, and lexicon peculiar to a national culture. She maintains that realia must be understood not only as objects, phenomena, and concepts, and not simply as a question of lexicon, but also in terms of multilevel national and cultural "conventions" (*obuslovlennost'*) derived from complex connotative differences between two languages. Realia constitute only one level of "the national-cultural conventions of lexicon." Just as important is "the level of the social signification of realia" and "the level of their emotional signification. In terms of information theory, even words of two different languages signifying the same object can convey completely different meaning to speakers belonging to different cultural environments, and the polysemic connotations can also differ completely" (1981:79, 90–91, 98–99).

In Western translation studies, realia have been placed in their broadest cultural-communicative context. They are seen as a problem of anthropology and ethnology, and especially of anthropological, ethnological, and cultural linguistics. Eugene Nida has done seminal work in this area by identifying five types of cultural knowledge needed by translators (1954), and H. Stephen Straight has elaborated Nida's system on the assumption that "translators must have considerable knowledge of both the source culture and the target culture of the languages in which they are working." According to Nida, the five types of cultural knowledge are ecology, material culture and technology, social categories, mythic patterns, and linguistic structures. According to Straight's elaboration, "a translator must be aware of the ecological differences between the culture of an original work and the culture into which it is being translated . . . variations in climate . . . terrain, flora, and fauna, and exploitation techniques." A translator must know the material culture, "the man-made things about which the people have first-hand awareness," including food, housing, transportation, clothing, the various tools by which the environment is exploited, and the state of technology. In addition, "social classes, kinship relations, and sex roles all vary according to different cultures, and the translator must recognize the different ways which the two cultures . . . have for making these distinctions." Again, under mythic patterns such phenomena as cosmology, taboos, and supernaturalism are important. Taboos are particularly difficult to handle because what is common place in one culture may be offensive in another. Finally, such linguistic components as phonology, morphology, syntax, and lexical semantics must be taken into account: the very sound, shape, and connotation of a word have cultural implications (1977:28–30).

Because of their orientation to lexical questions, Vlakhov and Florin's views are close to Nida's and Straight's fifth type of cultural knowledge, linguistic structures. This orientation enabled them to make a significant contribution to the Soviet school through carefully defined links between lexicon and realia. In their view, realia are adopted from one language into another by six methods, which they derived from analysis of Russian and Bulgarian translations and dictionaries. The first of these methods is transcription—for example, the English measure "foot" is conveyed into Russian and Bulgarian as *fut*, the Russian word *sputnik* is transcribed in English as "sputnik." Another method is calque—the English word "sky-scraper" is conveyed into Russian as *neboskrob*, the Spanish word *toreador* into Bulgarian as *bikoborets*. Creation of a new word constitutes another method to convey realia—English "seven-league boots" and German *Siebenmeilenstiefel* prompt, by analogy, the invention of Russian "seven-verst boots." Through assimilation, a word is adopted into a new culture with its object—the German *Windjacke* was assimilated into Russian as *vatnik* and into Bulgarian as *vatenka*. Through approximate translation, a simple word in one language has to be adopted into another language by a more complex word, usually a word-conjunction—the Russian *udarnik* had to be introduced into German as *Stossarbeiter* and into English as "shock-worker." The final method is descriptive translation —Russian *ukha* has to be explained in German as *Fischsuppe* and in English as "fish soup" (1970:439–40).

Vlakhov and Florin have also placed realia in their broadest cultural context. Their contribution is particularly valuable in that they have examined an implication not taken into account often enough by translators, namely, the harm that can be inflicted on one culture by another through indiscriminate transfer of words and the cultural phenomena they designate. In their opinion, translators are obliged to use words for realia, and must therefore introduce new words—calques—into their language. Realia are essential to the conveyance of national, local, or historical color; "that is, the atmosphere of the original environment and epoch in a work." On the one hand, the Italian word *gondolier* obviously should not be translated as "excursion leader" or "boat-rower." English "landlord," German *Junker*, Bulgarian *chorbadzhiia*, and Rumanian *plantateur* all designate distinctive national-cultural phenomena; they differ from each other and from the Russian *pomeshchik*. On the other hand, modern translators are overly disposed to introduce new words and realia into their language and thereby sometimes harm their language.

Translators ought to ask themselves rigorous questions before succumbing to this temptation. The most obvious of these questions is whether the words encountered constitute authentic realia. A translator might not realize that an object or phenomenon already exists or has been established in its new culture and might resort to a foreign adoption for which a word already exists. Translators must also ask themselves whether realia exist in their context. For example, the word for a Cossack chieftain, *ataman*, should be transcribed, but it would be a mistake to transfer the word from its medieval Russian context, where it means simply "leader" or "chief." And finally, translators should ask themselves whether borrowing is necessary or whether it is a hindrance to understanding. Above all, does the word sound so false in the new language as to be pretentious (1970:445–46, 441–43)?

The problem is actually twofold. As evidenced in the case of colloquial speech, realia should not be avoided. Their erasure from a foreign work results in blandscript or, even worse, in outright nationalization. Yet the immoderate introduction of realia can damage the native language and, simultaneously, make the translation ridiculous. A striking lexical example of the damage caused by the introduction of realia was once cited by Viktor

Khinkis, who ridiculed the atrocious transcription *"remarkabel'nye i mizerabel'nye ekzersisii"* for the English phrase "remarkable and miserable exercises" (1965:133).

Central Asian and Caucasian literatures are of utmost importance to the Soviet school. In regard to these literatures, considerable attention has been paid to the words and phrases that should or should not be introduced into Russian. A general rule is that only realia that do not exist in the new culture should be conveyed directly (transcribed). As V. M. Rossels says, "Only those foreign words which designate concepts, objects, phenomena, or more briefly speaking, realia, that do not exist in the culture of the language into which a work is being translated, should be allowed to stand in a translation." When Russians encounter the Caucasian words *churek* or *lavash* in a translation, they learn about kinds of bread that do not exist in their own culture and are not simply "bread." But they should not be obliged to contend with the Azeri word *khala*, since the word is no more than an "exotic hieroglyph" for the common word "aunt." A word designating a phenomenon common to both languages serves no literary function when introduced as a calque and may ruin the narrative by diverting the reader's attention (1955:169–70). The poet Pavel Antokolsky agrees. Words such as *aryk*, *aksakal*, and *ashug* should be transcribed into Russian since *aryk* does not signify a canal as Russians conceive of a canal, *aksakal* means not simply an old man but rather a kind of tribal elder, and *ashug* means not only a singer but also a poet and an improviser. But *gyz* means only "daughter," *oglu* means only "son," and *ioldash* means only "comrade" (Antokolsky et al. 1955:13–14).

Vlakhov and Florin's warning that excessive infusions of realia can be harmful is especially interesting because it touches on the present-day fate of the Russian language as a whole in addition to the problem of translation as communication. And this applies to languages other than Russian. In our time more than just a few nationalities have been complaining—and with good reason—about the powerful influence being exerted on the world by the English language, particularly its American variant. German, Italian, Spanish, and Japanese linguists have expressed concern, even alarm, over the "Americanization" of their languages, and the French Academy has even appointed a committee to explore ways of damming the flood of American words and expressions into the French language. This is a problem of culture, and specifically a problem of realia, for language impact goes inseparably with the spread of American culture and technology into all corners of the world. Russian linguists have expressed alarm over the seemingly uncontrolled flood of English words and primarily American realia into their language; those who are familiar with the Soviet Union know that the problem is acute in terms of the flood of realia into Russian and other Soviet cultures.

Indicative of this awareness is the Soviet translator and editor Nora Gal's book *The Word Alive and Dead*. This book, a study of bad usage in the Russian language as a whole rather than specifically realia, offers thousands of examples from Gal's lifelong experience as a translation editor. Translations are not the sole cause of bad language usage, Gal admits, but "no less than half of all that we read *is in translation*. It is in the language of *translation* that Marx and Engels, Dante and Goethe, Shakespeare and Stendhal, speak to us" (1972:155–56; emphasis in the original). Gal sounds a strong warning to Russians, for although hers are the complaints of any professional editor who becomes more than ordinarily aware of poor language habits, her examples show that many translators go far beyond reasonable limits to adopt foreign words into Russian. By poor usage Gal signifies the usual kind—slovenly grammar, misapplied lexicon, otiose syntax. But she also points to the fashionable penchant to use foreign words and expressions in place of clear and effective Russian resources.

Russian newspaper articles, stories, and novels are currently filled with such obviously foreign words as *intuitsiia, rezul'tat, moment, defekt, fiasko,* and *apogei,* even though each of these words has a perfectly good Russian counterpart. For example, Gal states, translators seem unable to say simply in Russian that circumstances need study; instead, they have to say *analizirovat' situatsiiu.* When Russians read translations, they find not easily accessible native Russian words but, inevitably, words with English origins such as *entuziazm, segregatsiia, privilegiia, momental'no, frontir, blokirovat', barrikadirovat', konfidentsial'no, diskreditirovat', reorganizatssia, argumentatsiia,* and *idealizirovat'.* Russians enter into a *diskussiia;* fall into a *panika* and behave *panicheski* feel *antipatiia, simpatiia,* and *terror;* reason with their *intellekt;* witness an *intsident;* face a *dilemma;* achieve *kompetentsiia* in their profession; request a *konsul'tatsiia;* and even find life *absurd.* Russians are more likely than not to read in a newspaper an *analiz situatsii* that considers all *faktory* and *fakty* and carefully measures the *balans riska.* It seems that a preference for foreign adoptions has spread into all areas of Russian culture (1972:27–48).

It must be stated that this is not the first time the Russian language has been heavily influenced by a foreign language. Peter the Great introduced a flood of Germanisms; the growth of the sciences in the eighteenth century saw as great an influence of Greek and Latin on Russian as on any other world language; and the "Frenchification" of the Russian language in the eighteenth and nineteenth centuries has been decried by Russians from Tolstoy to Solzhenitsyn. Many of the words of foreign origin listed above have existed in the Russian language for over a century. Many foreign words are so common in the Russian language as to seem natural to Russians. As Gal points out, the Russian language has been internationalized along with most other languages of the world, so it is understandable that the Russian ideological language is inundated with such calques as *kommunizm, sotsializm, kapitalizm, feodalizm,* and *klass, ekonomika, proletariat, respublika* (1972:50–51). The introduction of foreign words into a language is not a sin. Calques, neologisms, and cognates enrich both language and culture. Given that the Russian language has been many times influenced by many different languages, it is not surprising that ways of assimilating foreign influences are well developed in the very system of the language. The problem is not that foreign adoptions are something new and unprecedented for Russian but that the tendency to use a foreign word is compelling even in the most ordinary instance. The only impetus for this development—which is far more serious now than when Gal published her book in 1972—seems to be pretentiousness.

The problem of foreign adoptions has gone far beyond the niceties of realia as discussed by Vlakhov and Florin. Gal cites some striking instances of the use of foreign words purely for the sake of using foreign words. In one case, a translator should not have transliterated "boy," in the sense of a servant, as "*boi,*" because the word means "battle" in Russian, and the context leaves the Russian reader wondering how and why a battle entered a room behind a little table on wheels. In another case, a writer reporting on his visit to the United States used the exclamation "*Ai!*" in a description of a public meeting even though the exclamation could mean to Russians only that Americans shout "Ouch!" when they vote (1972:55; see also 48–49, 137).

Realia are not a problem exclusively of harm, however. Since realia are essential to translation as communication and the words for realia *contain* the cultural values that one nation gives to another, the problem of conveying them is essential. In many cases, realia would lose their impact, if not their absolutely necessary original meaning, if they were not transliterated. The word "satellite" could not begin to convey the trauma inflicted on the United States when the Soviets launched sputnik in 1957. The current terms *glasnost* and *perestroika* would be devoid of relevance to the current Soviet condition if they were translated as "frankness" and "reconstruction." American understanding of the Soviet Union would not be especially facilitated by transliteration of such bureaucratic acronyms as *Gosplan, MTS, Narkom,* or *Mossovet,* but the realium *KGB* would lose impact if it were translated as *CSS.* And the Russian word *Sovet,* transliterated phonetically as *Soviet,* would be meaningless if it were translated as "Council."

Soviet translators refer to realia most often when discussing the demand for translators to know everything. If translators do not know the significance of a particular object or phenomenon, they must learn it in order to convey it to their readers. Kashkin has said in this regard that the translator "must sometimes be both a historian and a sociologist." The Russian translator must know what is happening in the United States at any given time and must understand the implications of the terms that express objects, phenomena, conditions, or concepts. "The translator is two beings in one. He is both a philologist-encyclopedist and a writer-stylist. He is his author's thoughtful researcher and creative surrogate." The encyclopedist must never become a pedant, but neither must the artist hesitate to be an indefatigable student (1959:115, 113; also Ozerov 1959:285).

Rita Rayt, whose translations are models of a translator's quest for the meaning of the realia of other cultures, is an especially good example of the translator as scholar and researcher. She confronted the problem of realia with great ingenuity when she translated Kurt Vonnegut's novels. Given that she has never visited the United States, it is remarkable that she could decipher the words for many American realia. Where, for example, did she learn what is meant by "zap-guns," "contract labor," "barbershop quartet," or the myriads of other cultural paraphernalia that fill her subject's novels? In her translation of *Cat's Cradle*, Rayt made the words *karass* and *kalipso* bywords in the Soviet Union; she also taught Russian readers of *Breakfast of Champions* that Holiday Inns are likely to have a restaurant named Tally-Ho that serves a Number Five Breakfast.

Occasionally, Rayt introduces errors. West Virginia is given once as South Virginia, and the "founding fathers" are given as the "Pilgrim fathers." However, slips of culture are rare in Rayt's work, and she is generally a reliable source of insights into American culture. Rayt does not overdo the realia of Vonnegut's novels. In many instances, she does not explain American realia to her readers. She lets them wonder about the meaning of "contract labor," for example, and she does not explicate the Olympian etiology of the name of American truck companies. Sometimes she overlooks realia. Her Vonnegut-narrator does not light up a Pall Mall; rather, he simple lights up his favorite brand of cigarette. Very often, Vonnegut helps to define realia through his penchant for explaining the obvious. Rayt occasionally resorts to a footnote, but, knowing that too many realia can distract the reader without adding information necessary for literary appreciation, she most often lets logic work for her and does not translate, transcribe, explain, or even offer many realia.

Rayt's work serves to show that translators must know everything even though they do not use everything. One sensible aspect of this rule is that knowledge of context saves the translator from foolish errors. This is especially important for handling realia in view of Roothaer's note that translatory failings may be traced most often to cultural, not linguistic, ignorance. A translator poorly informed about Russian culture might encounter the name Derzhavin in context with the name of Catherine the

Great, might not know that G. R. Derzhavin was the greatest poet of Catherine's reign, and might asume that the poet's name, which has the same root as *derzhatel'* 'ruler' or 'magnate,' refers to a political entity. This would be a good guess, but it is precisely from such guesses about cultural context that slips most often result.

Informed modern translators seem to deal in two ways with realia. Adherents of the faithful translation prefer not to resort to anything that approaches scholarliness. They transliterate when realia resist conveyance out of cultural milieu, sometimes inserting an elaboration or gloss, sometimes obliging the reader to deal with meaning and cultural implication by deciphering the context. Or, they may, as Holman notes, convey a realium by resorting to "calque, adaptation, approximation or description." Whether they translate or transliterate, faithful translators only occasionally follow Vladimir Nabokov's advice that a footnote is in order. Scholarly translators, in contrast, are more receptive to Nabokov's solution. The preparation of authoritative texts has always required scholarly apparatus, of course. Nabokov's four-volume translation of Pushkin's *Eugene Onegin,* replete with commentary, definitive index, preface, introductions, original Russian text, and appended studies, is only the most glorious example of a standard scholarly translation. Reference here, however, is not to scholarly editions, but to the increasingly accepted large-audience translations that offer, together with a faithful text, an extra-functional apparatus. Quite often, a literary work is so text-conscious and so steeped in cultural context that its translation demands an apparatus. Nabokov's novels are notorious for their invitations to exegetes—thus the various annotated texts of his novels. In Russian literature, one work that demands such attention is the Symbolist poet and writer Andrey Bely's novel *Petersburg,* available in a popular translation by John Cournos (1959) and a scholarly translation by Robert A. Maguire and John E. Malmstad (1978).

It has already been pointed out in the discussion of Dostoyevsky's *Crime and Punishment* that Petersburg literature, "that other Russian literature," is peculiar to specific time, place, and cultural-historical associations. Even Bely's Symbolist novel, filled with abstract other-world allusions, links, and hints, is determinedly oriented to exact place—a street, a square, a monument, an architectural masterpiece. Color, geometric shape, light effect—these and other "physiological" aspects of this novel enter into the novel's complex, abstract, symbolic system. But these aspects also remain material, so that specific phenomenon and location are as important, in the realistic sense, as the location of things and events in *Crime and Punishment.* Bely's *Petersburg* is the epitome of the Petersburg theme in Russian literature. His Symbolist Petersburg is "an infinitely tiny locus in time and space expanding in ever-widening concentric circles into the green mists of the nth dimension." Bely's novel belongs to the Russian literature of phantasmagoria, illusion, irreality. It is symbolic in the grandiose historical manner of Pushkin's verse tale *The Bronze Horseman;* sinister as Pushkin's supernatural prose tale "The Queen of Spades"; preposterous as Gogol's Petersburg tales; and elevated to a "higher reality" like Dostoyevsky. But Bely's novel is also oriented to the reality of this eerie subarctic city; in some ways it is as sociologial and naturalistic as the myriads of "physiological sketches" that also belong to the Petersburg tradition. Realia are an essential aspect of this novel, just as the city's many parallelipopeds are its definitive sign. The translator of *Petersburg* must indeed know everything about this city: its history, its art and architecture, its literature, and its realia. This novel's translators must be cautious.

Maguire and Malmstad are cautious translators. In the sense of care for language and detail, caution is the strength of this translation; in the sense of timidity, caution is its weakness. Where the style of the Cournos translation is more easily readable, the Maguire and Malmstad translation is styled after Nabokovian literalism. As the translators state, "Our translation is literal in the sense that we have tried to find the most appropriate equivalent for a given work and have stuck to it throughout, bearing in mind that vital importance of repetition as one of Bely's principal devices" (1978:xxv). Perhaps Bely's idiosyncratic style demands accuracy over fidelity, for it comprises, to cite only a few of the translators' descriptions of it, "shifted grammatical categories, assaults on conventional syntax, quirky (some would say 'impossible') combinations of words, sudden compressions and ellipses, manipulations of sound and semantics" (1978:xxv). But even though the translators do not subscribe dogmatically to Nabokov's literalism—they balk when it comes to reproducing Bely's eccentric punctuation and speak of spirit as well as letter in their introduction—some of their conveyances are a bit too literal.

Where Cournos has, in the novel's prologue, "We shall dwell largely on Petersburg," Maguire and Malmstad have, more precisely, "Let us expatiate at greater length on Petersburg." Where Cournos has "By virtue of the same reasoning," his successors have "On the basis of these same judgments." Cournos aims for brevity and simplicity with "Our Russian Empire is a geographical entity, part of a well-known planet." Maguire and Malmstad strive for accurate reproduction of syntax with "This Russian Empire of ours is a geographical entity, which means: part of a certain planet."

This is not to say that the greater readability of the Cournos version is necessarily a correct attribute. Maguire and Malmstad are right when they stress the awkwardness of Bely's experimental prose, and they were in this respect astute to be literal. It can be argued that they should have used the more interesting second "Berlin" edition of 1916 for their text, instead of the considerably revised and more eccentric "Petrograd" text of

1922. They argue this point themselves and are considering using the 1916 text for any subsequent editions of their translation. Where Cournos does not justify his choice of text and does not identify what text he used (apparently he chose the first "Sirin" edition of 1913), Maguire and Malmstad provide a complete account of the difficulties of identifying a canonical text of any work by Bely and present sound arguments for rejecting both the 1913 text and the heavily censored Soviet editions of 1928/1935.

As for their approach to the task of translation, Maguire and Malmstad were careful to go through the text sequentially and systematically. They consulted native speakers, including the poet Nina Berberova and the scholar-translator Simon Karlinsky. They thoroughly analyzed their chosen text, even going so far as to collate their work with a Polish translation of the novel. Malmstad brought to their collaboration his authority as a Bely scholar and his familiarity with the manuscripts in the Leningrad archives. The thoroughness of their preparation is indicated not only by the care they took with the text but also in over sixty pages of notes. To identify and locate the myriads of Peterbourgeois realia in the novel, they used Karl Baedeker's superb 1914 edition of *Russia, with Teheran, Port Arthur, and Peking. A Handbook for Travellers*.

It is helpful to know, for example, that the "ambling and often bumbling" address to the reader in the Prologue, including "et cetera, et cetera, et cetera," is a parody of imperial proclamations that list the titles of the Russian Emperor; and that the epithet "Red Rus" provides not only political overtones but also the linguistic, cultural, and historical identities of the three East Slavic peoples who comprise the Empire. Notes are provided on Petersburg's embankments, islands, bridges, houses, squares, doors, streetlamps, churches, railway stations—both the physical reality of these and many other realia and their symbolic implications are thoroughly and pertinently described here.

The suggestion that the translator must know everything implicates more than just realia, and consideration of such "scholarly" matters as tsarist imperialism, Byzantinism, and Petersburg's architectural environment leads beyond discussions of realia as a problem of lexicon. Realia are always discussed as words or, at most, short phrases, but the possibility that realia go beyond lexicon to phraseology and syntax seems not to have been considered. An obvious example of realia as more than the word is those literary works, most pertinently Realist literary works, that rely to a great extent on the author's expert knowledge of a subject and intricate weaving of the words and syntax into the very style of a work—sports stories, for example, or sea adventures and war novels, or the myriads of Soviet Socialist Realist novels in which expert descriptions of and allusions to the process of work are central. Arthur Hailey's novels *Airport, Hotel*, and *Wheels* are an appropriate example of this, since the same kind of expertise that makes them popular in the United States—authoritative descriptions of "how things are done behind the scenes," including all the terms and syntactic formulations Hailey uses—have brought them great popularity in the Soviet Union too. Other examples are the Russian Realist writer Alexander Kuprin's novels and stories about circus performers, pirates, smugglers, musicians, actors, and tramps, the similarly expert works of Paul Gallico, Turgenev's *Notes of a Hunter*, Hemingway's novels about African safaris, and the deep sea fishing stories that Philip Wylie and Hemingway used to sell to *Collier's* and *Saturday Evening Post*.

The best example here is Ernest Hemingway, if only because of his high standing among Soviet readers (see Kashkin 1966). Hemingway is the epitome of the writer who made expert knowledge and skills the canon of modern Realist literature. Almost any novel or story could be chosen to illustrate this, but his short novel *The Old Man and the Sea*, rich in materials about the realia of expertise, is a good choice because the Russian translation offers telling examples of the pitfalls of dealing with realia. *The Old Man and the Sea* is one of Hemingway's most "expert" novels. The very feel and texture of its style derives from words for objects and phenomena, and especially words for skills that make it a delight both for connoisseurs of deep sea fishing and for those who have become amateur experts through Hemingway's novel. The story of the old man's victory over a giant marlin, his defeat by sharks, and the triumph of spirit is one of Hemingway's most concentrated and laconic works. Each sentence in the novel is as tight and to the point as a Hemingway could possibly make it—even the dream of the lions and the reflections on Joe DiMaggio—and there is no room for additions or elaborations of either syntax or overall form. Hemingway does not describe the intricacies of deep sea fishing in his work—the intricacies are the narrative itself. Nor does he bother to explain or to elaborate on his expertise—the reader understands the terms from the context.

The Russian version of Hemingway's *The Old Man and the Sea* appeared for the first time in 1952 in a translation by B. I. Izakov and Evgenya Kalashnikova. The translation was included that same year in the two-volume collection of Hemingway's works. It has seen nine editions to date. This canonical Russian text of the novel has been widely praised by Soviet critics and used for numerous Soviet critical studies and essays on the novel. In a recent critique of this translation, the Slavic scholar and editor Munir Sendich concludes that it meets many of the demands of Soviet artistic translation but nevertheless is marred by additions, concoctions, omissions, shortcomings of syntax, and chance errors (1986). Yet, so far as realia are concerned, the translators have handled individual lexical items quite well and in accordance with the methods specified by Vlakhov and Florin. Landlocked Russsians are unlikely to know technical terms for deep sea fishing, and many Russians are unlikely to know some of the Spanish terms, so the translators justifiably felt a need to insert glosses into the narrative. However, many lexical items did not require the glosses provided by these translators. When we look at conveyances of expertise in narrative phrases and sentences, it becomes apparent that Izakov and Kalashnikova added far too many explanations "aside" and inserted too many elaborations. Hemingway's terse narrative becomes prolix in such a protocol translation. Indeed, the Russian version of the novel is no longer a uniform narrative; rather, it is a narrative rudely enhanced by discursive addenda. This is not a poor translation—Russian critics have not erred in admiring Hemingway via this medium. But in too many instances the translators seem to have felt compelled to help Hemingway along his way to his Russian audience.

Where Hemingway says simply, "He was sorry for them all, even the great trunk backs that were as long as the skiff and weighed a ton," the translators have glossed the realium and otherwise elaborated the sentence to read, "The old man was sorry for them, even the great *shelled turtles called trunk backs* that were as long as the *whole* skiff and weighed a ton." Where Hemingway says, "His sword was as long as a baseball bat," the translators explain, "*In place of a nose* he had a sword as long as a baseball bat." Where Hemingway says, "He ate the white eggs to give himself strength," the translators gloss, "He ate the white *turtle* eggs to give himself strength." Experience of deep sea fishing is not required to understand from the simple statement "But the circles were much shorter now" that the Marlin is tiring. Nor does it take more than a brief consideration of the sentence to appreciate that what is meant (the fish is tiring) is well conveyed because what is said (the circles are getting smaller) is so laconic. This stylistic effect is lost and the narrative disrupted when the translators again elaborate and strengthen the sentence: "*For certain* the circles *the fish was making* had *become* much shorter now." Hemingway conveys the terrible size of the Marlin in one instance not by mentioning size but by having the old man wonder, "And who knows how old he is." But the stylistic effect is lost again when this bit of expertise (age means size to a fisherman) is explained, and even exaggerated: "And *God only* knows how long he has *lived on this earth*" (emphasis in the quotes added).

The mistake of these translators is their faulty strategy for dealing with Hemingway's style. Presumably, Hemingway's reader must be a hunter to comprehend the technical details and realia of "The Short Happy Life of Francis Macomber" or a fisherman to appreciate the Nick Adams stories or *The Old Man and Sea*. But most Hemingway fans, American and Russian alike, have never gone on a safari or fished for trout on the Upper Peninsula or for marlin in the Caribbean and still understand his expertise, lore, and realia without need of elaboration. The reader does not need to know anything about fishing to understand, for example, that the feel or smell of the hook inside the bait will turn a fish away. Hemingway does not need to say this in his novel, and he does not say it. Instead, he makes his reader feel it and understand it by working it into the narrative: "There was no part of the hook that a great fish could feel which was not sweet smelling and good tasting." It is apparent that any attempt to elucidate the sentence—to make the implicit explicit—will destroy its effect. Yet this is exactly what happens when the translators set about explaining—with ponderous syntax—what they apparently thought Hemingway failed to explain: "Approaching the hook the great fish would feel how sweet smelling and good tasting every last bit of it was." If writers have learned anything from Hemingway, it is that style need not "say" what is meant, but rather "show" what is meant. In trying to say for Hemingway what they think he should have said, the translators have missed what is said, what is meant, and what is shown all at once. A classic bit of Hemingwayan understatement—"What will I do if he decides to go down?"—is perfectly understandable to anyone who has never gone deep sea fishing. It shows, without saying, that if the marlin dies deep in the water, the old man will never be able to drag it to the surface. The very understatement makes the reader feel the old man's anxiety that he will lose his prize. There was no need for the translators to say all this out: "What will I do if he decides to go *like a stone to the bottom and die?*" (emphasis added).

Words for expertise are jargon. They become realia only when they are peculiar to a given culture (the Eskimo word for a particular kind of fishing spearhead, for example) or when they are new words for technology or other phenomena newly introduced to a culture. Realia are not only words, however; they exist also in phrases and whole sentences. This is especially apparent in expert descriptions of skills and practices. In the case of Hemingway's *The Old Man and the Sea*, we can see a clear connection between realia at the lexical level and realia at the syntactical level, because the translators chose to handle the problem of conveyance in the same way at both levels. Just as they glossed terms—identifying trunk backs as turtles, for example—they glossed syntax. In other words, new descriptions—that is, phrasings of technically difficult phenomena—gave the translators as much cause for insecurity as new words, and they responded with an identical solution, without reference to stratificational differences. That they undid much of the very essence of Hemingway's style is evident. More important than this particular case, however, is the need for linguists, especially translation linguists, to reconsider definitions of realia based exclusively on lexicon.

CONCLUSION

Russian and other Soviet translators have expended a great deal of effort to define their school of translation. The effort has always been to proclaim a new and unique world phenomenon—a multilingual All-Union school qualitatively different from anything that has happened previously. The effort began when Gorky, Chukovsky, Kashkin, and other founders tried to define a school even as they were still struggling with more basic questions of method, style, and terminology, and the effort continues to this day. Definitions of the Soviet school are as likely to appear in studies of specialized problems of translation as they are in book-length treatments of the school itself. Attempts at definition have had to be confronted throughout the present study, from Rossels's four commonly accepted postulates to Kashkin's, Fedorov's, and Gachechiladze's theories of artistic and realist translation, to Evgenya Kalashnikova's description of the school for the International Federation of Translators. Definitions of the Soviet school are based in most instances on attempts to articulate the Soviet method known as artistic translation. No other school or group in any national culture has gone to such lengths and into such detail to assert what translation should or should not be. One definition of Soviet artistic translation that will serve well as a basis for a final assessment of literary translation in Russia and America is particularly useful as a summary of the Soviet school.

In the 1968 edition of his major study of translation theory, A. V. Fedorov suggested that six "basic assumptions" about translation are so well established in Soviet scholarship and criticism that they would not be challenged by the majority of Soviet translators (see 1983). First, as a direct consequence of the demand for a full-valued representation of the original, Soviet translators accept ideological responsibility for the veracity of their work. Second, translators guarantee the high quality of the language used in their translations, in part by rejecting literalism and by defending their own language from unwanted inflictions of other languages. Third, Soviet translators accept the principle of the dialectical unity of form and content. Fourth, Soviet translators view the original as a semantic unity in which each separate element plays its own semantic role and which is linked with a specific national, social milieu and era. Translators view the whole and its elements in terms of artistic, as well as semantic, values. Fifth, Soviet translators approach their work through careful analysis of language and style and extensive study of the history of the author's people, language, culture, and literature—that is, translators apply the principle of study of phenomena and their interconnections. Translators know that each translation type— artistic, informational, commercial—has its own requirements, that no word or sentence is translated identically in every context, that rules and recipes are impossible, and that the absence of rules cannot be a license to change or to reinterpret the original. And sixth, Soviet translators accept the principle of translatability; for them, full-valued translation is possible (1968:142–44).

Fedorov's definition is important not only for what it says but also for what it reveals about the state of literary translation in Soviet letters. What should not be missed is that his definition, like Rossels's, Gachedchiladze's, or other definitions encountered in this study, is formulaic and decisive. One, two, three postulates, one, two, three assumptions—one-two-three, one-two-three—this is what the Soviet school is. Soviet theorists do not insist that translation is an art of perfection; they stress the importance of the word in its context, not as an absolute. But they assume common agreement among translators, work from a common perception of what literature is and what role translation plays in it, and are certain they will be heard. Inseparable from this propensity for authority is the ideological definition of the realist translation—a political definition that calls for authoritative centralized organization of social phenomena. No other definition of translation is so unabashedly ideological as this one. Tendencies of this method show up in Fedorov's definition, but only in his third assumption that Soviet translators accept the Marxist-Leninist principle of the dialectical unity of form and content. However, it has been seen earlier that Leninist principles and Marxist gnoseology are basic to definitions of realist translation—artistic translation as it was defined by Kashkin, Rossels, and Gachechiladze.

Other Soviet translators do not so readily ascribe ideological value to aesthetics, but prefer instead to define their art in ethical terms. Translations and translation methods are not simply right or wrong in the Soviet school; they are honest and dishonest, "principled" and "unprincipled." Note the principled character of Fedorov's definition: translators must accept ideological responsibility, of course, but they must also guarantee full value, take cultural and aesthetic traditions into account, apply the principle of study, combat literalism, honor the principle of translatability, and ensure that their products are adequate to the original and full-valued for the reader. Kashkin, Marya Lorie, Nora Gal, and Rita Rayt all assign specific moral and ethical responsibilities to translators, critics, editors, publishers, and readers. Nikolay Chukovsky and Kashkin are not alone when they say that translators ignorant of theory are unprincipled amateurs. Gal expresses moral indignation about pretentious use of calques and realia. Chukovsky severely criticizes inartistic translators.

Under no other national conditions are translation theorists so decisive, specific, formulaic, programmatic, ideological, and ethical about their art. In no other literary culture do translators speak so confidently about common agreement. No other school, group, or association of translators is so well organized, and no other translators are able to speak with such moral, ideological, or organizational authority. American translators do not have the means afforded by Soviet political and social conditions to establish a centralized authoritative organization, to create a monopoly, to speak from a national platform, and to define aesthetic principles in terms of a unifying ideology. This difference can be seen in the decisiveness of Soviet definitions as well as in the detail and extent to which they are developed.

Translators in most countries today subscribe to the charter of the International Federation of Translators and thereby agree on many important professional principles. In the United States, translation conditions have been at least somewhat rationalized by the efforts of organizations like PEN American Center, the American Translators Association, and the American Literary Translators Association. But no existing charter goes so far as to prescribe a method of translation. Seven of eight articles of a recent PEN publication (*Translation*, 26 Spring 1986, 273–74) deal with commercial relationships among author, publisher, and translator, including copyright arrangements. Only one article is concerned with matters that can be construed as ethical or aesthetic: "Translators should respect the original and refrain from making cuts or changes unless such alterations are permitted by the writers or their authorized representatives. Translators' texts should be respected." There are no prescriptions or definitions here, no mention of any translatory method and about adequate or full-valued translation, no prohibitions on literalism, no postulates or assumptions. Were a poll to be taken, it could very well turn out that the majority of translators subscribe to just these principles. Literalism is not respected in American letters, and most American translators probably just as decisively reject "scientific" methods of translation that, regardless of what they are called, result in lifeless language. But no American organization would attempt to define, for a majority or with any expectation of common agreement, what theory and practice of translation are and what they should be.

It seems fair to say again, however, that despite so much exertion of organizational, ideological, and moral authority to define a commonly accepted method of translation, Soviet theorists should not be labeled dogmatic. For all the specificity of their definitions, they are flexible and pragmatic. It would be difficult, for example, to find three translators more libertarian than Boris Pasternak, who decisively reinterpreted Shakespeare; Samuil Marshak, who did not let either formal or semantic demands disturb his versatile renditions of Robert Burns; or V. V. Levik, whose interlinear conveyances of European poets extend to the free end of the translation spectrum. It would be equally difficult to find a more dedicated adherent of the scientific method than Mikhail Lozinsky; and Valery Bryusov was as extremely literalist as Vladimir Nabokov. Yet these poets are featured prominently and for the most part with great favor in two of the best known books about artistic translation: Kornei Chukovsky's *A High Art* and E. G. Etkind's *Poetry and Translation*. The only clearly identifiable reason for this inclusion seems to be that despite the antipathy felt in the Soviet school toward literalism and libertarianism, translators do not hesitate to appreciate art where it is apparent.

Simply stated, the most greatly respected and ultimately decisive Russian assumption about translation is an intuitive admiration for translation as art, a conviction that translations should be judged on the basis of artistic criteria. Perhaps Evgenya Kalashnikova's statement that "a translation of a work of art should be a work of art and, if it passes this test, it becomes part and parcel of the literature into whose language it has been translated" (1966:9) and Kornei Chukovsky's assertion that "an artistic translation is always in all cases a creative act . . . precisely because translation is a matter of art, sweeping rules do not exist" (1969:9; 1984:141) speak most clearly on this point.

It should also be appreciated that the Soviet school is no longer as unique as its advocates believe. A better way to assess Soviet distinctiveness, particularly in regard to the American experience, is to consider that the rest of the world has only recently caught up to the Soviet school in theory and practice of translation. There is no doubt that the Soviet school led the way to the present state of the art of translation around the world, but neither in practice nor in theory is there a dramatic difference between the Soviet school and the rest of the world today. The basic argument of this comparative-critical study is that literary translation in the Russian and American worlds must be understood in context with the worldwide convergence of ideas and views of literary translation over the past several decades. This convergence can be most clearly seen in relation to Marilyn Gaddis Rose's autonomy spectrum. Literary translation, *literarische Ubersetzung, traduction littéraire*—these designations have entered into common usage in their respective languages and have been converging on an international scale. Translators in other countries are not as decisive as their Soviet colleagues, but they too accept the notion that translation properly defined and practiced belongs somewhere near the balanced center of the scale of gradations.

The Soviet school has banished the literalist translation and the scientific translation, whereas elsewhere in the world literalism has only been discredited. Soviet theorists and critics have been more decisive, too, about pushing the imitation, or adaptation, off its end of the translation spectrum. But it is not difficult to see that these actions are a matter of different pace, not different direction. Nor is it difficult to see that definitions of Soviet artistic translation can be reconciled with terms used elsewhere for translations that belong at the center of the spectrum. Lefevere's "organic translation," Cohen's "imitative" or "faithful" translation, Walter Arndt's "metrical" translation, Reiss's "expressive" translation—these descriptions of the *literary* translation process are well in keeping with the sense of balance, moderation, flexibility, creativity, fidelity, honesty, modesty, and morality that go into definitions of the Soviet artistic translation.

It is also possible to see the lines of the worldwide convergence elsewhere in relation to theory—namely, in the similarly swift and eclectic development of translation studies. Russian artistic and American literary translators share a common dislike of (and confusion about) linguistic studies of translation, but the Russian translators would hardly deny the powerful influence of Fedorov's linguistic studies on the Soviet school, and the American translators have not ignored such language-oriented theorists as Steiner or the contributions of linguists to such influential publications as *Babel*. Translation studies around the world, including in the Soviet Union, is indebted to the same mix of contributions from different areas of linguistics—psycholinguistics, sociolinguistics, anthropological linguistics, philosophy of language, semiotics. So far as semiotics is concerned, it is not likely that such mainline theorists as Gachechiladze would think to use the terms *signification* and *significant*, so important to Steiner and L. G. Kelly, but Soviet scholarship has taken a lead in semiotics through the so-called Moscow-Tartu school, and there are signs of the school's influence on Soviet theory of translation in such studies as L. Mikulina's analysis of realia in terms of information and communication theory (1981). Semiotics and structural linguistics have exerted a strong influence through Levý's work (1974), which in its turn is indebted to Jakobson (1966). Closely related here are Etkind's work in comparative stylistics (1959, 1963), Levin's work in historical stylistics (1963a, 1963b), and Papayan's work in comparative metrics (1975). Psycholinguistics, sociolinguistics, and anthropological linguistics are evident not only in the work of Mikulina but also in the influence of

Vlakhov and Florin's work on realia (1970). Soviet linguists have built a strong base for the development of computer translation in the work of Barkhudarov (1975) and Komissarov (1973).

Convergence does not mean that Soviet or American theory and practice conform to some impossible international model. So far as expressive literary theory is concerned, it is apparent that the rest of the world has been slow to emulate the Soviet school's decisive amelioration of the effects of the translator's own self-expression. Soviet theory provides a place in a translated work for the translator's personality, but a major ethical tenet of the Soviet school is that translators ought to express the original author's "I," and not the translator's. This development is not unknown elsewhere. Steiner is apparently the first modern theorist to make modesty an essential component of the translation process; disapproval of the translator's usurpation of the author's personality became apparent in American letters as early as the reaction to Robert Lowell's imitations at the Tate Address. But many American poets still believe that their own poetic gift can overcome all obstacles, even the language barrier—witness Burton Raffel's belief that the poet's control of his own language supersedes any need to know the language of the original.

Similarities and differences can also be seen in a mutual Russian and American convergence on mimetic value. Mimesis is nowhere as prominent in definitions of the translation process as in the Soviet school. True, Robert Adams often refers to translation as reflection, and Reuben Brower is committed to a view of translation as "mirror on mirror." But it is not likely that any American theorist would go so far as Kashkin, Rossels, and Gachechiladze do when they rest the very process of translation on Lenin's theory of reflection—the belief that a translation is a reflection of the original—and conduct such an elaborate method as the realist translation—the notion that a translation is a reflection of its original, which is in its turn a reflection of reality. The difference here is ideological, and there are other ideological differences. Despite their many contributions to poststructuralist theory, Western Marxists have ignored translation studies and seem not even to be aware of such Soviet Marxist-Leninist theoretical contributions as realist translation. Similarly, although Gachechiladze's attempt to imbed translation theory in a Marxist gnoseology is essentially a hermeneutics, Soviet hermeneutic theory is something quite different from Western hermeneutic approaches. A Marxist gnoseology is something quite different from Steiner's and Kelly's interpretations of the translation process, for example. The latter theorists emphasize exegesis, including textual analysis, in a search for truth and focus on what the text means as opposed to what it says or seems to say on the surface. In contrast, Gachechiladze assumes that the reality reflected by a work of art is knowable and that if the unity constituted by the original is faithfuly reproduced in all its relationships among the whole and its parts, and between the form and the content, the meaning of the text, both what it says and what it seems to say, will be preserved.

It is not appropriate to use the word *formalism* in reference to the Soviet school. The word carries too much ideological baggage and is blamed as the cause of literalist and scientific adventurism. But setting aside terminology, it might be possible to suggest that the deep respect in the Soviet school for textual analysis constitutes a faith in objective-text value. It is not possible to find in Soviet translation discussion any denigration of primacy of text. Kashkin, Rossels, Gachechiladze, and Fedorov all insist that the process of translation must begin with careful and exhaustive stylistic analysis; Koptilov makes analysis of text the very basis of the translation process. Formalist terms such as *norm, repetition, device*, and *dominant* constitute the basis and the substance of Soviet translation criticism. Indeed, the term *adequate* originates in objective-text theory, as does the concept's constituent terminology: *compensation, substitution, equivalence, correspondence, proportionality, effect, functionality.*

It is also not appropriate to suggest that Soviet translation theory is indebted to reception theory or reader-response criticism. A culture that has rejected formalism and structuralism can hardly be expected to have reached post-structuralism. Nevertheless, Soviet theorists have developed reader-oriented concepts and have used the notion of effect on the reader as a critical measure. The term *full-valued* has the same relevance to effect as the term *adequate* has to text, and it should be remembered that Smirnov made this an essential part of the first established definition of artistic translation: "By *adequate* we signify a translation which conveys all the author's intentions (unconscious, as well as intentional), *in the sense of its definitive ideological-emotional artistic effect on the reader*, and respects, as far as possible, all resources of imagery, coloration, rhythm, and so forth employed by the author, the latter being regarded not as an end in themselves, but only as *a means for achieving general effect*" (1934:527; emphasis added).

This close connection between the text of a translation and its effect on the reader has remained essential to definitions of artistic translation to this day. Thus, when Fedorov developed Smirnov's notion of adequacy into an analogous conveyance and added the term *full-valued*, he endorsed the assumption that the truest critical test of the quality of a translation is its "ideological-emotional artistic effect on the reader." When Gachechiladze fitted the terms *full-valued* and *adequate* to his Marxist-Leninist definition of realist translation, he added impetus to critical and theoretical shifts from text to reader and back, from analysis of the translation itself to tests of the translation against its readers' responses. When Rossels made functionality one of his four postulates of the Soviet school, he meant by this that the process of translation should result in a text that has the same effect on its new readers as the original had on its readers. Given the long history of this balance between text-oriented process and reader-oriented measure, it is not unreasonable to conclude that Soviet translation theory assumed some of the things about language and literature that were explicitly defined only later by German reception theory and by Anglo-American reader-response criticism.

Evidence for such a conclusion is not lacking. According to André Lefevere, there are essentially only two kinds of translation: "text-oriented translations" and "reader-oriented translations" (1977). Stephen Straight has stated that two questions ought to be answered whenever a translation is subjected to evaluation: "does the translator make the right choices of equivalence, is the translation 'faithful?'" and "does the translation evoke the same response?" (1981:43–48) Translation, Robert Adams has said, is "like a literary conversation with a fresh reader whose point of view is just odd enough to deepen a running dialogue now and then toward the possibility of fresh vision" (1973:180). Translators in the United States and elsewhere have been saying these things about reader and text for some time now. Levý, Steiner, Kelly, and many others whose ideas have been encountered in this study have also been saying these things about text and reader. Soviet theorists and critics have been saying essentially the same things. Etkind states that the translator has two options: he may "accommodate a foreign work of art to the perceptions of the reader, make the unfamiliar familiar, the remote near," or he may "reveal to the reader the richness of art, show him the beauty of diverse national forms, historical stratifications, individual creative systems" (1963:414). That is, the translator may be oriented to the text or to the reader, or may, as Soviet theorists of artistic translation have said all along, aim to strike a balance between the two. In either case, the reader is not only a measure but also a participant in the translation process itself.

But in addition to the author and the translator, Oleksy Kundzich has stated, "one more figure takes part in a translation—the reader." The reader's "active role begins long before he picks up the translation . . . the moment the translator bends over his desk he . . . feels the reader looking over his shoulder, sharing his doubts and decisions with him." There can be no creativity without the reader, for "every creativity is an address, and creativity is impossible without an addressee" (1968:12–13). Indeed, when they undertake to convey a work into their own language, translators not only make the reader a participant in the process, they also function as readers themselves. "Do we have to elaborate the well-known supposition," Kashkin has said, "that the translator unites in himself, first a *reader who indirectly receives the original,* then a *critic who analyzes the artistic side of the original,* and finally a *writer who artistically recreates the original*" (1955:141; emphasis in the original)?

Translation studies today are eclectic. Terms and concepts have been drawn from diverse areas of linguistics, language studies, literary theory, criticism, and philosophy. It is not yet fully clear where this rapid development of new knowledge into a new field has been leading us, but translation theorists have been moving in the same direction and reaching some of the same conclusions regardless of differing approaches and views. Despite their eclecticism, therefore, translation studies have begun to take shape, and translation theorists have begun to express coherently new ideas and concepts. The field will undoubtedly keep its eclectic character, and there is no reason to believe that it will become as specific as theory, practice, and criticism have been in the Soviet school. But the fact that Soviet and American ideas about text and effect have become similar without mutual awareness suggests that translation studies have been evolving toward a synthesis of text and response. The field will probably continue to develop in this direction. Possibly, it will assume shape through this synthesis. It can at least be said that new ideas, new knowledge, and new solutions to problems of translation will be found somewhere along the translation spectrum where text-oriented and reader-oriented value converge.

BIBLIOGRAPHY

▆▆▆▆▆▆ The reference-material or works-cited system of citation is used for documentation and evidence in this study. The following section of reference materials serves as both notes and bibliography. Russian titles are given in English wherever appropriate to discussion and cited in Russian in the reference materials section. No attempt has been made to cite canonical editions of translations or their originals. It is assumed that readers will want to consult the most available edition of works under discussion, and that it is easier to locate materials when cited by chapter, passage, scene, event, or other convenient means of identification. Another reason for this reference method is that analyses of translations would otherwise be subjected to a detrimental clutter of double citations in parentheses, sometimes after every word in a series. Care has been taken to identify, wherever possible, the text used for a translation. Otherwise, a translator's use of a differently edited text might be taken for an omission or error.

The modified Library of Congress method for transliteration of Russian is used for references and for words as words in text. This orthographic system facilitates location of Russian sources in most library catalogs and information retrieval systems and is sufficiently phonetic to provide a reliable indicator of sounds and shapes of words as words. The system recommended for transliteration of Russian by American publishers is used in the text; it is oriented to both pronunciation and simplified spelling for the general reader.

Adams, Robert M. 1973. *Proteus, His Lies, His Truth: Discussions of Literary Translation*. New York: W. W. Norton.

Ananiashvili, Elizbar. 1973. "Na novom etape." In *Khudozhestvennyi perevod*. Erevan: Erevan University Press, 50–77.

Andres, A. 1965. "Distantsiia vremeni i perevod (nekotorye mysli i nabliudeniia)." In *Masterstvo perevoda 1964*. Moscow: Sovetskii pisatel', 118–31.

Antokolsky, P. G. 1964. "Chernyi khleb masterstva." In *Masterstvo perevoda 1963*. Moscow: Sovetskii pisatel', 5–12.

Antokolsky, P. G., M. Auezov, and M. Rylsky. 1955. "Khudozhestvennye perevody literatur narodov SSSR." In *Voprosy khudozhestvennogo perevoda*. Moscow: Sovetskii pisatel', 5–44.

Arndt, Walter. 1972. *Pushkin Threefold*. New York: E. P. Dutton.

———. 1980. "Translating Faust." In J. W. von Goethe. *Faust: A Tragedy*. Tr. Walter Arndt. New York: W. W. Norton, 356–67.

Arnold, Matthew. 1905. *On Translating Homer*. London: John Murray.

Arrowsmith, William. 1961. "The Lively Conventions of Translation." In *The Craft and Context of Translation*. Austin, Tex.: University of Texas Press, 122–40.

Astley, George. 1971. "The Problem Seen from England." In *The World of Translation*. New York: PEN American Center, 307–11.

Balmont, K. D. 1904. "Pevets lichnosti i zhizni. Uol't Uitman." *Vesy*, no. 7, 11–32.

———. 1922. *Revoliutsionnaia poeziia Evropy i Ameriki. Uol't Uitman*. Moscow: Gosizdat; 2d ed. Moscow: Gosizdat, 1981.

Baltsezhan, Edvard. 1978. "Perevod kak tvorchestvo." *Babel*, 24, no. 3/4, 124–26.

Barkhudarov, L. S. 1975. *Iazyk i perevod. voprosy obshchei i chastnoi teorii perevoda*. Moscow: Vysshaia shkola.

Bassnett-McGuire, Susan. 1980. *Translation Studies*. London and New York: Methuen.

Bayley, John. 1983. "Looking in on Pushkin." *New York Review of Books*, 3 February, 35–38.

Bazhan, Mikola. 1973. "Tsennyi trud pisatelia–perevodchika." In *Khudozhestvennyi perevod*. Erevan: Erevan University Press, 19–26.

Beaugrande, Robert de. 1978. *Factors in a Theory of Poetic Translation*. Assen: Van Gorcum.

Bekker, M., ed. 1963. "Diskussiia o prostorechii." In *Masterstvo perevoda 1962*. Moscow: Sovetskii pisatel', 487–90.

Bely, Andrey. 1959. *St. Petersburg*. Tr. John Cournos. New York: Grove Press.

———. 1978. *Petersburg*. Tr. Robert A. Maguire and John E. Malmstad. Bloomington, Ind., and London: Indiana University Press.

Benjamin, Walter. 1968. "The Task of the Translator." *Illuminations*. Tr. Harry Zohn. New York: Harcourt, Brace and World.

Bennani, Ben. 1981. "Translating Arabic Poetry: An Interpretative Intertextual Approach." In *Translation Spectrum*. Albany, N.Y.: New York State University Press, 135–39.

Bethea, David. 1984. *Vladislav Khodasevich*. Princeton, N.J.: Princeton University Press.

———. 1984. Review of Pushkin 1981. *Slavic and East European Journal*, 28, no. 1, 112–14.

Block, Haskell M. 1981. "The Writer as Translator: Nerval, Baudelaire, Gide." In *Translation Spectrum*. Albany, N.Y.: State University of New York Press, 116–26.

Borges, Jorge Luis. 1973. "Translation." *Borges on Writing*. New York: E. P. Dutton, 103–60.

Bovie, Smith Palmer. 1961. "Translation as a Form of Criticism." In *The Craft and Context of Translation*. Austin, Tex.: University of Texas Press, 38–56.

Brower, Reuben. 1974. *Mirror on Mirror: Translation, Imitation, Parody.* Cambridge, Mass.: Harvard University Press.

Brown, Deming. 1954. "Soviet Taste in American Literature." In *A Guide to Soviet Russian Translations of American Literature.* New York: King's Crown Press, 3–27.

———. 1962. *Soviet Attitudes toward American Writing.* Princeton, N.J: Princeton University Press.

Carne-Ross, D. S. 1961. "Translation and Transposition." In *The Craft and Context of Translation.* Austin, Tex.: University of Texas Press, 3–21.

Carpovich, Vera. 1976. *Solzhenitsyn's Peculiar Vocabulary: Russian-English Glossary.* New York: Technical Dictionaries.

Cary, Edmond. 1957. "Théories soviétiques de la traduction." *Babel,* 3, no. 4, 179–90.

Chekhov, Anton. 1903. *The Black Monk, and Other Stories.* Tr. R. E. C. Long. London: Duckworth.

———. 1908. *The Kiss, and Other Stories.* Tr. R. E. C. Long. London: Duckworth; New York: Scribner's Sons.

———. 1914. *Stories of Russian Life.* Tr. Marian Fell. London: Duckworth; New York: Scribner's Sons.

———. 1915. *The Bet, and Other Stories.* Tr. S. S. Koteliansky and J. M. Murry. Dublin, London: Maunsel; Boston: J. W. Luce.

———. 1917. *The House with Mezzanine, and Other Stories.* Tr. S. S. Koteliansky and Gilbert Cannan. New York: Scribner's Sons.

———. 1917. *The Lady with the Dog, and Other Stories.* Tr. Constance Garnett. London: Chatto and Windus; New York: MacMillan.

———. 1920. *The Schoolmaster, and Other Stories.* Tr. Constance Garnett. London: Chatto and Windus; New York: MacMillan.

———. 1937. *Tchekoff's Plays and Stories.* Tr. S. S. Koteliansky. London: J. M. Dent.

———. 1959. *Great Stories.* Tr. Constance Garnett; ed. David H. Greene. New York: Dell.

———. 1963. *Selected Stories.* Tr. Ann Dunnigan. New York: Signet.

———. 1961. *Selected Tales of Tchehov.* 13 vols. Tr. Constance Garnett. Toronto: Clarke, Irwin.

———. 1963. *The Image of Chekhov: Forty Stories.* Tr. Robert Payne. New York: Knopf.

———. 1964. *Lady with Lapdog and Other Stories.* Tr. David Magarshack. Harmondsworth, Middlesex: Penguin.

———. 1965. *The Oxford Chekhov.* Tr. and ed. Ronald Hingley. 9 vols. Oxford, New York, Toronto, Melbourne: Oxford University Press.

———. 1968. *The Portable Chekov.* 2d. ed. New York: Viking.

———. 1979. *Anton Chekhov's Short Stories: Texts of the Stories. Background Criticism.* Ed. Ralph E. Matlaw. A Norton Critical Edition. New York: W. W. Norton.

———. 1983. *Chekhov: The Early Stories, 1883–1888.* Tr. Patrick Miles and Harvey Pitcher. London: John Murray; New York: MacMillan.

Chukovsky, K. I. 1906a. "Russkaia *Whitmaniana.*" *Vesy,* no. 10, 43–44.

———. 1906. "O pol'ze broma." *Vesy,* no. 12, 52–60.

———. 1923. *Poeziia griaduschei demokratii—Uot Uitman. Uot Uitman i ego "Listia travy."* Moscow–Petrograd: Gosizdat.

———. 1966. *Moi Uitmen.* Moscow: Progress; 2d ed. Moscow: Progress, 1968.

———. 1984. *The Art of Translation: Kornei Chukovsky's "A High Art."* Tr. and ed. Lauren G. Leighton. Knoxville, Tenn.: University of Tennessee Press.

——— and F. D. Batyushkov. 1919. *Teoriia i kritika perevoda.* Petrograd: Vsemirnaia literatura.

——— and N. Gumilev. 1918. *Printsipy perevoda.* Petrograd: Vsemirnaia literatura.

Chukovsky, N. K. 1970. "Desiataia muza." In *Masterstvo perevoda 1969.* Moscow: Sovetskii pisatel', 386–90.

Clayton, J. Douglas. 1983. "The Theory and Practice of Poetic Translation in Pushkin and Nabokov." *Canadian Slavonic Papers,* 24, no. 1, 90–100.

Cohen, J. M. 1970. "Dr. Waley's Translations." In *Madly Singing in the Mountains.* New York: Walker, 29–36.

Dagut, M. B. 1973. "Idioms." *Babel,* 19, no. 4, 168–69.

Donskoy, Mikhail. 1975. "Shekspir dlia russkoi stseny." In *Masterstvo perevoda 1974.* Moscow: Sovetskii pisatel', 187–228.

Doron, Marcia Nita, and Marilyn Gaddis Rose. 1981. "The Economics and Politics of Translation." In *Translation Spectrum.* Albany, N.Y.: State University of New York, 160–67.

Dostoyevsky, F. M. 1886. *Crime and Punishment.* [Tr. Frederick Whishaw]. London: Vizetelly and Co.

———. 1951. *Crime and Punishment.* Tr. Constance Garnett. New York: Modern Library.

———. 1951. *Crime and Punishment.* Tr. David Magarshack. Harmondsworth, Middlesex: Penguin Classics.

———. 1953. *Crime and Punishment.* Tr. Jessie Coulson. London, New York, Toronto: Oxford University Press.

———. 1963. *Crime and Punishment.* Tr. Michael Scammell. New York: Washington Square Press.

———. 1968. *Crime and Punishment.* Tr. Sidney Monas. New York and Scarborough, Ont.: New American Library; London: New English Library.

E. S. [interviewer]. 1977. "Gor Vidal—SShA. V sisteme paradoksov." *Inostrannaia literatura,* no. 10, 251–54.

Etkind, E. G. 1959. "Sopostavitel'naia stilistika." In *Masterstvo perevoda 1956–1958.* Moscow: Sovetskii pisatel', 71–86.

———. 1959. "Arkhiv perevodchicka." In *Masterstvo perevoda 1956–58.* Moscow: Sovetskii pisatel', 394–403.

———. 1963. *Poeziia i perevod.* Moscow–Leningrad: Sovetskii pisatel'.

———. 1968. "Slovo kak siuzhet." In *Masterstvo perevoda 1966.* Moscow: Sovetskii pisatel', 261–66.

———. 1978. *Notes of a Non-Conspirator.* Oxford, London, New York: Oxford University Press.

Falkonovich, G. 1970. "Mir poeta i dolg perevodchika." In *Masterstvo perevoda 1966*. Moscow: Sovetskii pisatel', 280–300.

Fedorov, A. V. 1968. *Osnovy obshchei teorii perevoda (Lingvisticheskii ocherk)*. 3d ed. rev. and suppl. Moscow: Vysshaia shkola.

———. 1978. "K istorii stanovleniia teorii perevoda v SSSR." *Babel*, 24, no. 3/4, 144–49.

———. 1983. *Osnovy obshchei teorii perevoda (lingvisticheskie problemy)*. 4th ed. rev. and enl. Moscow: Vysshaia shkola.

Fet, Afanasy. 1982. *I Have Come to Greet You: Selected Poems*. Tr. James Greer. London: Angel Books.

Fiene, Donald M. 1976. "Kurt Vonnegut's Popularity in the Soviet Union and his Affinities with Russian Literature." *Russian Literature Triquarterly*, no. 14, 166–90.

———. 1977. "Kurt Vonnegut as an American Dissident: His Popularity in the Soviet Union and his Affinities with Russian Literature." In *Vonnegut in America*. New York: Delacorte/Seymour Lawrence.

Forster, Leonard. 1958. "Translation: An Introduction." In *Aspects of Translation*. London: Secker and Warburg, 1–28.

Friedberg, Maurice. 1977. *A Decade of Euphoria: Soviet Reception of Western Literature after the Death of Stalin, 1953–1964*. Bloomington, Ind.: Indiana University Press.

Gachechiladze, G. R. 1967. "Realism and Dialectics in the Art of Translation." *Babel*, 13, no. 2, 87–91.

———. 1970. *Vvedenie v teoriiu khudozhestvennogo perevoda*. Tbilisi: Tbilisi University Press.

Gal, Nora. 1972. *Slovo zhivoe i mertvoe. iz opyta perevodchika i redaktora*. Moscow: Kniga.

Galantière, Lewis. 1970. "On Translation as a Profession." *Babel*, 16, no. 1, 30–33.

Galler, Meyer, and Harlan E. Marquess. 1972. *Soviet Prison Camp Speech: A Survivor's Glossary*. Madison, Wis.: University of Wisconsin Press.

Garvuk, Yu. 1968. "Nuzhen li novyi perevod 'Gamleta' na russkii iazyk?" In *Masterstvo perevoda 1966*. Moscow: Sovetskii pisatel', 19–34.

Gasparov, M. 1971. "Briusov i bukvalizm. po neizdannym materialam k perevodu 'Eneidy.'" In *Masterstvo perevoda 1971*. Moscow: Sovetskii pisatel', 88–128.

Ginsburg, Mirra. 1971. "Translation in Russia: The Politics of Translation." In *The World of Translation*. New York: PEN American Center, 351–60.

Ginzburg, L. A. 1959. "Vnachale bylo slovo." In *Masterstvo perevoda 1956–1958*. Moscow: Sovetskii pisatel', 287–94.

Gitovich, A. I. 1970. "Mysli i zametki ob iskusstve poeticheskogo perevoda." In *Masterstvo perevoda 1970*. Moscow: Sovetskii pisatel', 364–85.

Gogol, N. V. 1948. *Dead Souls*. Tr. Bernard Gilbert Guerney. New York: Holt, Rinehart and Winston.

———. 1961. *Dead Souls*. Tr. Andrew R. MacAndrew. New York: Signet Classics.

———. 1961. *Dead Souls*. Tr. David Magarshack. Baltimore: Penguin Books.

———. 1964. *Dead Souls.* Tr. Helen Michailoff. New York: Washington Square Press.

———. N.d. *Dead Souls.* Tr. Constance Garnett. New York: Modern Library.

Graves, Robert. 1965. "Moral Principles in Translation." *Encounter,* no. 4, 128–39.

Grayson, Jane. 1977. *Nabokov Translated: A Comparison of Nabokov's Russian and English Prose.* Oxford: Oxford University Press.

Gress, Elsa. 1971. "The Art of Translating." In *The World of Translation.* New York: PEN American Center, 53–59.

Gross, Gerald. 1971. "On Publishers and Translators." In *The World of Translation.* New York: PEN American Center, 153–60.

Guseynayev, A. 1975. "Khudozhestvennyi perevod i nashi nevzgody." In *Masterstvo perevoda 1974.* Moscow: Sovetskii pisatel', 34–46.

Hawkes, David. 1970. "From the Chinese." In *Madly Singing in the Mountains.* New York: Walker, 45–51.

Hefzallah, Ibrahim M. 1970. "The Art of Translation." *Babel,* 16, no. 4, 180–87.

Heidegger, Martin. 1971. *On the Way to Language.* Tr. Peter D. Hertz. New York, Evanston, San Francisco, and London: Harper and Row.

Heim, Michael Henry. 1982. "Pushkin Englished." *The Nation,* 235, 9 October 340–43.

Heller, Joseph. 1961. *Catch Twenty-Two.* New York: Simon & Schuster.

———. 1961. *Ulovka-22.* Tr. M. Vilensky and V. Titov. Moscow: Voenizdat.

Hemingway, Ernest. 1952. *Starik i more. Izbrannye proizvedeniia.* 2 vols. Moscow: Khudozhestvennaia literatura, 2: 577–633.

Hollander, John. 1966. "Versions, Interpretations, and Performances." In *On Translation.* New York: Oxford University Press, 205–31.

Holman, M. J. de K. 1983. "L. N. Tolstoy's *Resurrection:* Eighty Years of Translation into English. *Slavonic and East European Review,* 61, no. 1, 125–38.

Holmes, J. S., ed. 1972. *The Nature of Translation: Essays on the Theory and Practice of Literary Translation.* The Hague and Paris: Mouton.

House, Juliane. 1973. "On the Limits of Translatability." *Babel,* 19, no. 4, 166–67.

Howard, Richard. 1961. "A Professional Translator's Trade Alphabet." In *The Craft and Context of Translation.* Austin, Tex.: University of Texas Press, 163–71.

Jakobson, Roman. 1966. "On Linguistic Aspects of Translation." In *On Translation.* New York: Oxford University Press, 232–39.

Kalashnikova, Evgenya. 1966. "Translation in the USSR." *Babel,* 12, no. 1, 9–17.

Karlinsky, Simon. 1982. "Pushkin Re-Englished." *New York Times Book Review,* 26 September, 11, 25–26.

Kashkin, I. A. 1955. "V bor'be za realisticheskii perevod." In *Voprosy khudozhestvennogo perevoda.* Moscow: Sovetskii pisatel', 120–64.

———. 1959. "Tekushchie dela." In *Masterstvo perevoda 1956–1958.* Moscow: Sovetskii pisatel', 106–52.

———. 1964. "Perevod i realizm." In *Masterstvo perevoda 1963.* Moscow: Sovetskii pisatel', 451–65.

———. 1965. "Kritiki est' i net kritiki." In *Masterstvo perevoda 1964*. Moscow: Sovetskii pisatel', 5–11.

———. 1966. *Ernest Khemingue..* Moscow: Khudozhestvennaia literatura.

———. 1968a. "Lozhnyi printsip i nepriemlemye rezul'taty." *Dlia chitatelia-sovremennika*. Moscow: Sovetskii pisatel', 377–410.

———. 1968b. "Voprosy perevoda." *Dlia chitatelia-sovremennika*. Moscow: Sovetskii pisatel', 435–72.

Keene, Donald. 1970. "In Your Distant Street Few Drums Were Heard." In *Madly Singing in the Mountains*. New York: Walker, 52–62.

———. 1971. *Landscapes and Portraits: Appreciations of Japanese Culture*. Tokyo and Palo Alto, Calif.: Kodansha International.

Kelly, L. G. 1979. *The True Interpreter: A History of Translation Theory and Practice in the West*. New York: St. Martin's.

"Khartiia perevodchika—Mezhdunarodnaia federatsiia perevodchikov." 1965. In *Masterstvo perevoda 1964*. Moscow: Sovetskii pisatel', 496–500.

Khinkis, Viktor. 1965. "O pol'ze sorazmernosti i soobraznosti." In *Masterstvo perevoda 1964*. Moscow: Sovetskii pisatel', 132–48.

Klimoff, Alexis. 1973. "Solzhenitsyn in English: An Evaluation." In *Aleksandr Solzhenitsyn: Critical Essays and Documentary Materials*. New York: Collier.

Klöpfer, R. 1967. *Theorie der literarischen Übersetzung*. Munich: W. Fink.

Knox, R. A. 1949. *Trials of a Translator*. New York: Sheed and Ward.

———. 1957. *On English Translation*. Oxford: Clarendon Press.

Komissarov, V. N. 1973. *Slovo o perevode*. Moscow: Mezhdunarodnye otnosheniia.

Koptilov, V. V. 1970. "Oleksii Kundzich—teoretik i praktik." In *Masterstvo perevoda 1969*. Moscow: Sovetskii pisatel', 271–83.

———. 1971. "Etapy raboty perevodchika." In *Voprosy teorii khudozhestvennogo perevoda*. Moscow: Mezhdunarodnye otnosheniia, 148–66.

———. 1973. "I vshir' i vglub'." In *Masterstvo perevoda 1972*. Moscow: Sovetskii pisatel', 257–61.

Kozlovskii, V. E. 1981. *Sobranie slovarei russkogo vorovskogo iazyka*. Benson, Vt.: Chalidze Publications.

Kross, Jaan. 1970. "Bez liubvi khoroshii perevod nemyslim." In *Masterstvo perevoda 1969*. Moscow: Sovetskii pisatel', 89–96.

Kundzich, O. L. 1955. "Perevodcheskaia mysl' i perevodcheskoe nedomyslie." In *Voprosy khudozhestvennogo perevoda*. Moscow: Sovetskii pisatel', 213–58.

———. 1959. "Perevod i literaturnyi iazyk." In *Masterstvo perevoda 1956–1958*. Moscow: Sovetskii pisatel', 7–45.

———. 1968. "Perevodcheskii bloknot." In *Masterstvo perevoda 1966*. Moscow: Sovetskii pisatel', 199–238.

———. 1973. *Slovo i obraz*. Tr. V. M. Rossels. Moscow: Sovetskii pisatel'.

Kurella, A. 1959. "Teoriia i praktika perevoda." In *Masterstvo perevoda 1956–1958*. Moscow: Sovetskii pisatel', 407–37.

Laskov, Iv. 1973. "V neotshlifovannom zerkale." In *Masterstvo perevoda 1972*. Moscow: Sovetskii pisatel', 62–80.

Lattimore, Richard. 1966. "Practical Notes on Translating Greek Poetry." In *On Translation*. New York: Oxford University Press, 48–56.

Lefevere, André. 1970. "The Translation of Literature: An Approach." *Babel*, 16, no. 2, 75–79.

———. 1975. *Translating Poetry: Seven Strategies and a Blueprint*. Assen and Amsterdam: Van Gorcum.

———. 1977. *Translating Literature: The German Tradition from Luther to Rosenzweig*. Assen and Amsterdam: Van Gorcum.

Leighton, Lauren G. 1980. Review of Pushkin 1978. *Slavic and East European Journal*, 24, no. 3, 423–24.

———. 1982. "Whitman in Russia: Chukovsky and Balmont." *Calamus: Walt Whitman Quarterly, International*, 22, 1–17.

Levik, V. V. 1959. "O tochnosti i vernosti." In *Masterstvo perevoda 1956–1958*. Moscow: Sovetskii pisatel', 254–75.

———. 1964. "Vernoe slovo—na vernoe mesto." In *Masterstvo perevoda 1963*. Moscow: Sovetskii pisatel', 90–106.

———. 1968. "Nuzhny li novye perevody Shekspira?" In *Masterstvo perevoda 1966*. Moscow: Sovetskii pisatel', 93–104.

Levin, Yu. D. 1963a "Ob istorizme v podkhode k istorii perevoda." In *Masterstvo perevoda 1962*. Moscow: Sovetskii pisatel', 373–94.

———. 1963b. "Ob istoricheskoi evoliutsii printsipov perevoda." In *Mezhdunarodnye sviazi russkoi literatury*. Moscow-Leningrad: AN SSSR, 5–31.

———. 1968. "Russkie perevody Shekspira." In *Masterstvo perevoda 1966*. Moscow: Sovetskii pisatel', 5–25.

———. 1985. *Russkie perevodchiki XIX veka i razvitie khudozhestvennogo perevoda*. Leningrad: Nauka.

Levý, Jiří. 1967. "Translation as a Decision Process." In *To Honor Roman Jakobson*. The Hague: Mouton, 2: 1171–82.

———. 1974. *Isskusstvo perevoda*. Tr. V. M. Rossels. Moscow: Progress.

Leytes, A. 1955. "Khudozhestvennyi perevod kak iavlenie rodnoi literatury." *Voprosy khudozhestvennogo perevoda*. Moscow: Sovetskii pisatel', 97–119.

———. 1965. "Vvedenie v obshchuiu teoriiu khudozhestvennogo perevoda. Programma kursa. Literaturnyi institut imeni M. Gor'kogo." In *Masterstvo perevoda 1964*. Moscow: Sovetskii pisatel', 252–72.

Libman, V. A., comp. 1969. *Russian Studies of American Literature: A Bibliography*. Chapel Hill, N.C.: University of North Carolina Press.

———. 1977. *Amerikanskaia literatura v russkikh perevodakh i kritike. Bibliografiia, 1776–1976*. Moscow: AN SSSR.

Lipkin, S. I. 1964. "Perevod i sovremennost'." In *Masterstvo perevoda 1963*. Moscow: Sovetskii pisatel', 13–52.

Lorie, M. F. 1959. "O redakture khudozhestvennogo perevoda." In *Masterstvo perevoda 1956–1958*. Moscow: Sovetskii pisatel', 87–105.

———. 1965. "Ob odnom khoroshem perevode. 'Tiazhelye vremena' Dikkensa v perevode V. M. Toper." In *Masterstvo perevoda 1964*. Moscow: Sovetskii pisatel', 98–117.

———. 1970. "Bol'noi vopros. o sbornike 'Redaktor i perevod.'" In *Masterstvo perevoda 1969*. Moscow Sovetskii pisatel', 315–26.

————. 1970. *"Ulovki perevodchikov."* In *Masterstvo perevoda 1970.* Moscow: Sovetskii pisatel', 334–58.

Lundquist, James. 1977. *Kurt Vonnegut.* New York: Frederick Ungar.

Luplow, Richard. 1971. "Narrative Style and Structure in *One Day in the Life of Ivan Denisovich." Russian Literature Triquarterly,* no. 1, 399–412.

Lyubimov, N. M. 1983. "Perevod—iskusstvo." *Nesgoraemye slova.* Moscow: Khudozhestvennaia literatura, 5–89.

Makkai, Adam. 1972. *Idiom Structure in English.* The Hague and Paris: Mouton.

————. 1978. "Idiomaticity as a Language Universal." In *Universals of Human Language.* Vol. 3 (Word Structure). Stanford, Calif.: Stanford University Press.

"Manifesto on Translation." 1971. In *The World of Translation.* New York: PEN American Center, 376–84.

Markish, S. 1965. "Uchenym i perevodchikam." In *Masterstvo perevoda 1964.* Moscow: Sovetskii pisatel', 227–37.

Markish S., and M. Zand. 1970. "Voprosy i otvety." In *Masterstvo perevoda 1969.* Moscow: Sovetskii pisatel', 284–93.

Marshak, S. Ya. 1959. "Iskusstvo poeticheskogo portreta." In *Masterstvo perevoda 1956–1958.* Moscow: Sovetskii pisatel', 245–50.

Mathews, Jackson. 1966. "Third Thoughts on Translating Poetry." In *On Translation.* New York: Oxford University Press, 67–77.

Mehnert, Klaus. 1983. *The Russians and Their Favorite Books.* Stanford, Calif.: Hoover Institution Press.

Mendelson, M. 1965. *Zhizn' i tvorchestvo Uitmana.* Moscow: Khudozhestvennaia literatura.

Mikulina, L. 1981. "Natsional'no-kul'turnaia spetsifika i perevod." In *Masterstvo perevoda 1979.* Moscow: Sovetskii pisatel', 79–99.

Mikushevich, V. 1971. "Poeticheskii motiv i kontekst." In *Voprosy teorii khudozhestvennogo perevoda.* Moscow: Mezhdunarodnye otnosheniia, 6–80.

Mirsky, D. S. 1958. *A History of Russian Literature.* New York: Viking.

Mkrtchian, L. M. 1970. "Poeziia v perevode." In *Masterstvo perevoda 1969.* Moscow: Sovetskii pisatel', 5–46.

————. 1973. "O perevodakh bukval'nykh i podtiagivaiushchikhsia. . . " In *Masterstvo perevoda 1972.* Moscow: Sovetskii pisatel', 262–68.

Morris, Ivan. 1970. "The Genius of Arthur Waley." In *Madly Singing in the Mountains.* New York: Walker, 67–87.

Mounin, Georges. 1955. *Les Belles Infidèles.* Paris: Cahiers du Sud.

————. 1963. *Le problèmes théoriques de la traduction.* Paris: Gallimard.

————. 1967. *Die Übersetzung: Geschichte, Theorie, Anwendung.* Munich: Nymphenburger.

Mustafin, R. 1965. "Poeticheskaia intonatsiia perevodchika." In *Masterstvo perevoda 1964.* Moscow: Sovetskii pisatel', 34–50.

Nabokov, Vladimir. 1937. "Pouchkine, ou le vrai et le vraisembable." *La Nouvelle Revue francaise,* 48, no. 282. 362–78.

————. 1955. "Problems of Translation: *Onegin* in English." *Partisan Review,* 22, no. 4, 496–512.

———. 1957. "Zametki perevodchika." *Novyi zhurnal*, 49, 130–44.

———. 1958. "Translator's Foreword." In Mikhail Lermontov. *A Hero of our Time*. Garden City, N.Y.: Doubleday.

———. 1964a. "On Translating Pushkin: Pounding the Clavichord." *New York Review of Books*, 30 April, 14–16.

———. 1964b. "Postscript to W. Arndt's Article 'Goading the Pony.'" *New York Review of Books*, 30 April, 16.

———. 1966. "The Servile Path." In *On Translation*. New York: Oxford University Press, 97–110.

———. 1973. "Reply to My Critics." *Strong Opinions*. New York: McGraw-Hill.

Newmark, Peter. 1973. "An Approach to Translation." *Babel*, 19, no. 1, 3–19.

———. 1978. "Thought, Speech, and Translation." *Babel*, 24, no. 3/4, 127–29.

———. 1981. *Approaches to Translation*. Oxford, New York, Toronto, Sydney, Paris, Frankfurt: Pergamon Press.

Nida, Eugene A. 1954. *Customs and Cultures*. New York: Harper.

———. 1964. *Toward a Science of Translating*. United Bible Societies. E. J. Brill: Leiden.

———. 1978. "The Setting of Communication: A Largely Overlooked Factor." *Babel*, 24, no. 3/4, 114–17.

Nida, Eugene A., and Charles Taber. 1969. *The Theory and Practice of Translation*. United Bible Societies. E. J. Brill: Leiden.

Nims, John. 1971. "Poetry: Lost in Translation? *Sappho to Valéry: Poems in Translation*. Rutgers, N.J.: Rutgers University Press, xvii–xxxv.

Opulsky, A. 1973. "Prezhde chem perevodit'. . . " In *Masterstvo perevoda 1972*. Moscow: Sovetskii pisatel', 173–99.

Orlov, V. N. 1969. "Bal'mont. Zhizn' i poeziia." In K. D. Balmont, *Stikhotvoreniia*. Biblioteka poeta, bol'shaia seriia. Leningrad: Sovetskii pisatel', 5–74.

Ozerov, Lev. 1959. "Vtoroe rozhdenie." In *Masterstvo perevoda 1956–1958*. Moscow: Sovetskii pisatel', 276–86.

———. 1968. "Zametki Pasternaka o Shekspire." In *Masterstvo perevoda 1966*. Moscow: Sovetskii pisatel', 111–18.

Papayan, P. 1975. "K voprosu o metricheskikh ekvivalentakh. armianskaia i russkaia poeziia." In *Masterstvo perevoda 1974*. Moscow: Sovetskii pisatel', 254–77.

Paris, Jean. 1961. "Translation and Creation." In *The Craft and Context of Translation*. Austin, Tex: University of Texas Press, 57–67.

Pasternak, Boris. 1983. "Translating Shakespeare." *I Remember*. Cambridge, Mass., and London: Harvard University Press, 125–52.

Patterson, Rodney L. 1975. "Bal'mont." In K. D. Bal'mont, *Izbrannye stikhotvoreniia i poemy*. Munich: W. Fink, 15–80.

Paustovsky, K. G. 1969. *The Story of a Life*. Tr. Joseph Barnes. New York: Pantheon.

Pavlovskis, Zoja. 1981. "Translation from the Classics." In *Translation Spectrum*. Albany, N.Y.: State University of New York Press, 99–107.

Payne, Robert. 1971. "On the Impossibility of Translation." In *The World of Translation*. New York: PEN American Center, 361–65.

Petrov, S. M. 1963. "O pol'ze prostorechii." In *Masterstvo perevoda 1962*. Moscow: Sovetskii pisatel', 71–96.

Petrovsky, F. 1973. "Vozvrashchenie k bukvalizmu? (po povodu stat'i M. Gasparova)." In *Masterstvo perevoda 1972*. Moscow: Sovetskii pisatel', 253–56.

Popović, Anton. 1978. "The Contemporary State of the Theory of Literary Translation." *Babel*, 24, no. 3/4, 11–13.

Pound, Ezra. N.d. *Literary Essays of Ezra Pound*. Norfolk, Conn.: New Directions.

Proffer, Carl R. 1964. "*Dead Souls* in Translation." *Slavic and East European Journal*, 8, no. 4, 420–33.

———. 1972. *Soviet Criticism of American Literature in the Sixties: An Anthology*. Ann Arbor, Mich.: Ardis.

———. 1984. "Introduction." *The Barsukov Triangle, The Two-Toned Blond, and Other Stories*. Ann Arbor, Mich.: Ardis.

Purdy, Theodore M. 1971. "The Publisher's Dilemma." In *The World of Translation*. New York: PEN American Center, 9–13.

Pushkin, A. S. 1962. *The Penguin Book of Russian Verse*. Ed. and tr. Dimitri Obolensky. Harmondsworth, Middlesex: Penguin Books.

———. 1963. *Eugene Onegin*. Tr. Walter Arndt. New York: E. P. Dutton.

———. 1964a. *Eugene Onegin*. Ed. and tr. Vladimir Nabokov. 4 vols. Bollingen Series 72. New York: Pantheon, 1964.

———. 1964b. *Selected Verse*. Intr. and ed. John Fennell. Harmondsworth, Middlesex: Penguin Books.

———. 1975. *Eugene Onegin*. Ed. and tr. Vladimir Nabokov. New ed. rev. and tr. 4 vols. London: Routledge and Kegan Paul.

———. 1978. *Eugene Onegin*. Tr. Sir Charles Johnston. New York: Viking.

———. 1981a. *Eugene Onegin*. Tr. Sir Charles Johnston. 2d ed. rev. New York: Penguin Classics.

———. 1981b. *Eugene Onegin*. Tr. Walter Arndt. 2d ed. rev. New York: E. P. Dutton.

Pyman, Avril. 1963. "Ob angliiskikh perevodakh stikhotvorenii A. Bloka." In *Mezhdunarodnye sviazi russkoi literatury*. Moscow-Leningrad: AN SSSR, 417–33.

———. 1965. "Kak ia perevodila Turgeneva na angliiskii." In *Masterstvo perevoda 1964*. Moscow: Sovetskii pisatel', 377–404.

Raffel, Burton. 1971. *The Forked Tongue: A Study of the Translation Process*. The Hague: Mouton.

Rayt-Kovaleva, Rita. 1965. "Nit' ariadny." In *Redaktor i perevod*. Moscow: Kniga, 5–22.

Reid, R. 1983. "Pushkin Fivefold." *Irish Slavonic Studies*, no. 4, 112–19.

Reiss, Katharina. 1976. *Texttyp und Übersetzungsmethode*. Krönberg/Ts: Scriptor.

Rexroth, Kenneth. 1961. "The Poet as Translator." In *The Craft and Context of Translation*. Austin, Tex.: University of Texas Press, 22–37.

Roothaer, Roger. 1978. "Language, Thought and Translation." *Babel*, 24, no. 3/4, 130–35.

Rose, Marilyn Gaddis. 1977a. "From Literary Analysis to Literary Translation." In *Translation in the Humanities*. Binghamton, N.Y.: State University of New York at Binghamton, 34–37.

————. 1977b. "Introduction: The Translation Process." In *Translation in the Humanities*. Binghamton, N.Y.: State University of New York at Binghamton, 1–4.

————. 1981a. "Introduction: Time and Space in the Translation Process." In *Translation Spectrum*. Albany, N.Y.: State University of New York Press, 1–7.

————. 1981b. "Translation Types and Conventions." In *Translation Spectrum*. Albany, N.Y.: State University of New York Press, 31–40.

————. 1987. "Humanistic Translation Theory." In *Building Bridges*. Proceedings of the 27th Annual Conference of the American Translators Association.

Ross, Stephen David. 1977. "Translation as Judgment." In *Translation in the Humanities*. Binghamton, N.Y.: State University of New York at Binghamton, 5–14.

Rossels, V. M. 1955. "Perevod i natsional'noe svoeobrazie podlinnika." In *Voprosy khudozhestvennogo perevoda*. Moscow: Sovetskii pisatel', 165–212.

————. 1963. "Podspor'ia i pregrady. zametki o perevode s blizkogo iazyka." In *Masterstvo perevoda 1962*. Moscow: Sovetskii pisatel', 151–78.

————. 1964. "Nuzhna istoriia khudozhestvennogo perevoda v SSSR." In *Masterstvo perevoda 1963*. Moscow: Sovetskii pisatel', 53–62.

————. 1965. "Radi shumiashchikh zelenykh vetvei." In *Masterstvo perevoda 1964*. Moscow: Sovetskii pisatel', 12–33.

————. 1970. "Shory na glazakh." In *Masterstvo perevoda 1970*. Moscow: Sovetskii pisatel', 301–33.

————. 1972. *Estafeta slova*. Moscow: Sovetskii pisatel'.

————. 1974. "Opyt teorii khudozhestvennogo perevoda." In Jiří Levý, *Iskusstvo perevoda*. Moscow: Progress, 5–24.

Saudek, Erik A. 1971. "Endeavors for Fidelity." *Babel*, 17, no. 1, 12–13.

Savory, Theodore. 1968. *The Art of Translation*. 2d ed. Boston: The Writer.

Selver, Paul. 1966. *The Art of Translating Poetry*. London: John Baker.

Serdich, Munir. 1971. "The Translator's Kitchen." *Babel*, 17, no. 3, 110–21.

————. 1986. "The Russian Translation of Hemingway's *The Old Man and the Sea:* The Marlin and the Shark of the Soviet School of Translation." *Russian Language Journal*, 40, no. 105, 185–94.

Serman, I. Z. 1963. "Russkaia literatura XVIII veka i perevod." In *Masterstvo perevoda 1962*. Moscow: Sovetskii pisatel', 337–72.

Shaw, J. Thomas. 1965. "Translations of 'Onegin.'" *Russian Review*, 24, no. 2, 111–27.

Shuman, Mariia. 1964. "Slova perevodimye i slova neperevodimye." In *Masterstvo perevoda 1963*. Moscow: Sovetskii pisatel', 124–33.

Silman, T. 1963. "Kontseptsiia proizvedeniia i perevod." In *Masterstvo perevoda 1964*. Moscow: Sovetskii pisatel', 271–95.

Smirnov, A. A. 1934. "Perevod." In *Literaturnaia entsiklopediia*. 9 vols. Moscow-Leningrad: AN SSSR, 8: 527.

Smith, William Jay. 1985. "A Visit with Rita Rait." *Translation*, 25 (Fall), 300–309.

Snelly-Hornby, Mary. 1988. *Translation Studies: An Integrated Approach*, Amsterdam and Philadelphia: John Benjamins.

Sobolev, L. N. 1955. "O perevode obraza obrazom." In *Voprosy khudozhestvennogo perevoda*. Moscow: Sovetskii pisatel', 259–307.

———. 1973. "Perevod—zalog druzhby literatur." In *Khudozhestvennyi perevod*. Erevan: Erevan University Press, 27–42.

Solzhenitsyn, Alexander. 1963a. *One Day in the Life of Ivan Denisovich*. Tr. Bela von Block. New York: Lancer Books.

———. 1963b. *One Day in the Life of Ivan Denisovich*. Tr. Max Hayward and Ronald Hingley. New York: Praeger.

———. 1963c. *One Day in the Life of Ivan Denisovich*. Tr. Ralph Parker. New York: E. P. Dutton; London: Gollancz.

———. 1963d. *One Day in the Life of Ivan Denisovich*. Tr. Thomas P. Whitney. New York: Fawcett.

———. 1963e. "One Day." Tr. Ralph Parker. *Soviet Literature*, no. 2, 3–95.

———. 1970. *One Day in the Life of Ivan Denisovich*. Tr. Gillon Aitken. London: Sphere Books.

———. 1969. "Ne obychai degtem shchi belit', na to smetana." *Sobranie sochinenii*. 6 vols. Frankfurt: Possev, 5 261–67.

Stanevich, Vera. 1959. "Nekotorye voprosy perevoda prozy." In *Masterstvo perevoda 1956–1958*. Moscow: Sovetskii pisatel', 46–70.

———. 1971. "Ritm prozy i perevod." In *Voprosy teorii khudozhestvennogo perevoda*. Moscow: Mezhdunarodnye otnosheniia, 80–118.

Starostin, A. 1973. "Nekotorye soobrazheniia o bukvalizme i vol'nosti i o traktovke 'Eneidy' Valeriem Briusovym v osobennosti." In *Masterstvo perevoda 1972*. Moscow: Sovetskii pisatel', 269–74.

Steinbeck, John. 1957. *Grozd'ia gneva*. Tr. Natalya Volzhina. Moscow: Khudozhestvennaia literatura.

Steiner, George. 1968. "To Traduce or to Transfigure." *Encounter*, 27, 48–54.

———. 1975. *After Babel: Aspects of Language and Translation*. New York and London: Oxford University Press.

———. 1976. *Language and Silence: Essays on Language, Literature, and the Inhuman*. New York: Atheneum.

Straight, H. Stephen. 1977. "Translation: Some Anthropological and Psycholinguistic Factors." In *Translation in the Humanities*. Binghamton, N.Y.: State University of New York at Binghamton, 28–33.

———. 1981. "Knowledge, Purpose, and Intuition: Three Dimensions in the Evaluation of Translation." In *Translation Spectrum*. Albany, N.Y.: State University of New York Press, 41–51.

Sukharev, S. (Muryshkin). 1977. "Dva 'tigra.' o perevodcheskom stile i lichnosti perevodchika." In *Masterstvo perevoda 1976*. Moscow: Sovetskii pisatel', 296–317.

Tarkovsky, Arseny. 1973. "Vozmozhnosti perevoda." In *Khudozhestvennyi perevod*. Erevan: Erevan University Press, 263–68.

Tate, Allen. 1972. *The Translation of Poetry*. Published for the Library of Congress by the Gertrude Clarke Whitall Poetry and Literature Fund. Washington, D.C.

Thomas, D. M. 1982. "Letter to the Editor: D. M. Thomas on his Pushkin." *New York Times Book Review*, 24 October, 15, 22, 24.

Toper, P. M. 1955. "Traditsii realizma. russkie pisateli XIX veka o khudozh-estvennom perevode." In *Veprosy khudozhestvennogo perevoda*. Moscow: Sovetskii pisatel', 45–96.

———. 1959. "Vozrozhdennaia poeziia." In *Masterstvo perevoda 1956–1958*. Moscow: Sovetskii pisatel', 193–207.

Toper, V. M. 1968. "Iz arkhiva redaktora." In *Masterstvo perevoda 1966*. Moscow: Sovetskii pisatel', 337–62.

Twain, Mark. 1953. *Izbrannye proizvedeniia*. Moscow: Khudozhestvennaia literatura.

———. 1960. *Sobranie sochinenii v 12–i tomakh*. Moscow: Khudozhestvennia literatura.

———. 1961. *Prikliucheniia Toma Soiera. Prikliucheniia Gekl'beri Finna*. Moscow: Detskaia literatura.

———. 1971. *Prikliucheniia Toma Soiera. Prikliucheniia Gekl'beri Finna. Rasskazy.* Moscow: Detskaia literatura.

Tytler, Alexander. 1792. *Essay on the Principles of Translation*. London: T. Cadeell and W. Davies; 2d ed. 1797.

Valéry, Paul. 1961. "Variations on the 'Eclogues.'" *The Art of Poetry*. Tr. Denise Folliot. New York: Vintage Books, 295–312.

Venclova, Antanas. 1965. "Moia rabota nad Pushkinym." In *Masterstvo perevoda 1964*. Moscow: Sovetskii pisatel', 287–303.

Venclova, Tomas. 1983. "The Game of the Soviet Censor." *New York Review of Books*, 3 March, 34–45.

Vidal, Gore. 1977. "Berr. Roman." Tr. M. Bruk and A. Fayngar. *Inostrannaia literatura*, no. 7, 22–70; no. 8, 26–83; no. 9, 128–82; no. 10, 96–169.

Vinay, J.-P. 1975. "The Theory of Translation: Myth or Reality." In *Translation and Interpretation: A Symposium*. Vancouver: Vancouver University Press.

Vinograde, Ann C. 1972. "A Soviet Translation of *Slaughterhouse Five*." *Russian Language Journal*, 24, 14–18.

Vlakhov, Sergey and Sider Florin. 1970. "Neperevodimoe v perevode (realii)." In *Masterstvo perevoda 1969*. Moscow: Sovetskii pisatel', 432–56.

Vonnegut, Kurt, Jr. 1973. *Breakfast of Champions*. New York: Delacorte.

———. 1978. *Boinia nomer piat'. Kolybel' dlia koshki. Zavtrak dlia chempionov. Dai vam bog zdorov'ia, mister Rozuoter*. Tr. Rita Rait-Kovaleva. Moscow: Khudozhestvennaia literatura.

Waley, Allison. 1970. "Letter to Ivan Morris." In *Madly Singing in the Mountains*. New York: Walker, 114–28.

Wesling, Donald, and André Lefevere. 1970. "The Mystery of Translation." *Babel*, 16, no. 3, 124–34.

Will, F. 1973. *The Knife in the Stone*. The Hague and Paris: Mouton.

Winter, Werner. 1961. "Impossibilities of Translations." In *The Craft and Context of Translation*. Austin, Tex.: University of Texas Press, 68–82.

Yakolev, N. 1977. "Gor Vidal i Aaron Berr." *Inostrannaia literatura*, no. 8, 203–10.

Zabolotsky, N. A. 1959. "Zametki perevodchika." In *Masterstvo perevoda 1956–1958*. Moscow: Sovetskii pisatel', 251–53.

INDEX